MEDICAL

COMLEX-USA®
LEVEL 1
Lecture Notes
2015

Behavioral Science and Social Sciences

© 2015 by Kaplan, Inc.

Published by Kaplan Medical, a division of Kaplan, Inc.
395 Hudson Street
New York, NY 10014

Printed in the United States of America

10 9 8 7 6 5 4 3 2 1

Course ISBN: 978-1-62523-037-9 Item Number: CM4018M

Editors

Epidemiology, Statistics, Behavioral Science

Charles Faselis, M.D.
Chairman of Medicine
VA Medical Center
Washington, DC

Alina Gonzalez-Mayo, M.D.
Psychiatrist
Department of Veterans Administration
Bay Pines, FL

Mark Tyler-Lloyd, M.D., M.P.H.
Executive Director of Academics
Kaplan Medical
New York, NY

Basic Science of Patient Safety

Ted A. James, M.D., M.S., F.A.C.S.
Medical Director, Clinical Simulation and Patient Safety
Director, Skin & Soft Tissue Surgical Oncology
Associate Professor of Surgery
University of Vermont College of Medicine
Burlington, VT

Contents

Preface.. vii

Section I: Epidemiology and Biostatistics

Chapter 1: Epidemiology.. 3

Chapter 2: Biostatistics 19

Section II: Behavioral Science

Chapter 3: Life in the United States 43

Chapter 4: Substance-Related Disorders 55

Chapter 5: Human Sexuality..................................... 65

Chapter 6: Learning and Behavior Modification 75

Chapter 7: Defense Mechanisms 87

Chapter 8: Psychologic Health and Testing 99

Chapter 9: Human Development 103

Chapter 10: Sleep and Sleep Disorders 121

Chapter 11: Physician-Patient Relationship 131

Chapter 12: Diagnostic and Statistical Manual (DSM 5)............ 143

Chapter 13: Organic Disorders.................................. 167

Chapter 14: Psychopharmacology 181

Chapter 15: Ethical and Legal Issues 195

Chapter 16: Health Care Delivery Systems 209

Section III: Social Sciences

Chapter 17: Basic Science of Patient Safety............... 215

Index 245

Preface

These volumes of Lecture Notes represent the most-likely-to-be-tested material on the current COMLEX-USA Level 1 exam.

We want to hear what you think. What do you like about the Notes? What could be improved? Please share your feedback by e-mailing us at **medfeedback@kaplan.com**.

Best of luck on your COMLEX exam!

Kaplan Medical

Epidemiology and Biostatistics

EPIDEMIOLOGIC MEASURES

Epidemiology is the study of the distribution and determinants of health-related states within a population.

- Epidemiology sees disease as distributed within a group, not as a property of an individual.
- The tools of epidemiology are numbers. Numbers in epidemiology are ratios converted into rates.
- The denominator is key: who is "at risk" for a particular event or disease state.
- Compare the number of actual cases with the number of potential cases to determine the rate.

$$\frac{\text{Actual cases}}{\text{Potential cases}} = \frac{\text{Numerator}}{\text{Denominator}} = \textbf{RATE}$$

- Rates are generally, but not always, per 100,000 persons by the Centers for Disease Control and Prevention (*CDC*), but can be per any multiplier. (Vital statistics are usually per 1,000 persons.)

Incidence and Prevalence

1. Incidence rate (IR): the rate at which **new events** occur in a population. The numerator is the number of NEW events that occur in a defined period; the denominator is the population at risk of experiencing this new event during the same period.

$$\textbf{Incidence rate} = \frac{\text{Number of \textbf{new events} in a specified period}}{\text{Number of persons "exposed to risk" of becoming new cases during this period}} \times 10^n$$

Remember, IR:

- Should include only **new** cases of the disease that occurred during the specified period.
- Should **not** include cases that occurred or were diagnosed earlier.
- This is especially important when working with infectious diseases such as tuberculosis and malaria.

Examples:

a. Over the course of one year, 5 men are diagnosed with prostate cancer, out of a total male study population of 200 (who do not have prostate cancer at the beginning of the study period). We would then say the incidence of prostate cancer in this population was 0.025 (or 2,500 per 100,000 men-years of study).

Note

The COMLEX Requires You to Know:

- The definitions and use of rates
- Incidence and prevalence
- Standardized rates
- Use and computations for screening tests
- How to identify bias in research
- Common research study designs

b. A population at risk is composed of 100 medical students. Twenty-five medical students develop symptoms consistent with acute infectious diarrhea and are confirmed by laboratory testing to have been infected with campylobacter. If 12 students developed campylobacter in September and 13 developed campylobacter in October, what is the incidence rate of campylobacter for those 2 months?

In this case, the numerator is the 25 new cases.

The denominator (person-time at risk) could be calculated by:

[(100 students at risk at the beginning of Sept. + 75 students at risk at the end of Oct.) / 2] × 2 months
= [(175 / 2) × 2] months
= 175 person-months of risk

Since 25 students got campylobacter in September or October, there are 75 students remaining at risk at the end of October.

The incidence rate would then be:

(25 new cases) / (175 person-months of risk) = 14% of the students are getting campylobacter each month

- **Attack rate** is the cumulative incidence of infection in a group of people observed over a period of time during an epidemic, usually in relation to food borne illness. It is the number of exposed people infected with the disease divided by the total number of exposed people.

It is measured from the beginning of an outbreak to the end of the outbreak. It is often referred to as an attack ratio.

For instance, if there are 70 people taken ill out of 98 in an outbreak, the attack rate is 70/98 ~ 0.714 or about 71.4%.

Consider an outbreak of Norwalk virus in which 18 persons in 18 different households all became ill. If the population of the community was 1,000, then the overall attack rate was $18 / 1,000 \times 100\% = 1.8\%$.

2. Prevalence rate: all persons who experience an event in a population. The numerator is ALL individuals who have an attribute or disease at a particular point in time (or during a particular period of time); the denominator is the population at risk of having the attribute or disease at this point in time or midway through the period.

$$\text{Prevalence rate} = \frac{\text{All cases of a disease at a given point/period}}{\text{Total population "at risk" for being cases at a given point/period}} \times 10^n$$

Prevalence is the proportion of people in a population who have a particular disease at a specified point in time, or over a specified period of time.

- The numerator includes not only new cases, but also old cases (people who remained ill during the specified point or period in time). A case is counted in prevalence until death or recovery occurs.

- This makes prevalence different from incidence, which includes only new cases in the numerator.

- Prevalence is most useful for measuring the burden of chronic diseases such as tuberculosis, malaria and HIV in a population.

For example, the CDC estimated the prevalence of obesity among American adults in 2001 at approximately 20%. Since the number (20%) includes ALL cases of obesity in the United States, we are talking about *prevalence*.

Prevalence is distinct from incidence. Prevalence is a measurement of *all* individuals (new and old) affected by the disease at a particular time, whereas incidence is a measurement of the number of *new* individuals who contract a disease during a particular period of time.

Point vs. Period Prevalence The amount of disease present in a population changes over time. Sometimes, we want to know how much of a particular disease is present in a population at a single point in time, a sort of 'snapshot view'.

    a. **Point prevalence:** For example, we may want to find out the prevalence of Tb in Community A today. To do that, we need to calculate the **point prevalence** on a given date. The numerator would include all known TB patients who live in Community A that day. The denominator would be the population of Community A that day.

Point prevalence is useful in comparing different points in time to help determine whether an outbreak is occurring.

    b. Period prevalence: prevalence during a specified period or span of time

    c. Focus on *chronic* conditions

3. Understanding the relationship between incidence and prevalence

    a. Prevalence = Incidence × Duration (P = I × D)

    b. "Prevalence pot"

        i. Incident cases or new cases are monitored over time.

        ii. New cases join pre-existing cases to make up total prevalence.

        iii. Prevalent cases leave the prevalence pot in one of two ways: recovery or death.

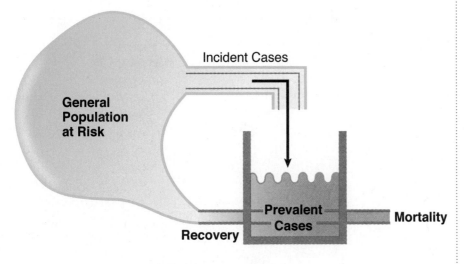

Figure 1-1. Prevalence Pot

4. Morbidity rate: rate of disease in a population at risk; refers to both incident and prevalent cases

5. Mortality rate: rate of death in a population at risk; refers to incident cases only

Table 1-1. Incidence and Prevalence

What happens to incidence and prevalence if:	Incidence	Prevalence
New effective treatment is initiated?	N	↓
New effective vaccine gains widespread use?	↓	↓
Number of persons dying from the condition increases?	N	↓
Additional Federal research dollars are targeted to a specific condition?	N	N
Behavioral risk factors are reduced in the population at large?	↓	↓
Contacts between infected persons and noninfected persons are reduced:		
For airborne infectious disease?	↓	↓
For noninfectious disease?	N	N
Recovery from the disease is more rapid than it was 1 year ago?	N	↓
Long-term survival rates for the disease are increasing?	N	↑

N = no change; ↓ = decrease; ↑ = increase

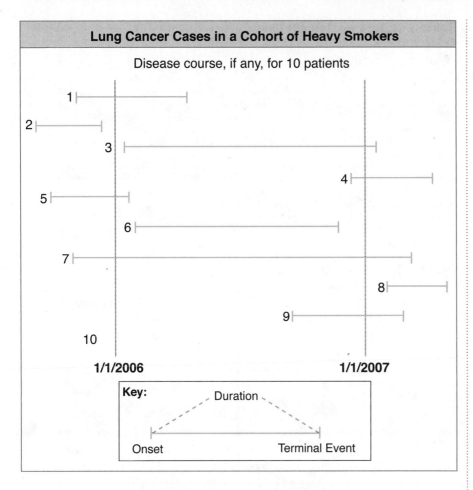

Lung Cancer Cases in a Cohort of Heavy Smokers

Disease course, if any, for 10 patients

1/1/2006   1/1/2007

Key: Duration

Onset   Terminal Event

Figure 1-2. Calculating Incidence and Prevalence

Crude, Specific, and Standardized Rates

1. <u>Crude rate</u>: actual measured rate for **whole population**

2. <u>Specific rate</u>: actual measured rate for **subgroup of population**, e.g., "age-specific" or "sex-specific" rate. A crude rate can be expressed as a weighted sum of age-specific rates. Each component of that sum has the following form:

(proportion of the population in the specified age group) $\times$ (age-specific rate)

3. <u>Standardized rate (or adjusted rate)</u>: adjusted to make groups equal on some factor, e.g., age; an "as if" statistic for comparing groups. The standardized rate adjusts or removes any difference between two populations based on the standardized variable. This allows an "uncontaminated" or unconfounded comparison.

Table 1-2. Types of Mortality Rates

Crude mortality rate	$\dfrac{\text{Deaths}}{\text{Population}}$
Cause-specific mortality rate	$\dfrac{\text{Deaths from cause}}{\text{Population}}$
Case-fatality rate	$\dfrac{\text{Deaths from cause}}{\text{Number of persons with the disease/cause}}$
Proportionate mortality rate (PMR)	$\dfrac{\text{Deaths from cause}}{\text{All deaths}}$

Practice Question

1. Why does Population A have a higher crude rate of disease compared with Population C? (Hint: Look at the age distribution.)

Table 1-3. Disease Rates Positively Correlated with Age

	Population A		Population B		Population C	
	Cases	Population	Cases	Population	Cases	Population
Younger	1	1,000	2	2,000	3	3,000
Intermediate	4	2,000	4	2,000	4	2,000
Older	9	3,000	6	2,000	3	1,000
Total	14	6,000	12	6,000	10	6,000
Crude Rates per 1,000	2.3		2.0		1.6	

UNDERSTANDING SCREENING TESTS

Table 1-4. Screening Results in a 2 × 2 Table

Screening Test Results		Disease		
		Present	Absent	Totals
	Positive	TP 60	FP 70	TP+FP
	Negative	FN 40	TN 30	TN+FN
	Totals	TP+FN	TN+FP	TP+TN+FP+FN

TP=true positives; TN=true negatives; FP=false positives; FN=false negatives

Pre-test Probabilities

Sensitivity and **specificity** are measures of the performance of different tests (and in some cases physical findings and symptoms). Why do we need them? We can't always use the gold-standard test to diagnose or exclude a disease so we usually start off with the use imperfect tests that are cheaper and easier to use. Think about what would happen if you called the cardiology fellow to do a cardiac catheterization (the gold standard test to diagnose acute myocardial ischemia) on a patient without having an EKG.

But these tests have their limitations. That's what sensitivity and specificity measures: the limitations and deficiencies of our every-day tests.

a. <u>Sensitivity</u>: the probability of correctly identifying a case of disease. Sensitivity is the **proportion of truly diseased persons** in the screened population who are **identified as diseased** by the screening test. This is also known as the "true positive rate."

Sensitivity = TP/(TP + FN)

= true positives/(true positives + false negatives)

 i. Measures only the distribution of persons with disease

 ii. Uses data from the left column of the 2 × 2 table (Table 1-4)

 iii. Note: 1-sensitivity = false negative rate

If a test has a high sensitivity then a negative result would indicate the absence of the disease. Take for example temporal arteritis (TA), a large vessel vasculitis involving predominantly branches of the external carotid artery which occurs in patients age >50, has elevated ESR in every case. So, 100% of patients with TA have elevated ESR. The sensitivity of an abnormal ESR for TA is 100%. If a patient you suspect of having TA has a normal ESR, then the patient does not have TA.

Mnemonic for the clinical use of sensitivity: **SN-N-OUT (<u>s</u>ensitive test-<u>n</u>egative-rules <u>out</u> disease)**

b. <u>Specificity</u>: the probability of correctly identifying disease-free persons. Specificity is the **proportion of truly nondiseased persons** who are **identified as nondiseased** by the screening test. This is also known as the "true negative rate."

Specificity $= TN/(TN + FP)$

$$= \text{true negatives}/(\text{true negatives} + \text{false positives})$$

   i. Measures only the distribution of persons who are disease-free

   ii. Uses data from the right column of the 2×2 table

   iii. Note: 1-specificity = false positive rate

If a test has a high specificity then a positive result would indicate the existence of the disease. Example: CT angiogram has a very high specificity for pulmonary embolism (97%). A CT scan read as positive for pulmonary embolism is likely true.

Mnemonic for the clinical use of specificity: **SP-I-N** (**sp**ecific test-positive-rules **in** disease)

Remember SNOUT and SPIN!

For any test, there is usually a trade-off between the two. This trade-off can be represented graphically as the screening dimension curves (figure 1-3) and ROC curves (figure 1-4).

Post-test Probabilities

a. <u>Positive predictive value</u>: the probability of disease in a person who receives a positive test result. The probability that a **person with a positive test is a true positive.** (i.e., has the disease) is referred to as the "predictive value of a positive test."

Positive predictive value $= TP/(TP + FP)$

$$= \text{true positives}/$$
$$(\text{true positives} + \text{false positives})$$

   i. Measures only the distribution of persons who receive a positive test result

   ii. Uses data from the top row of the 2×2 table

b. <u>Negative predictive value</u>: the probability of no disease in a person who receives a negative test result. The probability that a **person with a negative test is a true negative** (i.e., does not have the disease) is referred to as the "predictive value of a negative test."

Negative predictive value $= TN/(TN + FN)$

$$= \text{true negatives}/$$
$$(\text{true negatives} + \text{false negatives})$$

   i. Measures only the distribution of persons who receive a negative test result

   ii. Uses data from the bottom row of the 2×2 table

c. <u>Accuracy</u>: total percentage correctly selected; the degree to which a measurement, or an estimate based on measurements, represents the true value of the attribute that is being measured.

Accuracy $= (TP + TN)/(TP + TN + FP + FN)$

$$= (\text{true positives} + \text{true negatives})/\text{total screened patients}$$

Practice Questions

1. What is the effect of increased incidence on sensitivity? On positive predictive value?

   (None; screening does not assess incidence.)

2. What is the effect of increased prevalence on sensitivity? On positive predictive value?

   (Sensitivity stays the same, positive predictive value increases.)

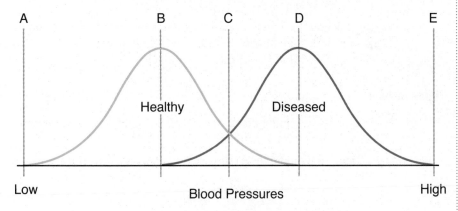

Figure 1-3. Healthy and Diseased Populations Along a Screening Dimension

1. Which cutoff point provides optimal sensitivity? (B) Specificity? (D) Accuracy? (C) Positive predictive value? (D)

2. Note: point of optimum sensitivty = point of optimum negative predictive valuepoint of optimum specificity = point of optimum positive predictive value

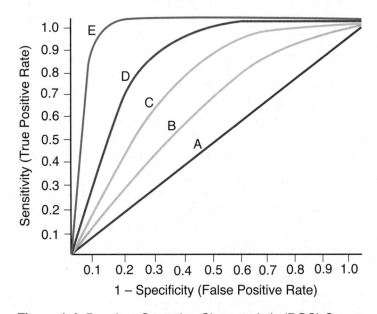

Figure 1-4. Receiver Operating Characteristic (ROC) Curves

Practice Question

1. Which curve indicates the best screening test?

STUDY DESIGNS

Bias in Research: Deviation from the Truth of Inferred Results

1. <u>Reliability</u>: ability of a test to **measure something consistently**, either across testing situations (test-retest reliability), within a test (split-half reliability), or across judges (inter-rater reliability). Think of the clustering of rifle shots at a target. (Precision)

2. <u>Validity</u>: degree to which a test **measures that which was intended**. Think of a marksman hitting the bull's-eye. Reliability is a necessary, but insufficient, condition for validity. (Accuracy)

Types of bias

1. <u>Selection bias</u> (sampling bias): the **sample selected is not representative** of the population. Examples:
   a. Predicting rates of heart disease by gathering subjects from a local health club
   b. Berkson bias: using only hospital records to estimate population prevalence
   c. Nonrespondent bias: people included in a study are different from those who are not
   d. Solution: random, independent sample; weight data

2. <u>Measurement bias</u>: information is **gathered in a manner that distorts the information**. Examples:
   a. Measuring patients' satisfaction with their respective physicians by using leading questions, e.g., "You don't like your doctor, do you?"
   b. Hawthorne effect: subjects' behavior is altered because they are being studied. Only a factor when there is no control group in a prospective study
   c. Solution: have a control group

3. <u>Experimenter expectancy</u> (Pygmalion effect): **experimenter's expectations inadvertently communicated** to subjects, who then produce the desired effects. Solution: **double-blind design**, where neither the subject nor the investigators who have contact with them know which group receives the intervention under study and which group is the control

4. <u>Lead-time bias</u>: gives a **false estimate of survival rates**. Example: Patients seem to live longer with the disease after it is uncovered by a screening test. Actually, there is no increased survival, but because the disease is discovered sooner, patients who are diagnosed *seem* to live longer. Solution: use life-expectancy to assess benefit

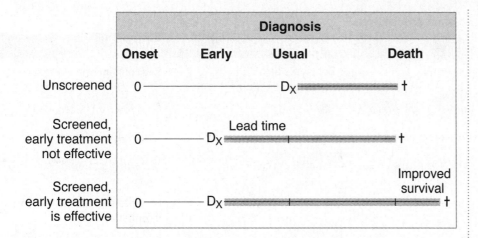

Figure 1-5. Diagnosis, Time, and Survival

5. <u>Recall bias</u>: subjects **fail to accurately recall events** in the past. Example: "How many times last year did you kiss your mother?" Likely problem in retrospective studies. Solution: confirmation

6. <u>Late-look bias</u>: **individuals with severe disease are less likely to be uncovered** in a survey **because they die first**. Example: a recent survey found that persons with AIDS reported only mild symptoms. Solution: stratify by disease severity

7. <u>Confounding bias</u>: **factor being examined is related to other factors** of less interest. Unanticipated factors obscure a relationship or make it seem like there is one when there is not. More than one explanation can be found for the presented results. Example: comparing the relationship between exercise and heart disease in two populations when one population is younger and the other is older. Are differences in heart disease due to exercise or to age? Solution: combine the results from multiple studies, meta-analysis

8. <u>Design bias</u>: **parts of the study do not fit together** to answer the question of interest. Most common issue is non-comparable control group. Example comparing the effects of an anti-hypertensive drug in hypertensives versus normotensives. Solution: random assignment. Subjects assigned to treatment or control group by a random process.

Table 1-5. Type of Bias in Research and Important Associations

Type of Bias	Definition	Important Associations	Solutions
Selection	Sample not representative	Berkson's bias, nonrespondent bias	Random, independent sample
Measurement	Gathering the information distorts it	Hawthorne effect	Control group/placebo group
Experimenter expectancy	Researcher's beliefs affect outcome	Pygmalion effect	Double-blind design
Lead-time	Early detection confused with increased survival	Benefits of screening	Measure "back-end" survival
Recall	Subjects cannot remember accurately	Retrospective studies	Multiple sources to confirm information
Late-look	Severely diseased individuals are not uncovered	Early mortality	Stratify by severity
Confounding	Unanticipated factors obscure results	Hidden factors affect results	Multiple studies, good research design
Design	Parts of study do not fit together	Non-comparable control group	Random assignment

Note

- Random error is unfortunate but okay and expected (a threat to reliability).
- Systematic error is bad and biases result (a threat to validity).

Types of Research Studies: Observational Versus Clinical Trials

Observational studies: nature is allowed to take its course, no intervention

1. Case report: brief, objective report of a **clinical characteristic or outcome from a single clinical subject** or event, $n = 1$. E.g., 23-year-old man with treatment-resistant TB. No control group

2. Case series report: objective report of a **clinical characteristic or outcome from a group of clinical subjects**, $n > 1$. E.g., patients at local hospital with treatment-resistant TB. No control group

3. Cross-sectional study: the **presence or absence of disease and other variables** are determined in each member of the study population or in a representative sample **at a particular time**. The co-occurrence of a variable and the disease can be examined.

   a. Disease prevalence rather than incidence is recorded.

   b. The temporal sequence of cause and effect cannot usually be determined in a cross-sectional study

   c. Example: who in the community now has treatment-resistant TB

4. Case-control study: identifies **a group of people with the disease** and **compares them with a suitable comparison group without the disease**. Almost always retrospective. E.g., comparing cases of treatment-resistant TB with cases of nonresistant TB

   a. Cannot assess incidence or prevalence of disease

   b. Can help determine causal relationships

   c. Very useful for studying conditions with very low incidence or prevalence

5. Cohort study: population group of those who have been **exposed to risk factor** is identified and followed over time and **compared with a group not exposed to the risk factor**. Outcome is disease incidence in each group, e.g., following a prison inmate population and marking the development of treatment-resistant TB.

a. Prospective; subjects tracked forward in time

b. Can determine incidence and causal relationships

c. Must follow population long enough for incidence to appear

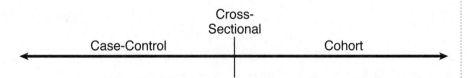

Figure 1-6. Differentiating Study Types by Time

Analyzing observational studies

1. For cross-sectional studies: use *chi*-square (x^2)

2. For cohort studies: use relative risk and/or attributable risk

   - Relative risk (RR): comparative probability asking "How much more likely?"

     a. Incidence rate of **exposed group divided by** the incidence rate of the **unexposed group**

     b. How much greater chance does one group have of contracting the disease compared with the other group?

     c. E.g., if infant mortality rate in whites is 8.9 per 1,000 live births and 18.0 in blacks per 1,000 live births, then the relative risk of blacks versus whites is 18.0 divided by 8.9 = 2.02. Compared with whites, black infants are twice as likely to die in the first year of life.

     d. For statistical analysis, yields a *p*-value

   - Attributable risk (AR): comparative probability asking "How many more cases in one group?"

     a. Incidence rate of **exposed group minus** the incidence rate of the **unexposed group**

     b. Using the same example, attributable risk is equal to 18.0 minus 8.9 = 9.1. Of every 1,000 black infants, there were 9.1 more deaths than were observed in 1,000 white infants. In this case attributable risk gives the excess mortality.

     c. Note that both relative risk and attributable risk tell us if there are differences, but do not tell us why those differences exist.

     d. Number Need to Treat (NNT) = Inverse of attributable risk (if looking at treatment)

     How many people do you have to do something to stop one case you otherwise would have had?

     Note that the Number Needed to Harm (NNH) is computed the same way. For NNH, inverse of attributable risk, where comparison focuses on exposure.

     NNH = Inverse of attributable risk (if looking at exposure)

     - 18/1,000 – 8/1,000 = 10/1,000 = AR

     - Inverse of 10/1,000 = 100 = NNT or NNH

     - Interpretations: for every 100 people treated, 1 case will be prevented

Cohort Study

	Disease	No Disease
Risk Factor	60 A	240 B
No Risk Factor	60 C	540 D

3. For case-control studies: use odds ratio (OR)

- <u>Odds ratio</u>: looks at the increased odds of getting a disease with exposure to a risk factor versus nonexposure to that factor

  a. Odds of **exposure for cases divided by** odds of **exposure for controls**

  b. The odds that a person with lung cancer was a smoker versus the odds that a person without lung cancer was a smoker

Table 1-6. Case-Control Study: Lung Cancer and Smoking

	Lung Cancer	No Lung Cancer
Smokers	659 (A)	984 (B)
Nonsmokers	25 (C)	348 (D)

  c. Odds ratio $= \dfrac{A/C}{B/D} = \dfrac{AD}{BC}$

  d. Use OR = AD/BC as working formula

  e. For the above example:

$$OR = \frac{AD}{BC} = \frac{659 \times 348}{984 \times 25} = 9.32$$

  f. Interpretation: the odds of having been a smoker are more than nine times greater for someone with lung cancer compared with someone without lung cancer.

  g. Odds ratio does not so much predict disease as estimate the strength of a risk factor.

Practice Question

How would you analyze the data from this case-control study?

Table 1-7. Case-Control Study: Colorectal Cancer and Family History Practice

	No Colorectal Cancer	Colorectal Cancer	TOTALS
Family History of Colorectal Cancer	120	60	180
No Family History of Colorectal Cancer	200	20	220
TOTALS	320	80	400
ANSWER:	$\dfrac{AD}{BC}$	$\dfrac{(60)(200)}{(120)(20)}$	OR = 5.0

Interpretation: this means that the odds of having a family history of colorectal cancer are five times greater for those who have the disease than for those who do not.

Table 1-8. Differentiating Observational Studies

Characteristic	Cross-Sectional Studies	Case-Control Studies	Cohort Studies
Time	One time point	Retrospective	Prospective
Incidence	NO	NO	YES
Prevalence	YES	NO	NO
Causality	NO	YES	YES
Role of disease	Prevalence of disease	Begin with disease	End with disease
Assesses	Association of risk factor and disease	Many risk factors for single disease	Single risk factor affecting many diseases
Data analysis	*Chi*-square to assess association	Odds ratio to estimate risk	Relative risk to estimate risk

Clinical trials (intervention studies): research that involves the administration of a test regimen to evaluate its safety and efficacy

1. Control group: subjects who **do not receive the intervention under study**; used as a **source of comparison** to be certain that the experiment group is being affected by the intervention and not by other factors. In clinical trials, this is most often a placebo group. Note that control group subjects must be **as similar as possible to intervention group** subjects.

2. For Food and Drug Administration (FDA) approval, three phases of clinical trials must be passed.

   a. Phase One: testing **safety in healthy volunteers**

   b. Phase Two: testing **protocol and dose levels** in a small group of **patient volunteers**

   c. Phase Three: testing **efficacy and occurrence of side effects** in a larger group of **patient volunteers**. Phase III is considered the definitive test.

   d. Post-marketing Survey: collecting reports of drug side-effects when out in common usage (post-FDA approval)

3. Randomized controlled clinical trial (RCT)

   a. Subjects in the study are **randomly allocated** into "intervention" and "control" groups to receive or not receive an experimental preventive or therapeutic procedure or intervention.

   b. Generally regarded as the **most scientifically rigorous** studies available in epidemiology

   c. **Double-blind RCT** is the type of study **least subject to bias**, but also the **most expensive** to conduct. Double-blind means that neither subjects nor researchers who have contact with them know whether the subjects are in the treatment or comparison group.

   • Two types of control groups
     – Placebos
       * Often 25 to 40% of patients show improvement in placebo group
     – Standard of care
       * Current treatment versus new treatment

4. Community trial: experiment in which the unit of allocation to receive a preventive or therapeutic regimen is an **entire community or political subdivision**. Does the treatment work in real-world circumstances?

5. Cross-over study: for ethical reasons, no group involved can remain untreated. **All subjects receive intervention**, but at different times. Also makes recruitment of subjects easier.

Example: AZT trials. Assume double-blind design. Group A receives AZT for 3 months, Group B is control. For second 3 months, Group B receives AZT and Group A is control.

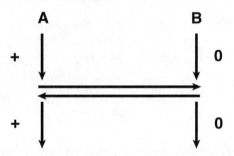

Figure 1-7. Cross-Over Study

Biostatistics 2

KEY PROBABILITY RULES

Independence: across Multiple Events

a. Combine probabilities for independent events by **multiplication**

   i. Events are **independent if** the **occurrence of one tells you nothing about the occurrence of another**. The issue here is the intersection of two sets.

   ii. E.g., if the chance of having blond hair is 0.3 and the chance of having a cold is 0.2, the chance of meeting a blond-haired person with a cold is: $0.3 \times 0.2 = 0.06$ (or 6%)

b. If events are nonindependent

   i. Multiply the probability of one event by the probability of the second, assuming that the first has occurred.

   ii. E.g., if a box has 5 white balls and 5 black balls, the chance of picking 2 black balls is: $(5/10) \times (4/9) = 0.5 \times 0.44 = 0.22$ (or 22%)

Mutually Exclusive: within a Single Event

a. Combine probabilities for mutually exclusive events by **addition**

   i. Mutually exclusive means that the **occurrence of one event precludes the occurrence of the other**. The issue here is the union of two sets.

   ii. E.g., if a coin lands on heads, it cannot be tails; the two are **mutually exclusive**. If a coin is flipped, the chance that it will be either heads or tails is: $0.5 + 0.5 = 1.0$ (or 100%)

b. If two events are not mutually exclusive

   i. The combination of probabilities is accomplished by adding the two together and subtracting out the multiplied probabilities.

   ii. E.g., if the chance of having diabetes is 10% and the chance of being obese is 30%, the chance of meeting someone who is obese or has diabetes or both is: $0.1 + 0.3 - (0.1 \times 0.3) = 0.37$ (or 37%)

Note

The COMLEX Requires You to Know:

- Rules governing joint probability
- Uses of central tendency
- Measures of variation
- Constant percentages under the normal curve
- Computing and using confidence intervals, including standard errors and z-scores
- The logic of statistics, including p-values and Type I and Type II errors
- Types of scales
- How to choose among very basic statistical tests.

You do not need to know all of statistics, but just enough to answer the presented questions

Mutually Exclusive	Nonmutually Exclusive
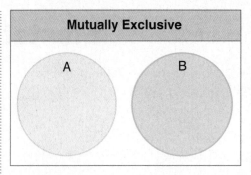	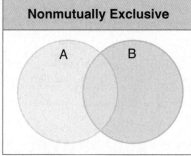

Figure 2-1. Venn Diagram Representations of Mutually Exclusive and Nonmutually Exclusive Events

Practice Questions

1. If the prevalence of diabetes is 10%, what is the chance that 3 people selected at random from the population will all have diabetes? $(0.1 \times 0.1 \times 0.1 = 0.001)$

2. Chicago has a population of 10,000,000. If 25% of the population is Latino, 30% is African American, 5% is Arab American, and 40% is of European extraction, how many people in Chicago are classified as other than of European extraction? $(25\% + 30\% + 5\% = 60\%.\ 60\% \times 10,000,000 = 6,000,000)$

3. At age 65, the probability of surviving for the next 5 years is 0.8 for a white man and 0.9 for a white woman. For a married couple who are both white and age 65, the probability that the wife will be a living widow 5 years later is:
   (A) 90%
   (B) 72%
   (C) 18%
   (D) 10%
   (E) 8%

Answer: **C.** This question asks for the joint probability of independent events; therefore, the probabilities are multiplied. Chance of the wife being alive: 90%. Chance of the husband being dead: 100% – 80% = 20%. Therefore, $0.9 \times 0.2 = 18\%$.

4. If the chance of surviving for 1 year after being diagnosed with prostate cancer is 80% and the chance of surviving for 2 years after diagnosis is 60%, what is the chance of surviving for 2 years after diagnosis, given that the patient is alive at the end of the first year?
   (A) 20%
   (B) 48%
   (C) 60%
   (D) 75%
   (E) 80%

Answer: **D.** The question tests knowledge of "conditional probability." Out of 100 patients, 80 are alive at the end of 1 year and 60 at the end of 2 years. The 60 patients alive after 2 years are a subset of those that make it to the first year. Therefore, $60/80 = 75\%$.

DESCRIPTIVE STATISTICS: SUMMARIZING THE DATA

Distributions

Statistics deals with the world as distributions. These distributions are summarized by a **central tendency and variation around that center**. The most important distribution is the **normal or Gaussian curve**. This "bell-shaped" curve is **symmetric**, with one side the mirror image of the other.

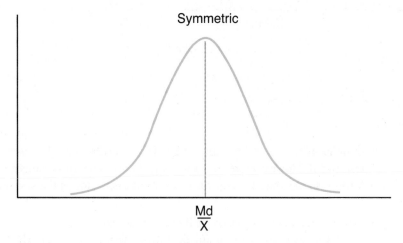

Figure 2-2. Measures of Central Tendency

Central tendency

a. Central tendency is a general term for several characteristics of the distribution of a set of values or measurements around a value **at or near the middle of the set**.

- **Mean ($\overline{X}$) (a synonym for average)**: the sum of the values of the observations divided by the numbers of observations
- **Median (Md)**: the simplest division of a set of measurements is into two parts — the upper half and lower half. The **point on the scale that divides the group** in this way is the median. The measurement below which half the observations fall: the 50th percentile
- **Mode**: the **most frequently occurring value** in a set of observations

Given the distribution of numbers: 3, 6, 7, 7, 9, 10, 12, 15, 16

The mode is 7, the median is 9, the mean is 9.4

- Skewed curves: not all curves are normal. Sometimes the curve is skewed either positively or negatively. A **positive skew** has the tail to the right and the **mean greater than the median**. A **negative skew** has the tail to the left and the **median greater than the mean**. For skewed distributions, the median is a better representation of central tendency than is the mean.

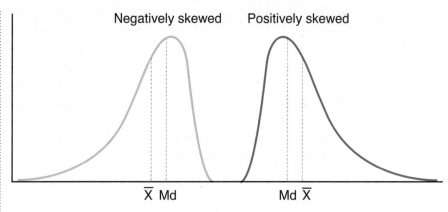

Figure 2-3. Skewed Distribution Curves

Measures of variability

The simplest measure of variability is the **range**, the difference between the highest and the lowest score. But the range is unstable and changes easily. A more stable and more useful measure of dispersion is the **standard deviation**.

a. To calculate the standard deviation, we first subtract the mean from each score to obtain **deviations from the mean**. This will give us both positive and negative values. But squaring the deviations, the next step, makes them all positive. The *squared* deviations are added together and *divided by the number of cases*. The square root is taken of this average, and the result is the standard deviation (S or SD).

$$s = \sqrt{\frac{\sum(X - \overline{X})^2}{n - 1}}$$

The square of the standard deviation (s^2) equals the **variance**.

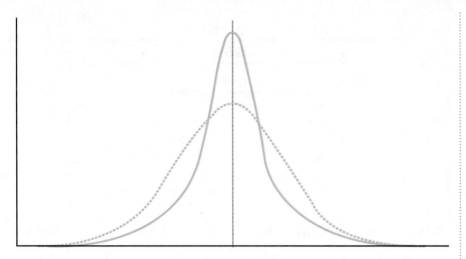

Figure 2-4. Comparison of 2 Normal Curves with the Same Means, but Different Standard Deviations

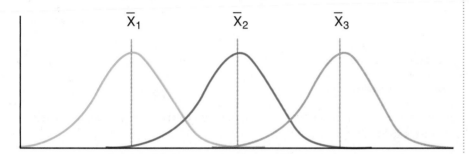

Figure 2-5. Comparison of 3 Normal Curves with the Same Standard Deviations, but Different Means

b. You will not be asked to calculate a standard deviation or variance on the exam, but you do need to know what they are and how they relate to the normal curve. In ANY normal curve, a constant proportion of the cases fall within one, two, and three standard deviations of the mean.

    i. Within one standard deviation: 68%

    ii. Within two standard deviations: 95.5%

    iii. Within three standard deviations: 99.7%

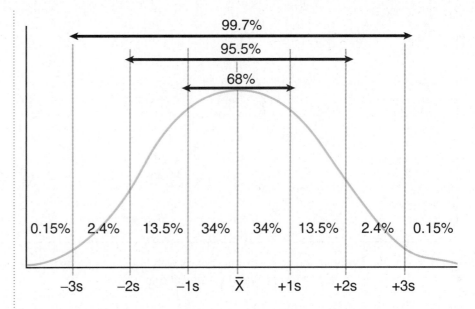

Figure 2-6. Percentage of Cases within 1, 2, and 3 Standard Deviations of the Mean in a Normal Distribution

Know the constants presented in Figure 2-6 and be able to combine the given constants to answer simple questions.

Practice Questions

1. In a normal distribution curve, what percent of the cases are below 2s below the mean? (2.5%)

2. In a normal distribution curve, what percent of the cases are above 1s below the mean? (84%)

3. A student who scores at the 97.5 percentile falls where on the curve? (2s above the mean)

4. A student took two tests:

	Score	Mean	Standard Deviation
Test A	45%	30%	5%
Test B	60%	40%	10%

On which test did the student do better, relative to his classmates? (On Test A, she scored 3s above the mean versus only 2s above the mean for Test B.)

INFERENTIAL STATISTICS: GENERALIZATIONS FROM A SAMPLE TO THE POPULATION AS A WHOLE

The purpose of inferential statistics is to designate **how likely it is that a given finding is simply the result of chance**. Inferential statistics would not be necessary if investigators studied all members of a population. However, because we can rarely observe and study entire populations, we try to select samples that are representative of the entire population so that we can **generalize the results from the sample to the population**.

Confidence Intervals

Confidence intervals are a way of admitting that any measurement from a sample is only an **estimate** of the population. Although the estimate given from the sample is likely to be close, the true values for the population may be above or below the sample values. A confidence interval **specifies how far above or below a sample-based value the population value lies** within a given range, from a possible high to a possible low. Reality, therefore, is most likely to be somewhere within the specified range.

Practice Questions

1. Assuming the graph (Figure 2-7) presents 95% confidence intervals, which groups, if any, are statistically different from each other?

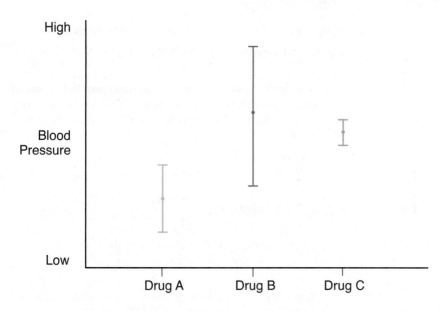

Figure 2-7. Blood Pressures at End of Clinical Trial for 3 Drugs

Answer: When comparing two groups, any overlap of confidence intervals means the groups are not significantly different. Therefore, if the graph represents 95% confidence intervals, Drugs B and C are no different in their effects; Drug B is no different from Drug A; Drug A has a better effect than Drug C.

Confidence intervals for relative risk and odds ratios

If the given confidence interval contains 1.0, then there is no statistically significant effect of exposure.

Example:

Relative Risk	Confidence Interval	Interpretation
1.77	(1.22 – 2.45)	Statistically significant (increased risk)
1.63	(0.85 – 2.46)	NOT statistically significant (risk is the same)
0.78	(0.56 – 0.94)	Statistically significant (decreased risk)

- If RR > 1.0, then subtract 1.0 and read as percent increase. So 1.77 means one group has 77% more cases than the other.
- If RR < 1.0, then subtract from 1.0 and read as reduction in risk. So 0.78 means one group has a 22% reduction in risk.

Understanding Statistical Inference

The goal of science is to define reality. Think about statistics as the referee in the game of science. We have all agreed to play the game according to the judgment calls of the referee, even though we know the referee can and will be wrong sometimes.

Basic steps of statistical inference

a. Define the research question: what are you trying to show?

b. Define the null hypothesis, *generally the opposite of what you hope to show*

    i. Null hypothesis says that the **findings are the result of chance or random factors**. If you want to show that a drug works, the null hypothesis will be that the drug does NOT work.

    ii. Alternative hypothesis says what is left after defining the null hypothesis. In this example, that the drug does actually work.

c. Two types of null hypotheses

    i. One-tailed, i.e., directional or "one-sided," such that one group is *either* greater than, or less than, the other. E.g., Group A is not < than Group B, or Group A is not > Group B

    ii. Two-tailed, i.e., nondirectional or "two-sided," such that two groups are not the same. E.g., Group A = Group B

Hypothesis testing

At this point, data are collected and analyzed by the appropriate statistical test. How to run these tests is not tested on COMLEX, but you may need to be able to interpret results of statistical tests with which you are presented.

a. *p*-value: to interpret output from a statistical test, focus on the *p*-value. The term *p*-value refers to two things. In its first sense, the *p*-value is a standard against which we compare our results. In the second sense, the *p*-value is a result of computation.

i. The **computed *p*-value is compared with the *p*-value criterion to test statistical significance**. If the computed value is less than the criterion, we have achieved statistical significance. In general, the smaller the *p* the better.

ii. The *p*-value criterion is traditionally set at $p \leq 0.05$. (Assume that these are the criteria if no other value is explicitly specified.) Using this standard:

- If $p \leq 0.05$, reject the null hypothesis (reached statistical significance)
- If $p > 0.05$, do not reject the null hypothesis (has not reached statistical significance).

Note

We never accept the null hypothesis. We either reject it or fail to reject it. Saying we do not have sufficient evidence to reject it is not the same as being able to affirm that it is true.

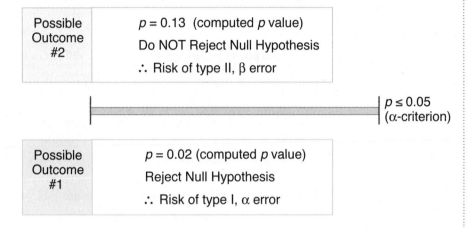

Figure 2-8. Making Decisions Using *p*-Values

- If $p = 0.02$, reject the null hypothesis, i.e., decide that the drug works
- If $p = 0.13$, fail to reject the null hypothesis, i.e., decide that the drug does not work

Types of errors

Just because we reject the null hypothesis, we are not certain that we are correct. For some reason, the results given by the sample may be inconsistent with the full population. If this is true, any decision we make on the basis of the sample could be in error. There are two possible types of errors that we could make:

i. Type I error (α error): **rejecting the null hypothesis when it is really true**, i.e., assuming a statistically significant effect on the basis of the sample when there is none in the population, e.g., asserting that the drug works when it doesn't. The chance of type I error is given by the *p*-value. If $p = 0.05$, then the chance of a type I error is 5 in 100, or 1 in 20.

ii. Type II error (β error): **failing to reject the null hypothesis when it is really false**, i.e., declaring no significant effect on the basis of the sample when there really is one in the population, e.g., asserting the drug does not work when it really does. The chance of a type II error cannot be directly estimated from the *p*-value.

Note

- If the null hypothesis is rejected, there is no chance of a type II error. If the null hypothesis is not rejected, there is no chance of a type I error.

- Type I error (error of commission) is generally considered worse than type II error (error of omission).

Meaning of the p-value

    i. Provides criterion for making decisions about the null hypothesis

    ii. Quantifies the chances that a decision to reject the null hypothesis will be wrong

    iii. Tells statistical significance, not clinical significance or likelihood of benefit

    iv. Limits to the *p*-value: the *p*-value does NOT tell us

        – The chance that an individual patient will benefit

        – The percentage of patients who will benefit

        – The degree of benefit expected for a given patient

Statistical power

    i. In statistics, **power** is the capacity to detect a difference if there is one.

    ii. Just as increasing the power of a microscope makes it easier to see what is going on in histology, increasing statistical power allows us to detect what is happening in the data.

    iii. Power is directly related to type II error: $1 - \beta =$ Power

    iv. There are a number of ways to increase statistical power. The most common is to increase the sample size.

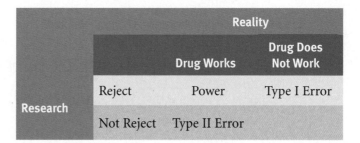

NOMINAL, ORDINAL, INTERVAL, AND RATIO SCALES

To convert the world into numbers, we use 4 types of scales. Focus on nominal and interval scales for the exam.

Table 2-1. Types of Scales in Statistics

Type of Scale	Description	Key Words	Examples
Nominal (Categorical)	Different groups	This or that or that	Gender, comparing among treatment interventions
Ordinal	Groups in sequence	Comparative quality, rank order	Olympic medals, class rank in medical school
Interval	Exact differences among groups	Quantity, mean, and standard deviation	Height, weight, blood pressure, drug dosage
Ratio	Interval + true zero point	Zero means zero	Temperature measured in degrees Kelvin

Nominal or Categorical Scale

A nominal scale puts people into boxes, without specifying the relationship between the boxes. Gender is a common example of a nominal scale with two groups, male and female. Anytime you can say, "It's either this or that," you are dealing with a nominal scale. Other examples: cities, drug versus control group.

Ordinal Scale

Numbers can also be used to express ordinal or rank order relations. For example, we say Ben is taller than Fred. Now we know more than just the category in which to place someone. We know something about the relationship between the categories (quality). What we do not know is how different the two categories are (quantity). Class rank in medical school and medals at the Olympics are examples of ordinal scales.

Interval Scale

Uses a scale graded in equal increments. In the scale of length, we know that one inch is equal to any other inch. Interval scales allow us to say not only that two things are different, but also by how much. If a measurement has a mean and a standard deviation, treat it as an interval scale. It is sometimes called a "numeric scale."

Ratio Scale

The best measure is the ratio scale. This scale orders things and contains equal intervals, like the previous two scales. But it also has one additional quality: a **true zero point**. In a ratio scale, zero is a floor, you can't go any lower. Measuring temperature using the Kelvin scale yields ratio scale measurement.

Note

The scales are hierarchically arranged from least information provided (nominal) to most information provided (ratio). Any scale can be degraded to a lower scale, e.g., interval data can be treated as ordinal.

For the COMLEX, concentrate on identifying nominal and interval scales.

STATISTICAL TESTS

Table 2-2. Types of Scales and Basic Statistical Tests

Name of Statistical Test	Variables		Comment
	Interval	Nominal	
Pearson Correlation	2	0	Is there a linear relationship?
Chi-square	0	2	Any # of groups
t-test	1	1	2 groups only
One-way ANOVA	1	1	2 or more groups
Matched pairs *t*-test	1	1	2 groups, linked data pairs, before and after
Repeated measures ANOVA	1	1	More than 2 groups, linked data

ANOVA = Analysis of Variance

Correlation Analysis (r, ranges from −1.0 to +1.0)

a. A **positive value** means that **two variables go together in the same direction,** e.g., MCAT scores have a positive correlation with medical school grades.

b. A **negative value** means that the **presence of one variable is associated with the absence of another variable,** e.g., there is a negative correlation between age and quickness of reflexes.

c. The further from 0, the stronger the relationship (r = 0)

d. A **zero correlation** means that **two variables have no linear relation to one another,** e.g., height and success in medical school.

e. Graphing correlations using scatterplots

    i. Scatterplot will show points that approximate a line.

    ii. Be able to interpret scatterplots of data: positive slope, negative slope, and which of a set of scatterplots indicates a stronger correlation.

Strong, Positive Correlation	Weak, Positive Correlation	Strong, Negative Correlation	Weak, Negative Correlation	Zero Correlation (r = 0)

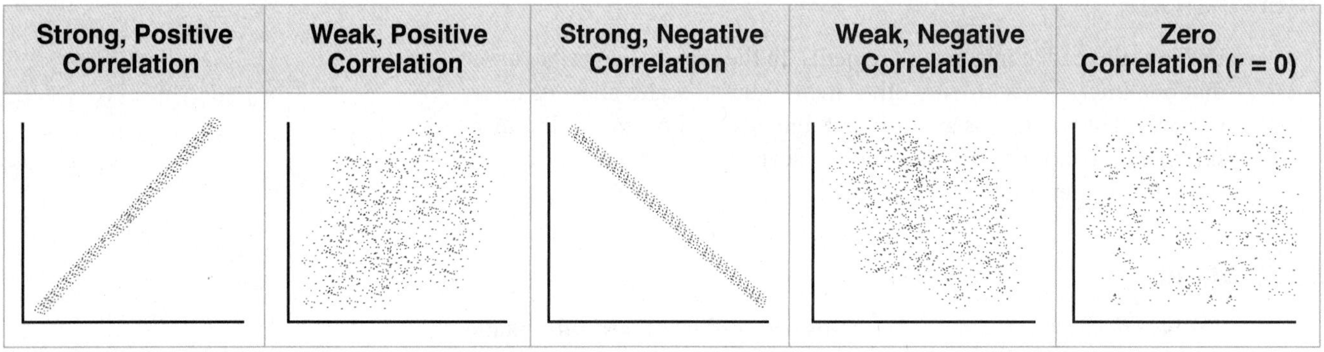

Figure 2-9. Scatterplots and Correlations

f. NOTE: Correlation, by itself, does not mean causation.

A correlation coefficient indicates the **degree to which two measures are related,** not why they are related. It does not mean that one variable necessarily causes the other. There are 2 types of correlations.

a. Pearson correlation: compares 2 interval level variables

b. Spearman correlation: compares 2 ordinal level variables

t-tests

a. Output of a *t*-test is a "*t*" statistic

b. **Comparing the means of 2 groups** from a single nominal variable, using means from an interval variable to see whether the groups are different

c. Used for two groups only, i.e., compares 2 means. E.g., do patients with MI who are in psychotherapy have a reduced length of convalescence compared with those who are not in therapy?

d. "Pooled *t*-test" is regular *t*-test, assuming the variances of the 2 groups are the same

e. Matched pairs *t*-test: each person in one group is matched with a person in the second. Applies to before and after measures and linked data

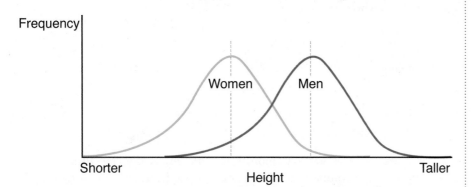

Figure 2-10. Comparison of the Distributions of Two Groups

Analysis of Variance (ANOVA)

a. Output from an ANOVA is one or more "F" statistics

b. One-way: **compares means of many groups** (two or more) **of a single nominal variable** using an interval variable. Significant p-value means that at least two of the tested groups are different.

c. Two-way: **compares means of groups generated by two nominal variables** using an interval variable. Can test effects of several variables at the same time.

d. Repeated measures ANOVA: multiple measurements of same people over time

Chi-square

a. Nominal data only

b. Any number of groups (2×2, 2×3, 3×3, etc.)

c. Tests to see whether two nominal variables are independent, e.g., testing the efficacy of a new drug by comparing the number of recovered patients given the drug with those who are not

Table 2-3. *Chi*-Square Analysis for Nominal Data

	New Drug	Placebo	Totals
Recovered	45	35	80
Not Recovered	15	25	40
Totals	60	60	120

Review Questions

1. A recent study found a higher incidence of SIDS for children of mothers who smoke. If the rate for smoking mothers is 230/100,000 and the rate for nonsmoking mothers is 71/100,000, what is the relative risk for children of mothers who smoke?

    (A) 159
    (B) 32
    (C) 230
    (D) 3.2
    (E) 8.4

2. A researcher wishing to demonstrate the efficacy of a new treatment for hypertension compares the effects of the new treatment versus a placebo. This study provides a test of the null hypothesis that the new treatment has no effect on hypertension. In this case, the null hypothesis should be considered as

    (A) positive proof that the stated premise is correct
    (B) the assertion of a statistically significant relationship
    (C) the assumption that the study design is adequate
    (D) the probability that the relationship being studied is the result of random factors
    (E) the result the experimenter hopes to achieve

3. A standardized test was used to assess the level of depression in a group of patients on a cardiac care unit. The results yielded a mean of 14.60 with confidence limits of 14.55 and 14.65. This presented confidence limit is

    (A) less precise, but has a higher confidence than 14.20 and 15.00
    (B) more precise, but has a lower confidence than 14.20 and 15.00
    (C) less precise, but has a lower confidence than 14.20 and 15.00
    (D) more precise, but has a higher confidence than 14.20 and 15.00
    (E) indeterminate, because the degree of confidence is not specified

4. A recently published report explored the relationship between height and subjects' self-reported cholesterol levels in a sample of 44- to 65-year-old males. The report included a correlation of +0.02, computed for the relationship between height and cholesterol level. One of the possible interpretations of this correlation is:

    (A) The statistic proves that there is no definable relationship between the two specified variables.
    (B) There is a limited causal relationship between the two specified variables.
    (C) A real-life relationship may exist, but the measurement error is too large.
    (D) A scatterplot of the data will show a clear linear slope.
    (E) The correlation is significant at the 0.02 level.

Items 5 through 7

The Collaborative Depression study examined several factors impacting the detection and treatment of depression. One primary focus was to develop a biochemical test for diagnosing depression. For this research, a subpopulation of 300 persons was selected and subjected to the Dexamethasone Suppression Test (DST). The results of the study are as follows:

	Actual Depression	
	NO	YES
DST Results		
Depressed	87	102
Nondepressed	63	48

Using this table, the following ratios were computed:

(A) 102:150

(B) 102:189

(C) 63:150

(D) 87:150

(E) 63:111

5. Which of these ratios measures specificity?

6. Which of these ratios measures positive predictive value?

7. Which of these ratios measures sensitivity?

8. Initial research supported a conclusion that a positive relationship exists between coffee consumption and heart disease. However, subsequent, more extensive research suggests that this initial conclusion was the result of a Type I error. In this context, a Type I error

(A) means there is no real-life significance, but statistical significance is found

(B) suggests that the researcher has probably selected the wrong statistical test

(C) results from a nonexclusionary clause in the null hypothesis

(D) indicates that the study failed to detect an effect statistically, when one is present in the population

(E) has a probability in direct proportion to the size of the test statistic

9. A survey of a popular seaside community (population =1,225) found the local inhabitants to have unusually elevated blood pressures. In this survey, just over 95% of the population had systolics between 110 and 190. Assuming a normal distribution for these assessed blood pressures, the standard deviation for systolic blood pressure in this seaside community is most likely

(A) 10

(B) 20

(C) 30

(D) 40

(E) 50

10. A report of a clinical trial of a new drug for herpes simplex II versus a placebo noted that the new drug gave a higher proportion of success than the placebo. The report ended with the statement: *chi*-sq = 4.72, p <0.05. In light of this information, we may conclude that

    (A) fewer than one in 20 will fail to benefit from the drug

    (B) the chance that an individual patient will fail to benefit is less than 0.05

    (C) if the drug were effective, the probability of the reported finding is less than one in 20

    (D) if the drug were ineffective, the probability of the reported finding is less than 0.05

    (E) the null hypothesis is false

11. A recent study was conducted to assess the intelligence of students enrolled in an alternative high school program. The results showed the IQs of the students distributed according to the normal curve, with a mean of 115 and a standard deviation of 10. Based on this information it is most reasonable to conclude that

    (A) 50% of the students will have an IQ below the standard mean of 100

    (B) 5% of the students will have IQs below 105

    (C) students with IQs of 125 are at the 84th percentile

    (D) 2.5% of the students will have IQs greater than 125

    (E) all of the students' scores fall between 85 and 135

12. A correlation of +0.56 is found between alcohol consumption and systolic blood pressure in men. This correlation is significant at the 0.001 level. From this information we may conclude that:

    (A) There is no association between alcohol consumption and systolic pressure.

    (B) Men who consume less alcohol are at lower risk for increased systolic pressure.

    (C) Men who consume less alcohol are at higher risk for increased systolic pressure.

    (D) High alcohol consumption can cause increased systolic pressure in men.

    (E) High systolic pressure can cause increased alcohol consumption in men.

Questions 13-15

To assess the effects of air pollution on health, a random sample of 250 residents of Denver, Colorado, were given thorough checkups every 2 years. This same procedure was followed on a matched sample of persons living in Fort Collins, Colorado, a smaller town located about 60 miles north. Some of the results, presented as percent mortality, are displayed in the table below.

Table 1. Cumulative Mortality in Two Communities Over 10 Years

	1975	1977	1979	1981	1983	1985
Denver	4%	6%	10%	15%	22%	28%
Fort Collins	2%	3%	7%	10%	12%	14%

13. This type of study can be best characterized as a

    (A) cross-sectional study
    (B) clinical case trial design
    (C) cross-over study
    (D) cohort study
    (E) case-control study

14. According to the data presented in the table, the cumulative relative risk for living in Denver by the year 1981 was

    (A) 0.67
    (B) 5%
    (C) 1.5
    (D) 2.0
    (E) 1.33

15. What statistical test would you run to test whether there was a difference between the cumulative mortality rate for Denver and Fort Collins in 1985?

    (A) *t*-test
    (B) ANOVA
    (C) Regression
    (D) Correlation coefficient
    (E) *Chi*-square

16. A study is conducted to examine the relationship between myocardial infarctions and time spent driving when commuting to and from work. One hundred married males who had suffered infarcts were selected and their average commuting time ascertained from either the subject, or if the infarct had been fatal, their spouse. A comparison group of 100 married males who had not suffered infarcts was also selected and their average commuting time recorded. When examining this data for a possibly causal relationship between commuting time and the occurrence of myocardial infarcts, the most likely measure of association is

   (A) odds ratio
   (B) relative risk
   (C) incidence rate
   (D) attributable risk
   (E) correlation coefficient

17. A particular association determines membership based on members' IQ scores. Only those people who have documented IQ scores at least two standard deviations above the mean on the Wechsler Adult Intelligence Scale, Revised (WAIS-R), are eligible for admission. Out of a group of 400 people randomly selected from the population at large, how many would be eligible for membership in this society?

   (A) 2
   (B) 4
   (C) 6
   (D) 8
   (E) 10

18. A physician wishes to study whether moderate alcohol consumption is associated with heart disease. If, in reality, moderate alcohol consumption leads to a relative risk of heart disease of 0.60, the physician wants to have a 95% chance of detecting an effect this large in the planned study. This statement is an illustration of specifying

   (A) alpha error
   (B) beta error
   (C) a null hypothesis
   (D) criterion odds
   (E) statistical power

19. Public health officials were examining a suspicious outbreak of diarrhea in an inner city community child-care center. Center workers identified children with diarrhea and all children at the center were studied. Officials discovered that children who drank liquids from a bottle were more likely to have diarrhea than children who drank from a glass. They concluded that drinking from unclean bottles was the cause of the outbreak. The use of bottles was subsequently banned from the center. The outbreak subsided. Which of the following is the most likely source of bias in this study?

   (A) Recall bias
   (B) Lead-time bias
   (C) Measurement bias
   (D) Confounding
   (E) Random differences as to the identification of diarrhea

20. Suicides in teenagers in a small Wisconsin town had been a rare event before 11 cases were recorded in 1994. This unusual occurrence led to the initiation of an investigation to try to determine the reason for this upsurge. The researchers suspect that the suicides are linked to the increasing numbers of new families who have recently moved to the town. The best type of study to explore this possibility would likely be a

(A) cohort study

(B) case-control study

(C) cross-over study

(D) cross-sectional study

(E) community trial study

Items 21-30

Which statistical test will most likely be used to analyze the data suggested by the following statements?

(A) *t*-test

(B) *Chi*-square test

(C) One-way ANOVA

(D) Two-way ANOVA

(E) Pearson correlation

(F) Matched pairs *t*-test

21. Comparing the blood sugar levels of husbands and wives.

22. Comparing the number of staff who do or do not call in sick for each of three different nursing shifts.

23. Is there a relationship between time spent on studying and test score?

24. A researcher believes that boys with same-sex siblings are more likely to have higher testosterone levels.

25. A doctor believes that drawing blood is faster with a vacutainer for someone once that person is trained, but faster with a standard syringe for someone with no training.

26. Twenty rats are coated with margarine and 20 with butter as part of a study to explore the carcinogenic effects of oleo.

27. To assess the efficacy of surgical interventions for breast cancer, the quality of life, measured on a ten-point scale, of 30 women who underwent radical mastectomies was compared with 30 women who received radiation treatments and 15 women who refused any medical intervention.

28. Comparison of passing and failure rates at each of three test sites.

29. Comparison of actual measured test scores for students at each of three test sites.

30. Assessing changes in blood pressure for a group of 30 hypertensives 1 week before and 3 months after beginning a course of antihypertensive medication.

31. In a study of chemical workers, 400 workers with respiratory disease and 150 workers without respiratory disease were selected for examination. The investigators obtained a history of exposure to a particular solvent in both groups of workers. Among workers with the respiratory disease, 250 gave a history of exposure to the solvent, compared to 50 of the workers without respiratory disease. The study design can best be described as a

    (A) case-control study
    (B) cohort study
    (C) cross-sectional study
    (D) community trial
    (E) comparative clinical trial

32. The air quality is assessed in two Midwestern cities, one in which a government program has instituted reducing the amount of carbon monoxide emissions allowed, and one without the government program. The rates of respiratory problems in both cities are recorded over a 5-year period. Given the design of this study, an appropriate one-tailed null hypothesis would be

    (A) air quality is related to respiratory problems in both of the cities under study.
    (B) air quality is related to respiratory problems in the city with the government program but not in the other city.
    (C) no evidence will be found for differences in air quality between the two cities.
    (D) the rate of respiratory problems in the city with the government program will not be any lower than that of the other city.
    (E) air quality will be inversely related to the rate of respiratory problems in both cities.

Answers

1. **Answer: D.** Relative risk means divide, compute the ratio between the two groups. [230/71 = 3.2]

2. **Answer: D.** Definition question. Null hypothesis is a statement of chance, the opposite of what the researcher hopes to find.

3. **Answer: B.** Smaller interval is more precise, but less confident. Precise means narrower interval. 95% confidence yields a smaller interval than 99% confidence.

4. **Answer: C.** One reason for a near-zero correlation is that the error of measurement is so large that it obscures an underlying relationship. Shows no linear relationship. Does not mean cause. Number given is coefficient, not p-value.

5. **Answer: C.** True negatives, out of all nondiseased. [TN/(TN+FP)] = [63/(87+63)]. Note, divided by number ending in "0".

6. **Answer: B.** True positives, out of all positives. [TP/(TP+FP)] = [102/(102+87)]. Note, divided by number ending in "9".

7. **Answer: A.** True positives, out of all diseased. [TP/(TP+FN)] = [102/(102+48)]. Note, divided by number ending in "0".

8. **Answer: A.** Type I error means the researcher rejected the null hypothesis, but should not have. This means that although statistical significance is found, there is no real-world significance. By reversing the clauses in the answer, the correct answer becomes more apparent. Answer D is a good definition of a Type II error.

9. **Answer: B.** If 95% of cases fall between 110 and 190 and the distribution is symmetrical, then the mean must be 150, and the numbers given are two standard deviations above and below the mean. This means that two standard deviations must equal 40 and that one standard deviation equals 20.

10. **Answer: D.** Key here is the "p-value." Ignore the *chi*-square value. If less than 0.05, this gives the chance of a Type I error. Therefore, the probability of the finding if the drug was ineffective.

11. **Answer: C.** This is one standard deviation above the mean. [115 + 10]. Below this point are 84% of the cases using the normal curve.

12. **Answer: B.** The given correlation is statistically significant at the 0.001 level and can therefore be interpreted. It is a positive correlation, suggesting that high goes with high and low goes with low. Avoid answers that suggest a causal relationship.

13. **Answer: D.** People in the two communities are followed forward in time and incidence (mortality) is the outcome.

14. **Answer: C.** Key is to focus only on 1981. Relative risk means divide. [15%/10% = 1.5] or 1.5 times the risk.

15. **Answer: E.** Denver versus Fort Collins is one nominal variable with two groups. Dead versus alive is the second nominal variable. Two nominal variables with $n > 25$ = *chi*-square.

16. **Answer: A.** This is a case-control study (infarcts versus no infarcts). Therefore, use an odds ratio. The data is not incidence data, so relative risk does not apply.

17. **Answer: E.** The IQ is scaled to have a mean of 100 and a standard deviation of 15. What percent of the cases are above two standard deviations above the mean? (2.5%)
Therefore, what is 2.5% of 400? (10)

18. **Answer: E.** Power is the chance of detecting a difference in the study if there really is a difference in the real world. The question tells us what chance the researcher will have of finding a difference.

19. **Answer: D.** Bottle versus glass is confounded with age or maturity. The other options, while possible, are unlikely.

20. **Answer: B.** Select suicide cases and compare with nonsuicides (controls).

21. **Answer: F.** Blood sugar levels are ratio data, treated as interval data. Husbands and wives are nominal, but are nonindependent, matched pairs; therefore, matched pairs t-test.

22. **Answer: B.** Staff either call in sick or do not (nominal variable) over three shifts (nominal variable). Two nominal variables with a 2×3 design, *chi*-square.

23. **Answer: E.** "Is there a relationship?" between two interval level variables. Pearson correlation.

24. **Answer: A.** Same sex versus no same sex (nominal variable). Testosterone level is assessed as ratio and treated as interval. Therefore, simple t-test.

25. **Answer: D.** Vacutainer versus standard syringe (nominal), training versus no training (nominal), and time (interval). Two nominal and one interval = two-way ANOVA.

26. **Answer: B.** Margarine versus butter (nominal), cancer versus no cancer (nominal). Therefore, *chi*-square.

27. **Answer: C.** Three types of treatment: surgery, radiation, and none (nominal variable, three groups), quality of life on the given scale (interval). Therefore, one-way ANOVA.

28. **Answer: B.** Passing versus failure (nominal), three sites (nominal). Therefore, *chi*-square.

29. **Answer: C.** Three sites (nominal) with actual test scores (interval). Therefore, one-way ANOVA.

30. **Answer: F.** Before and after (nominal, two-groups, matched pairs), and blood pressure (interval). Therefore, matched pairs t-test.

31. **Answer: A.** Respiratory (cases) versus nonrespiratory disease (controls), looking at history.

32. **Answer: D.** The correct statement needs to be a one-directional statement of no effect. "Not any lower than" satisfies this criterion.

Behavioral Science

Life in the United States 3

FAMILY LIFE

Marriage and Divorce

1. The divorce rate has been rising steadily for more than 40 years.
2. It is estimated that nearly half of all marriages in the United States today will end in divorce.
3. As recent as 2012, the United States has had the sixth highest rate of divorce worldwide.
4. Women who are college graduates are less likely to divorce than women who do not complete high school.
5. Married individuals are associated with a higher Well-Being Index Score than individuals associated with unmarried categories.
6. The divorce rate among physicians is higher than for people of other occupational groups.
7. Marriage has a better chance of success if both partners are of similar backgrounds, race, intelligence, and education.
8. Divorce rates are higher for children of divorced parents, couples who marry young, lower socioeconomic status (SES), very high SES.
9. Divorced persons have the highest rates of hospitalization for mental disorders.
10. Divorce is hard on children: more behavior problems, delayed physical and mental development. However, staying in a hostile environment can be even harder on children.
11. Marital satisfaction is higher for couples without children.

2011 Latest U.S. Separation, Divorce and Married Data

Marital Status	Well-Being Index Score
Married	68.8
Single	65.0
Windowed	63.5
Domestic Partner	63.3
Divorced	59.7
Separated	55.9
National Adults	66.2

Note

The COMLEX Requires You to Know:

Some basic facts about life in the United States, including:

- Family life
- Suicide
- Use of health care
- AIDS

(General patterns and trends are more important than specific numbers.)

Age at marriage for those who divorce in America (2011)

Age	Women	Men
Age < 20	27.6%	11.7%
Age 20 to 24	36.6%	38.8%
Age 25 to 29	16.4%	22.3%
Age 30 to 34	8.5%	11.6%
Age 35 to 39	5.1%	6.5%

SOCIOECONOMIC STATUS (SES)

1. SES: weighted combination of occupation and education. Income is *not* used as a direct determinant of SES.

2. In general, there is a positive correlation between SES and good things such as good mental health, life satisfaction, freedom from illness, and life expectancy. Exceptions to this are anxiety disorders and breast cancer in women, and more bipolar in either gender. High-SES people marry later and have children later.

3. Lower SES is also associated with more sharply defined sex-role expectations, more rigidity in expectations of individuals, and more action-oriented language rather than conceptual language.

4. Most low-SES families are single-parent families. More than 80% of single families are headed by women.

SUICIDE

Statistics

a. Annually, more than 35,000 commit suicide in the United States and more than one million worldwide.

b. Annually, as many as 600,000 (2.9% of those older than 18) attempt suicide.

c. Suicide rate in the U.S. is nearly 12 per 100,000

d. Between 10 and 20 suicide attempts for every one that succeeds
    i. Men commit suicide 4 times as often as women
    ii. Women attempt suicide 3 times as often as men

e. Firearms are the most likely method by which <u>either</u> men or women *commit* suicide. Pills/poisons most likely method for women to *attempt* suicide

f. For people aged 15 to 24, suicide is the third leading cause of death; for those aged 25 to 35, it is the second.

g. Suicides outnumber homicides in the U.S.

Teen Suicide

a. 2009 was 6.3%. 2011 rate was 7.8%. These increasing numbers reflect more teen suicides related to bullying.

b. Lifetime prevalence of suicide ideation: 54%; past 12 months: 26%; specific method: 10%

   c. 60% say they had a friend who committed suicide.

   d. For this age group only: ethnic group with the highest suicide rate is Native Americans. This age group has the highest rate for all ages of Native Americans.

   e. Psychological autopsy studies show that almost all had some prior mental illness, although most were undetected. 50% had been identified or had sought help.

      i. Highest risk: boys aged 15 to 19 who are depressed and/or drink heavily

      ii. Higher rates in single-parent families

      iii. Precipitating event is some shameful or humiliating experience

   f. Educational prevention programs: increased knowledge but no demonstrated change on rates.

   g. Best prevention: identify and address the underlying mental illness or substance abuse. Treat cause, not symptom.

Epidemiologic Facts

   a. Elderly: 40 per 100,000 for men older than 65

      i. Rates 3 to 4 times rest of the population

      ii. Attempt suicide less often but succeed more often

      iii. 25% of suicides are older than 65

      iv. Native American elderly have lower suicide rates than other elderly. The rate is also lower than younger Native Americans.

   b. More than 25% of all suicides are alcohol related.

   c. Roughly 80% have given some warning.

      i. 80% have seen a physician in the past 6 months.

      ii. 50% have seen a physician in the past month.

   d. Rates are higher for:

      i. Protestants versus Catholics (although how religious is more important than which religion)

      ii. Upper or middle classes versus lower classes

      iii. Whites versus blacks

      iv. Separated, divorced, widowed, or unemployed (Note: singles are not at higher risk)

      v. During harder economic times and after national crises

   e. Persons discharged from mental hospitals: 34 times more likely to commit suicide than the general population

      i. Depression: 15%

      ii. Alcoholism: 15%

      iii. Schizophrenia: 10%

      iv. Borderline personality disorder: 5%

   f. Higher concordance in monozygotic twins than in dizygotic twins.

   g. Physicians have a higher suicide rate than the general population

      i. Psychiatry is the highest subspecialty (although recent data suggest that surgeons and family practice rates are comparable)

ii. When SES is controlled for, physicians' rate is the same as the general population

iii. However, suicide rate for female physicians is four times greater than general population. Stays high even after controlling for SES.

h. Highest "on-the-job" mortality: taxi drivers

i. Suicide (especially violent suicide) is associated with lower serotonin levels.

Table 3-1. Risk Factors for Suicide

Previous suicide attempt(s) (#1 risk factor)
Family history of suicide
Male gender
Family history of child abuse
History of mental disorders, particularly clinical depression
History of alcohol and substance abuse
Feelings of hopelessness
Impulsive or aggressive tendencies
Cultural and religious beliefs (e.g., belief that suicide is noble resolution of a personal dilemma)
Local epidemics of suicide
Isolation, a feeling of being cut off from other people
Living alone
Barriers to accessing mental health treatment
Loss (relational, social, work, or financial)
Physical illness
Easy access to lethal methods
Unwillingness to seek help because of the stigma attached to mental health and substance abuse disorders or to suicidal thoughts

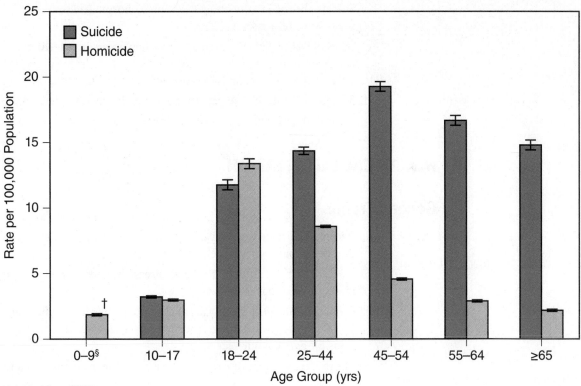

Adapted from CDC.gov

US Deaths and Mortality
- Number of deaths: 2,468,435
- Death rate: 799.5 deaths per 100,000 population
- Life expectancy: 78.7 years
- Infant Mortality rate: 6.15 deaths per 1,000 live births

Number of deaths for leading causes of death:
- Heart disease: 597,689
- Cancer: 574,743
- Chronic lower respiratory diseases: 138,080
- Stroke (cerebrovascular diseases): 129,476
- Accidents (unintentional injuries): 120,859
- Alzheimer's disease: 83,494
- Diabetes: 69,071
- Nephritis, nephrotic syndrome, and nephrosis: 50,476
- Influenza and Pneumonia: 50,097
- Intentional self-harm (suicide): 38,364

Clinical Issues

    a. Clinical signs

        i. Previous suicide attempt

       ii. Sense of hopelessness

      iii. Having a plan

b. Suicide threats are the clearest reason to hospitalize someone for psychiatric reasons.

c. IMPORTANT: Suicide often occurs when a person is feeling better after coming out of a deep depressive episode (more likely just after admission to hospital for psychiatric reasons).

d. Suicide is common in patients faced with chronic, painful, or hopeless condition

HEALTH CARE UTILIZATION

General Trends

a. Recent years have seen a rise in chronic conditions, decline in the number of patients with acute conditions.

b. Since 1960, the death rate for heart disease has declined, while the rate for cancer has increased.

c. People age >65 visit the physician about twice as often as those age <45. This pattern is strongest for men because women see physicians for gynecologic reasons.

d. The most common principal diagnosis resulting in an office visit to a physician

    i. For men: essential hypertension

    ii. For women: pregnancy

e. The average length of hospital stay has been declining slowly but steadily since 1970. Now 4.9 days.

f. Average hospital occupancy rate is about 69% nationwide.

    i. 50% is the break-even point for a hospital.

    ii. Largest portion of hospital budget is for personnel

g. Whites have 10 times the number of physician visits as blacks.

h. More malpractice suits involve breast cancer than any other diagnosis.

i. Physicians are regulated by State Medical Boards; hospitals are accredited by the Joint Commission for Accreditation of Healthcare Organizations (JCAHO).

Mental Illness

a. Over the past 30 years there has been a decrease in the number of persons who occupy hospital beds for mental illness.

b. Admissions have not changed: stays are shorter; more outpatient treatment and serial admissions.

c. Reasons for shorter stays:

    i. Development of medication

    ii. Movement to deinstitutionalize people

d. Most psychiatric care hospitals are run by states.

e. One in 10 persons will be hospitalized at some time in their lives for psychiatric reasons (includes substance-related disorders).

Hospitalization

a. Most admissions: psychiatric reasons

b. Most days in hospital: diseases of cardiovascular system

c. Most days lost from work: diseases of upper respiratory system

d. Ambulatory clinics: back pain 30% of cases

e. Most work-related disability: muscle/skeletal problems

Health Care Payments

a. Capitation: prospective payment system. Payments are made for number of people the provider is responsible for, not care delivered.

b. Medicare: federal government program that provides insurance payment for the elderly, the disabled, and dependents of the disabled.

   i. Medicare does not generally cover routine physical exams, nursing home care, or prescription drugs.

   ii. Medicare does cover ambulance transport, dialysis, and speech and occupational therapy.

HIV/AIDS

1. About 1,000,000 adults and 200,000 children in the U.S. are HIV-positive (male 1:100, female 1:800)

2. One in 5 living with HIV is unaware of their infection.

3. In some inner-city areas, as many as 50% of males are HIV-positive.

4. AIDS is now the *9th* leading cause of death for all men aged 25 to 34.

   a. Better treatments have reduced mortality.

   b. Unintended injuries is #1

5. Most dangerous sexual practice: anal intercourse

6. Recent evidence that HIV can be transmitted by oral sex

7. If the patient has AIDS today, most likely homo/bisexual man

8. If recently became HIV-positive, most likely IV drug user

9. Fastest growing method of HIV transmission: heterosexual contact (especially for blacks and Hispanics)

   a. Heterosexual transmission is easier from men to women than from women to men

   b. Risk of acquiring for men is greater if contact occurs during menses.

   c. Uncircumcised men are more likely to be seropositive and contract HIV during sex.

10. HIV transmission rates

   a. Risk from single sexual encounter with man who is not a member of a risk group: 1 in 5 million

   b. Risk from single encounter with man who is a member of a high risk group: 1 in 20 to 1 in 2

   c. Needle-stick (with HIV-positive blood): 1 in 100 to 1 in 1,000 (average 1 in 250)

d. Seroconversion from blood transfusion: 2 of 3

e. If the mother is HIV-positive, 100% of children will test positive at birth

    i. About 20% of these remain HIV-positive after 1 year.

    ii. Breast-feeding increases transmission rate to 50%.

    iii. AZT reduces risk by half (to about 10%). AZT + C-section reduces transmission rate to 5%.

MORBIDITY AND MORTALITY

For this section, patterns—not specific numbers—are what matter.

Disease Rates

Mandatory reportable diseases

When mandatory reportable diseases are encountered, they must be reported to the local Public Health Department, who will inform the CDC.

Table 3-2. Selected Mandatory Reportable Diseases

Diagnosis	Rank Order
Chlamydia	1
Gonorrhea	2
Chicken pox	3
AIDS	4
Syphilis	5
Salmonella	6
Hepatitis A	7
Tuberculosis	8
Lyme	9
Hepatitis B	10
Pertussis	11
Hepatitis-Other	12
Legionnaires	13
Mumps	14
Rubella	15
Measles	16

Table 3-3. Top 3 Non-genetic Causes of Death in the U.S.

	% of Total Deaths
Tobacco	19%
Diet/Activity	14%
Alcohol	5%

Cancer rates

a. Female lung cancer rates are increasing:
   i. 5.1 per 100,000 in 1965
   ii. More than 30 per 100,000 in 2008
b. Most common cancer for either sex
   i. Basal cell or squamous cell cancers: 900,000 cases per year
   ii. Basal cell 90% of skin cancers
   iii. Melanoma: 42,000 cases per year, more than 7,000 deaths
   iv. Incidence rate 16 times higher for whites than blacks

Mortality rates per 100,000

Table 3-4. Leading Sites of Cancer Incidence and Death

Types of Cancer	Incidence	Deaths
Males		
Prostate	1	2
Lung	2	1
Colorectal	3	3
Females		
Breast	1	2
Lung	2	1
Colorectal	3	3

Table 3-5. U.S. Mortality Rates per 100,000

Cause of Death	Rate per 100,000
Heart disease	191
Cancer	184
Chronic lower respiratory disease	41.4
Stroke (cerebrovascular diseases)	46.0
Accidents (unintentional injuries)	39.4 (approx. 50% vehicles)
Alzheimer's disease	27.2
Diabetes mellitus	23.5
Nephritis, nephrotic syndrome, and nephrosis	14.7
Influenza and Pneumonia	17.2
Intentional self-harm (suicide)	12.3

U.S. Deaths and Mortality

- Number of deaths: 2,468,435
- Death rate: 799.5 deaths per 100,000 population
- Life expectancy: 78.7 years
- Infant Mortality rate: 6.15 deaths per 1,000 live births

Number of deaths for leading causes of death:

- Heart disease: 597,689
- Cancer: 574,743
- Chronic lower respiratory diseases: 138,080
- Stroke (cerebrovascular diseases): 129,476
- Accidents (unintentional injuries): 120,859
- Alzheimer's disease: 83,494
- Diabetes: 69,071
- Nephritis, nephrotic syndrome, and nephrosis: 50,476
- Influenza and Pneumonia: 50,097
- Intentional self-harm (suicide): 38,364

Table 3-6. Top 3 Leading Causes of Death by Age Group

Rank	Less than 1	1 to 4	4 to 9	10 to 14	15 to 24	25 to 34	35 to 44	45 to 54	55 to 65	over 65
#1	Congenital anomalies	Unintended injuries	Unintended injuries	Unintended injuries	Unintended injuries	Unintended injuries	Neoplasia	Neoplasia	Neoplasia	Heart disease
#2	Short gestation	Congenital anomalies	Neoplasia	Neoplasia	Homicide	Suicide	Unintended injuries	Heart disease	Heart disease	Neoplasia
#3	SIDS	Neoplasia	Congenital anomalies	Suicide	Suicide	Homicide	Heart disease	Unintended injuries	Bronchitis, asthma, emphysema	Cerebro-vascular

Table 3-7. Causes of Death Patterns in Minority Groups Compared with Whites

Disease/Problem	African Americans	Latinos	Native Americans	Asian/Pacific Islanders
Cancer	+	×	×	×
Cardiovascular disease	+	×	×	×
Chemical dependency	+	+	+	×
Diabetes mellitus	+	+	+	×
Infant mortality	+	×	+	×
Violence	+	+	+	×
Homicide	+	+	+	×
Suicide	×	×	+	×
Unintentional injury	+	+	+	×
AIDS/HIV	+	+	×	×

+ = higher than whites; x = not higher than whites

Infant mortality

   a. Rates per 1,000 live births

      i. Whites: 6.0

      ii. African Americans: 14.3

      iii. Hispanics:

         • Puerto Ricans: 8.6

         • All other Hispanics: 6.1

      iv. Native Americans: 8.8

      v. Overall: 7.2

   b. Top 3 reasons for death:

      i. Birth defects: 24%

      ii. Low birth weight (1,500 g) and respiratory distress: 18%

      iii. Sudden infant death syndrome (SIDS): 16%

   c. Key facts

      i. African Americans have the highest rates of infant mortality from low birth weight and infections.

         • #1 killer of African American infants is low birth weight

         • SIDS is #2 for African Americans

      ii. Native Americans have the highest SIDS rate.

Substance-Related Disorders

4

PHYSIOLOGY OF SUBSTANCE-RELATED DISORDERS

The addiction pathway in the brain is a dopamine pathway. Activation of this pathway accounts for the "positive reinforcement" feeling and makes us want to repeat the action that triggered that feeling.

Mesolimbic pathway

Stimulus → Cerebral Cortex → Ventral Tegmental Area → Nucleus Accumbens
- food
- drugs
- sex
- kindness

Dopamine   Serotonin

(↑ desire   (gives body the impression
for stimulus)   of satisfaction so cravings
                   are reduced)

<u>Drugs working in nucleus accumbens</u>

Amphetamines

Cocaine

Opiates

TCH

PCP

Nicotine

Ketamine

<u>Drugs working in ventral tegmental area</u>

Opiates

Alcohol

Barbiturates

Benzodiazepines

Note

The COMLEX Requires You to Know:

- Susceptibility to alcohol problems and the most common interventions

- Presenting signs and symptoms for intoxication and withdrawal reactions for commonly abused substances

- Basic facts about substance abuse and health status

ALCOHOL AND ALCOHOLISM

1. Costs the United States more than $100 billion a year; the most costly health problem; includes costs due to death and illness
   a. Nevertheless, tobacco accounts for more loss of life. The best way to reduce long-term mortality is to eliminate smoking.
   b. Crime is the major cost issue for illegal drugs.

2. Alcohol is the most abused drug for all ages.

    a. Approximately 10% of all adults (12 million people) are problem drinkers.

    b. M > W

    c. Most widely used illicit drug for teenagers and marijuana most widely used illicit drug.

3. Since 1980, per capita consumption of alcohol has declined. Binge drinking is becoming more common. The proportion of heavy drinkers younger than 20 has increased.

4. Alcoholism rates are higher for the low-SES groups, but they recover sooner.

5. Alcohol use has been implicated in 15% of all auto accidents.

6. Alcohol use implicated in 50% of all

    a. Auto accidents not involving a pedestrian

    b. Auto accident deaths

    c. Homicides (killer or victim)

    d. Hospital admissions

7. Fetal alcohol syndrome (FAS)

    a. The leading known cause of intellectual disability (Down syndrome is second)

    b. Characterized by developmental and intellectual disability, craniofacial abnormalities, limb dislocation

    c. Consumption of large quantities of alcohol needed to produce FAS

8. Increasing evidence for genetic contribution

    a. Concordance rates: MZ > DZ (MZ = 60%, DZ = 30%)

    b. Marked ethnic-group differences: Asians, Jewish Americans, and Italian Americans much less likely to develop alcoholism than Americans with northern European roots

    c. Capacity to tolerate alcohol is the key (enzyme induction, lack of tyrosine kinase)

    d. If biologic father was an alcoholic, the incidence of alcoholism in males adopted into nonalcoholic families is equal to the incidence of alcoholism in sons raised by biologic alcoholic fathers.

    e. Family history of alcoholism increases likelihood of major depression in offspring.

9. CAGE questions

    a. Have you ever tried to **C**ut down on alcohol intake and not succeeded?

    b. Have you ever been **A**nnoyed about criticism concerning your drinking?

    c. Have you ever felt **G**uilty about your drinking behavior?

    d. Have you ever had to take a drink as an **E**ye-opener in the morning to relieve the anxiety and shakiness?

10. Medical complications of alcohol abuse

    Cirrhosis, alcoholic hepatitis, pancreatitis, gastric or duodenal ulcer, esophageal varices, middle-age onset of diabetes, gastrointestinal cancer, hypertension, peripheral neuropathies, myopathies, cardiomyopathy, cerebral vascular accidents, erectile dysfunction, vitamin deficiencies, pernicious anemia, and brain disorders, including Wernicke-Korsakoff syndrome (mortality rate of untreated Wernicke is 50%; treatment is with thiamine)

11. Chronic alcohol use can lead to cognitive decline.

12. Treatment issues

   a. Most successful way to get person into treatment is to be referred by employer

   b. Alcoholics Anonymous: largest source of alcohol treatment in U.S.

      i. The original 12-step program. Grassroots movement

      ii. Provides substitute dependency, social support, inspiration and hope, and external reminders that drinking is aversive. Meetings and sponsors

      iii. Spiritual program

   c. Al-Anon for family and friends: deals with codependence and enabling behaviors

13. Stages of behaviorial change

      i. Precontemplation: unaware of problem

      ii. Contemplation: aware of problem but ambivalent about action

      iii. Preparation: first decision to change. Small steps taken.

      iv. Action: change begins. Trial and error.

      v. Maintenance: new behaviors practiced. Focus on relapse prevention.

      vi. Relapse: efforts to change abandoned

   Cycle may repeat until sobriety is established.

14. Pharmacologic treatments

   a. Disulfiram (Antabuse)

      i. Decreases alcohol consumption

      ii. Interferes with aldehyde dehydrogenase and produces symptoms of nausea, chest pain, hyperventilation, tachycardia, vomiting

      iii. Should be used with psychotherapy (or 12-step program)

      iv. Aversive conditioning

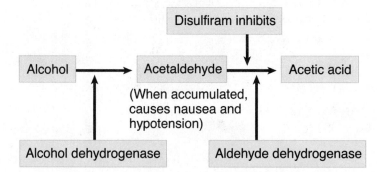

Figure 4-1. Disulfiram Treatment

   b. Naltrexone

      i. Reduces craving

COMMON ABUSED SUBSTANCES

Table 4-2. Summary of Substance Abuse

Substance	Intoxication	Withdrawal	Treatment	Psychopharmacology
Amphetamines (release DA) Cocaine (prevent re-uptake of DA)	Euphoria, hypervigilance, anxiety, stereotyped behavior, grandiosity, paranoia, tachycardia, pupillary dilation	Depression, fatigue, increased appetite unpleasant dreams, suicide	Antipsychotics or benzodiazepines for intoxication; bromocriptine, amantadine, bupropion for withdrawal	Noradrenaline system, NAC pathway (dopaminergic)
Caffeine	Restlessness, agitation, insomnia, diuresis, GI disturbances, excitement	Headache, fatigue, drowsiness, nausea or vomiting (1–4 days)	Analgesics for withdrawal	Antagonist of adenosine receptors, increased cAMP in neurons that have adenosine receptors
Cannabis (e.g., marijuana, hashish)	Impaired motor coordination, anxiety, slowed reaction time, impaired judgment, conjunctival injection, dry mouth, increased appetite, psychosis	None	Abstinence and support	Inhibitory G protein, GABA, increased serotonin, lower level of NAC activation
Hallucinogens (e.g., LSD, mescaline, ketamine)	Hallucinations, illusions, anxiety, ideas of reference, depersonalization, pupillary dilation, tremors, uncoordination	None	Supportive counseling, talking down, antipsychotics or benzodiazepines for intoxication	Partial agonist at postsynaptic 5-HT receptors
Inhalants (glue, paint thinner)	Belligerence, impaired judgment, nystagmus, uncoordination, lethargy, unsteady gait, crusting around nose/mouth	None	Education and counseling	GABA, cross tolerance, cerebellum (versus basal ganglia for Parkinson's)
Nicotine	None in usual doses but more depression (2×), impotency, traffic accidents, and more days lost from work	Irritability, depressed mood and heart rate, increased appetite, insomnia, anxiety	Nicotine patch, education, bupropion, varenicline, bromocriptine	Agonist at Ach receptors, activates dopaminergic pathway (positive reinforcer), speeds and intensifies flow of glutamate
Opiates (heroin, codeine, oxycodone)	Pupillary constriction, constipation, drowsiness, slurred speech, respiratory depression, bradycardia, coma, death	"Flu-like" muscle aches, nausea or vomiting, yawning, piloerection, lacrimation, rhinorrhea, fever, insomnia, pupillary dilation (7–10 days)	For intoxication naloxone (short half-life); clonidine, methadone, buprenorphine for withdrawal	Opiate receptors, locus cereleus pathway (noradrenergic), NAC pathway
Phencyclidine (PCP, angel dust)	Assaultive, combative, impulsive, agitated, nystagmus, ataxia, hypersalivation, muscle rigidity, decreased response to pain, hyperacusis, paranoia, unpredictible violence, psychosis	None	Nonstimmulating environment, restraints, vitamin C, benzodiazepines, or antipsychotics for intoxication	Antagonist of *N*-methyl D-aspartate glutamate receptors, prevents influx of calcium ions, activates dopaminergic neurons
Sedative hypnotics (barbituates, benzodiazepines)	Impaired judgment, slurred speech, uncoordination, unsteady gait, stupor, coma, death–barb confusion, falls, memory problems for benzos	Autonomic hyperactivity tremors, hyperactivity; hallucinations, anxiety, grand mal seizures, death	Mechanical ventilation in overdose; sodium bicarbonate to alkanize urine in barbituate overdose	GABA, cross-tolerance, delirium

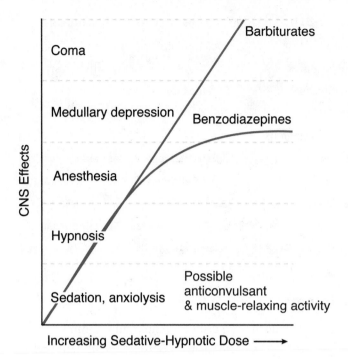

OTHER ABUSED SUBSTANCES

Ecstasy (MDMA)

a. Also called "E", X or XTC

b. Acts as a hallucinogen combined with an amphetamine

c. Effects begin in 45 minutes and last 2 to 4 hours.

d. Symptoms include derealization, hallucinations, mania-like mood, hyperthermia, hypertension, convulsions, and death.

e. Fatigue the day after use

Anabolic Steroids

a. Taken by male and female athletes to increase performance and physique

b. With chronic use, can cause cardiomyopathy, bone mineral loss with later osteoporosis, hypertension, diabetes, atrophy of testes, mood lability, depression, atypical psychosis

c. Presenting signs include skin atrophy, spontaneous bruising, acne, low serum potassium levels

    i. Men: breast development, scrotal pain, premature baldness

    ii. Women: disrupted menstrual cycle, deepening of voice, excessive body hair

Table 4-3. Helpful Hints of Substance-Related Disorders

Paranoia	Cocaine/amphetamine intoxication
Depression	Cocaine/amphetamine withdrawal
Arrhythmias	Cocaine intoxication
Violence	PCP
Vertical nystagmus	PCP
Pinpoint pupils	Opiate overdose (treatment = naloxone)
Flu-like	Opiate withdrawal (treatment = clonidine)
Flashbacks	LSD
Seizures	Benzodiazepine/alcohol withdrawal
Death	Barbiturate withdrawal

Epidemiology

    a. Most illicit drug users are employed full-time.

    b. About 33% of psychiatric disorders are substance-related disorders.

        i. Men outnumber women roughly 2.5 times.

        ii. Prevalence of substance-related disorders in newly admitted psychiatric inpatients or outpatients is roughly 50%.

        iii. These "dual diagnosis" patients are very difficult to treat and tend to continue use when on inpatient wards.

    c. Substance-related disorders adds to the suicide risk of any underlying psychiatric diagnosis.

    d. 50% of emergency department visits are substance related.

    e. Physicians tend to underdiagnose substance-related problems of all types, especially those in women, high-SES patients (and other physicians).

SUBSTANCE-ABUSING PHYSICIANS

1. Psychiatrists and anesthesiologists have highest rates.

2. Physician impairment issues are dealt with by the State Licensing Boards.

3. If you suspect that a colleague has a substance-related problem do the following and <u>in this order</u>:

    a. Get the colleague to suspend patient contact.

    b. You must report it to hospital administration and the State Board.

    c. Ideally, get the colleague into treatment.

Review Questions

33. Suicide has increased incidence in a wide range of psychiatric disorders. In others, the association is closer to that of the general population. The suicide rate for which of the following disorders is most likely to be closest to that of the general population?

    (A) Schizophrenia

    (B) Alcoholism

    (C) Schizoid personality disorder

    (D) Major affective disorders

    (E) Borderline personality disorder

34. A 39-year-old divorced Hispanic woman presents with lethargy and fatigue. When questioned, she complains of diffuse physical aches, although her health appears to be generally good. She confesses that she finds herself crying "for no reason." She reports not really feeling like seeing any of her usual friends and has difficulty sleeping, especially waking up early in the morning. She is given a preliminary diagnosis of uni-polar depression. In addition to this diagnosis, the strongest risk factor for suicide in this patient would be the patient's

    (A) age

    (B) gender

    (C) marital status

    (D) overall health

    (E) visit to the physician

    (F) fatigue

35. Mr. Jones has been complaining of a depressed mood for several months. His wife informs you that he tried to kill himself last month when he reported hearing voices that told him to kill himself. He was hospitalized for 21 days and given a diagnosis of a major psychiatric disorder. When questioned, he reported having "given up." Upon further questioning, you learn that he has a 10-year history of alcoholism. Which of the following would pose the greatest risk for future completed suicide?

    (A) Feelings of helplessness

    (B) Marital status

    (C) Affective disorders

    (D) Past suicide attempt

    (E) Schizophrenia

36. The medical record of a 65-year-old white male details a long list of medical conditions, including diabetes, gastric ulcer, recurrent headaches, and peripheral neuropathies. In addition, the record indicates that the patient has a history of substance-related disorder, although no specifics are provided. When interviewing the patient, the physician is most likely to discover that the substance abused by the patient most likely was

    (A) alcohol

    (B) cocaine

    (C) caffeine

    (D) ecstasy

    (E) hallucinogens

    (F) inhalants

    (G) opiates

    (H) sedative hypnotics

37. A 21-year-old male patient is brought to the emergency department by his parents, who are concerned because he was stumbling around their house, waving his arms in the air, and would not respond verbally to their questions. When examined, the patient appears anxious, with elevated heart rate and clammy skin. A slight tremor is evident in his hands and his pupils are dilated. Over time, he becomes verbal and reports that he felt like he was floating out of his body and that words spoken to him seemed like insects that should be swatted away. He also admits to having recently taken an illegal substance. The patient's behavior and physiology are most consistent with intoxication due to

    (A) cocaine

    (B) inhaled paint thinner

    (C) marijuana

    (D) mescaline

    (E) phencyclidine

    (F) phenobarbital

38. The police bring a 22-year-old white male to the emergency department. From the outset, he is belligerent, aggressive, and violent, requiring the efforts of several officers to restrain him. When questioned, the patient is paranoid. Physical exam shows him to have muscle rigidity and pupils that move up and down rapidly. The patient had previously been treated for opiate overdose. What neurochemical mechanisms are most likely to account for the patient's current behavior?

    (A) Reduction in levels of GABA

    (B) Antagonism of the glutamate receptors

    (C) Partial agonist of the postsynaptic serotonin receptors

    (D) Antagonism of the locus cerelose pathway and blocking of substance P

    (E) Increases in GABA and inhibitory G protein

39. Parents who are concerned because their 17-year-old son is "just not himself" bring him to the emergency department. Preliminary examination shows the boy to be drowsy, with slurred speech, pupillary constriction, lethargy, and generally positive affect. Based on this initial presentation, the boy is most likely intoxicated with

   (A) caffeine

   (B) cannabis

   (C) cocaine

   (D) LSD

   (E) alcohol

   (F) inhalants

   (G) phencyclidine

   (H) nicotine

   (I) opiates

   (J) sedative hypnotics

Answers

33. **Answer: C.** All options presented have suicide rates higher than the general population, but schizoid personality disorder has the lowest associated rate. Alcoholism and depression = 15%, schizophrenia = 10%, borderlines = 5 to 7%.

34. **Answer: C.** Being over age 45, male, in poor health and emerging from depression are all risk factors for suicide, but none of these are true for this patient. The fact that she is divorced, and the social isolation that may bring, is the strongest risk factor alongside the diagnosed depression.

35. **Answer: D.** Past suicide attempt is the strongest risk factor. Sense of hopelessness is second.

36. **Answer: A.** Alcohol is the most abused drug for any age. Note that the patient's symptoms, with the exception of the headache, are all linked to long-term alcohol use.

37. **Answer: D.** The patient presents behavior and symptoms of someone high on hallucinogens. Although cocaine may also induce anxiety, the case lacks the other cocaine-related symptoms.

38. **Answer: B.** The presenting profile is most suggestive of PCP intoxication, which produces its behavioral effects by antagonism of the glutamate receptors and the activation of dopamine neurons.

39. **Answer: I.** Pupillary constriction and lethargy are the key features here.

SEXUAL BEHAVIOR IN THE UNITED STATES

In the United States, 95% of people have their first sexual experience outside of marriage.

Adolescent Sexual Behavior

a. Nearly 70% of all unmarried females are nonvirgins by age 19 (80% of males).

   i. Nearly 4 in 10 teenage girls whose first intercourse experience happened at age 13–14 report that the sex was unwanted or involuntary.

   ii. Average age of first sexual experience: 16

b. Adolescents in the aggregate still drift into sexual activity rather than decide to have sex.

   i. Most adolescent sexual activity still takes place in the context of one primary relationship.

   ii. Most adolescents are not promiscuous, but "serially monogamous."

c. Recent survey: 57% of adolescents claim to have used a condom the last time they had sex.

   i. Other research suggests that they do not do as they say.

   ii. More than 50% of sexually active adolescents do not use birth control regularly.

Teenage Pregnancy

The Centers for Disease Control and Prevention reports that 305,388 babies were born to women age 15–19 in 2012. This reflects a decrease for U.S. teens in this age group. Teens seem to be less sexually active, and more of those who are sexually active seem to be using birth control than in previous years.

- Despite declines in rates of teen pregnancy in the U.S., about 820,000 teens become pregnant each year.
- Nearly 80 percent of teenagers who become pregnant are unmarried.
- 80 percent of teenage pregnancies are unintended.
- The main rise in the teen pregnancy rate is among girls younger than 15
- Close to 25 percent of teen mothers have a second child within two years of the first birth.

a. About 1 million U.S. teenagers become pregnant each year.

   i. 10% of all teenage girls

   ii. 50% of all unwed mothers are teenagers.

Note

The COMLEX Requires You To Know:

- Sexual behavior in the United States
- Paraphilias
- Differential diagnosis among sexual dysfunctions
- Facts about sexual practices

    b. 50% have the child.

        i. 33% have elective abortions.

        ii. The remainder are spontaneously aborted.

    c. About 33% of girls aged 15–19 have at least 1 unwanted pregnancy.

    d. Single mothers account for 70% of births to girls aged 15–19.

    e. Consequences of teenage pregnancy

        i. For mother:

          ● Leading cause of school dropout

          ● High risk for obstetric complications

        ii. For child:

          ● Neonatal deaths and prematurity are common.

          ● Possible lower level of intellectual functioning

          ● Problems of single-parent family (increased risk of delinquency, suicide)

Sexually Transmitted Diseases

    a. One in 5 teenagers will have a sexually transmitted disease: rates for gonorrhea and chlamydia are higher for adolescents than for any older group.

    b. Highest incidence: most common sexually transmitted disease is human papilloma virus (HPV).

    c. Highest prevalence: one in 5 Americans has herpes simplex virus, type 2 (HSV-2).

        i. Chlamydia is the most commonly reported STD in women.

        ii. Gonorrhea is the most commonly reported STD in men.

    d. Syphilis (primary and secondary):

        i. Cases have doubled since 1970.

        ii. Rate now more than 20/100,000

    e. Gonorrhea:

        i. Number of cases has declined by half since 1975.

        ii. Since 1975, increase in resistant strains

Table 5-1. Male Sexual Response Cycle

Body Area	Excitement Phase	Orgasm Phase	Resolution Phase
Skin	Sexual flush	3–15 seconds	Disappears
Penis	Vasocongestion, penile erection	Ejaculation	Detumescence
Scrotum	Tightening and lifting	No change	Decrease to baseline size
Testes	Elevation and increase in size	No change	Decrease to baseline size, descent
Breasts	Nipple erection	No change	Return to baseline

During the excitement and orgasm phase, there is an increase in respiration, tachycardia up to 180 beats per minute, a rise in systolic blood pressure 20–100 mm Hg and diastolic blood pressure of 10–50 mm Hg.

Table 5-2. Female Sexual Response Cycle

Body Area	Excitement Phase	Orgasm Phase	Resolution Phase
Skin	Sexual flush	3–15 seconds	Disappears
Breasts	Nipple erection, areolas enlarge	May become tremulous	Return to normal
Clitoris	Enlargement, shaft retracts	No change	Detumescence, shaft returns to normal
Labia majora	Nulliparous: elevate and flatten Multiparous: congestion and edema	No change	Nulliparous: increase to normal size Multiparous: decrease to normal size
Labia minora	Increase in size, deeper in color	Contractions of proximal portion	Return to normal
Vagina	Transudate, elongation	Contractions in lower third	Congestion disappears, ejaculate forms seminal pool in upper 2/3
Uterus	Ascends into false pelvis "Tenting effect"	Contractions	Contractions cease and uterus descends

1. Plateau phase is a stage of sustained excitement.
2. Only men have a refractory period.

PARAPHILIC DISORDERS

1. <u>Pedophilia</u>: sexual urges toward children. Most common paraphilia
2. <u>Exhibitionism</u>: recurrent desire to expose genitals to stranger
3. <u>Voyeurism</u>: sexual pleasure from watching others who are naked, grooming, or having sex. Begins early in childhood
4. <u>Sadism</u>: sexual pleasure derived from others' pain
5. <u>Masochism</u>: sexual pleasure derived from being abused or dominated
6. <u>Fetishism</u>: sexual focus on objects, e.g., shoes, stockings
   a. Transvestite fetishism: fantasies or actual dressing by heterosexual men in female clothes for sexual arousal
7. <u>Frotteurism</u>: male rubbing of genitals against fully clothed woman to achieve orgasm; subways and buses
8. <u>Zoophilia</u>: animals preferred in sexual fantasies or practices
9. <u>Coprophilia</u>: combining sex and defecation
10. <u>Urophilia</u>: combining sex and urination
11. <u>Necrophilia</u>: preferred sex with cadavers
12. <u>Hypoxyphilia</u>: altered state of consciousness secondary to hypoxia while experiencing orgasm. Autoerotic asphyxiation, poppers, amyl nitrate, nitric oxide

Table 5-3. Gender Identity and Preferred Sexual Partner of a Biologic Male

Common Label	Gender Identity	Preferred Sexual Partner
Heterosexual	Male	Female
Transvestite fetishism	Male	Female
Gender dysphoria (transsexual)	Female	Male
Homosexual	Male	Male

Gender identity: sense of maleness or femaleness, established by the age of 3 years.

SEXUAL DYSFUNCTIONS

Sexual Desire Disorders

a. <u>Male hypoactive sexual desire disorder</u>: deficiency or absence of fantasies or desires. Reasons: low testosterone, CNS depressants, common postsurgery, depression, marital discord.

Sexual Arousal Disorders

a. <u>Female sexual interest/arousal disorder</u>
  i. Women unable to achieve adequate vaginal lubrication
  ii. May be hormonally related: many women report peak sexual desire just prior to menses
  iii. Antihistamine and anticholinergic medications cause decrease in vaginal lubrication

b. <u>Male erectile disorder</u> (impotence)
  - 10 to 20% lifetime prevalence, point prevalence is 3%
  - 50% of men treated for sexual disorders have this complaint
  - Incidence 8% young adult, 75% of men older than 80
  - 50% more likely in smokers
  - Be sure to check alcohol usage, diabetes, marital conflict
  - Must determine if organic versus psychological
  i. Assessment: postage stamp test, snap gauge (to test physiological versus phychological)
  ii. Treatment: sildenafil (Viagra), vardenafil (Levitra), tadalafil (Cialis)

Orgasm Disorders

a. <u>Female orgasm disorder</u>
  i. Inability to achieve orgasm
  ii. 5% of married women older than 35 have never achieved orgasm
  iii. Overall prevalence from all causes: 30%
  iv. Treatment: fantasy, vibrators

b. <u>Premature ejaculation</u>

    i. Male ejaculates before or immediately after entering vagina

    ii. More common if early sexual experiences were in back seat of car or with prostitute, anxiety about sexual act

    iii. Treatment: stop and go technique, squeeze technique, SSRIs

Genitopelvic Pain/Penetration Disorders

a. Psychological in origin

b. Recurrent and persistent pain before, during, or after intercourse

    i. Only diagnosed in women

    ii. Not diagnosed if due to medical problems

c. Involuntary muscle constriction of the outer third of the vagina that prevents penile insertion

    i. Treatment: relaxation, Hegar dilators

MASTURBATION

1. Normal activity from infancy to old age

2. Reasons

    a. In adults: lonely, tired, bored, relieve stress, help sleep

    b. In children: normal, feels good

3. Frequency: 3–4 times weekly for adolescents, 1–2 times weekly for adults, once a month for married people

4. Equally common in men and women

5. Abnormal only if interferes with sexual or occupational functioning

6. Can lead to premature ejaculation in males who use it primarily to reduce tension

HOMOSEXUALITY

1. Not considered a mental illness

2. 4 to 10% of all males, 1 to 3% of all females

3. Issue is partner preference, not behavior

    a. Behavioral patterns of homosexuals are as varied as those of heterosexuals.

    b. Same level and variations in sexuality as for heterosexuals

4. Male–male relationships are less stable than are female–female relationships

5. Over 50% of homosexuals have children

6. Distinguish between ego-syntonic and ego-dystonic homosexuality

    a. Ego-syntonic: agrees with sense of self, person is comfortable

    b. Ego-dystonic: disagrees with sense of self, makes person uncomfortable

    c. If ego-dystonic: sexual orientation distress. NOT considered pathologic unless ego-dystonic

7. Increasing evidence of biologic contribution. Higher concordance rates for MZ twins (52%) than for DZ (22%)

8. Preference well established by adolescence

    a. Feelings of preference emerge 3 or more years before first encounter

    b. Describe duration of feelings with "As long as I can remember"

9. Similar number of heterosexual experiences reported in childhood and adolescence

    a. Report experiences as "ungratifying"

    b. 30 to 40% of all people report at least 1 same-gender sexual experience

SEXUALITY AND AGING

1. Sexual interest does not decline significantly with aging.

2. Continued sexual activity means sexual activity can continue.

3. Best predictor of sexual activity in the elderly is availability of a partner.

4. After myocardial infarction (MI), sexual position that puts least strain on the heart: partner on top

5. Changes in men:

    a. Slower erection

    b. Longer refractory period

    c. More stimulation needed

6. Changes in women:

    a. Vaginal dryness

    b. Vaginal thinning

    c. Can be reduced by estrogen replacement

Review Questions

40. A young couple comes to you for counseling soon after they are married. They say they have read that marital satisfaction changes over the course of the marriage and want to know what they should expect over the course of their own marriage. The physician tells them that, although their personal experience may be different, overall marital satisfaction tends to

    (A) increase with length of time married

    (B) decrease with length of time married

    (C) increase gradually, reaching a high point when children are in adolescence, then decline rapidly

    (D) decrease gradually during the childbearing years, then increases after all children have left home

    (E) increase during the preschool years, decreasing during grammar school, then rise again during adolescence

41. Your schedule indicates that you have an initial appointment with a patient who is a 50-year-old white male. Following the examination, the most likely resultant diagnosis for this man is

    (A) gastrointestinal problems

    (B) upper respiratory distress

    (C) essential hypertension

    (D) obesity

    (E) urinary problems

42. According to surveys by the Centers for Disease Control and Prevention, as of 2000, the most common health problem in the United States is

    (A) cancer

    (B) heart disease

    (C) substance-related disorder

    (D) obesity

    (E) dental caries

43. A 32-year-old white woman appears at your office for her annual physical exam. The physical exam shows the patient to be in good health, although she is slightly overweight and has moderately elevated blood pressure. If the patient were to die at some point in the next 10 years, the most likely cause of death would be

    (A) unintended injuries

    (B) neoplasms

    (C) heart disease

    (D) homicide

    (E) AIDS

44. During a 1-year period, a physician practicing medicine in the United States would be most likely to encounter a patient suffering from which of the following mandatory reportable diseases?

    (A) Hepatitis A
    (B) Lyme disease
    (C) HIV/AIDS
    (D) Chicken pox
    (E) Syphilis

45. An earthquake recently devastated a town in Northern California. Electricity was shut off for several days, and many of the people in the area were homeless. The most likely pattern of response of the affected population would be

    (A) widespread emotional aftereffects that are usually mild and transitory
    (B) disintegration of social organization
    (C) incidence of post-traumatic stress syndrome in close to 20% of those affected
    (D) children adapt to the new circumstances more quickly than do adults
    (E) increased divorce in the following 6 months

46. You have been appointed to provide an assessment of the general health status of your local community. You have a limited budget and must, therefore, focus on the most likely determinant of community health status. Based on this information, your assessment should focus on

    (A) hospital bed:population ratio
    (B) infant mortality rate
    (C) physician:patient ratio
    (D) general mortality rate
    (E) quality of the physical and social environment

47. Following surgery for the removal of her appendix, a female patient comes to see you complaining of a lack of interest in sexual contact with her husband. "We have been fighting so much lately," she says. "Between that and the pressure I feel at work, I just don't know what to do anymore." Medical history shows that she has been taking diazepam for the past 2 years and oral contraceptives for the past 5 years. Which of the following can be safely excluded as unlikely to result in the reported suppression of libido?

    (A) Oral contraceptives
    (B) Marital discord
    (C) Postoperative recovery
    (D) Work stress
    (E) Diazepam

48. At the conclusion of her annual gynecologic exam, a 34-year-old married Hispanic woman confides to her physician that her interest in sex has been "spotty" lately. Although she has sexual relations with her husband at least once a week, she reports feeling "really passionate" only in the week just prior to the onset of menses. She refrains from sexual intercourse during menses. The woman wants to know what is wrong with her. The physician's best response would be

(A) "What medications are you taking?"

(B) "Is your husband sometimes abusive?"

(C) "This is a normal pattern of sexual arousal reported by many women."

(D) "You may find that an erotic movie will stimulate your sexual desire at times when you do not feel passionate."

(E) "How often does your husband want to have sex?"

(F) "I'm going to have you talk to a friend of mine who specializes in this sort of thing."

(G) "You might consider abstaining from sex for awhile until you feel more sure that you want it."

49. A woman reports to her physician that she can achieve orgasm only when recalling a previous, abusive boyfriend. Suspecting the presence of a paraphilia, the physician should explore for further evidence of

(A) coprophilia

(B) transvestitism

(C) sadism

(D) frotteurism

(E) voyeurism

(F) exhibitionism

(G) pedophilia

(H) fetishism

(I) masochism

(J) zoophilia

(K) necrophilia

50. A 72-year-old married man who is being treated for elevated cholesterol asks his physician about normal sexual function in the elderly. At this point, the physician should inform the patient that

(A) loss of interest in sex is a natural part of aging

(B) although men maintain interest in sexual activity, women lose interest as they age

(C) more mental and physical stimulation may be required to achieve erection

(D) sexual activity should be limited to once a month to reduce cardiovascular stress

(E) he will be provided with a prescription for an anti-impotence drug so that it is available when he needs it

Answers

40. **Answer: D.** Marital satisfaction tends to be lower for couples with children, and to rise when the children leave home.

41. **Answer: C.** Essential hypertension is the most likely diagnosis resulting from an office visit by a male to his physicians.

42. **Answer: E.** The key here is the phrase "health problem." More people have dental cavities than anything else listed.

43. **Answer: B.** For males in the same age range, the leading cause of death is accidents.

44. **Answer: D.** In order from most to least likely: chicken pox, HIV/AIDS, syphilis, salmonella, hepatitis A.

45. **Answer: A.** The aftermath of natural disasters finds many people suffering from distress reactions. These reactions, however, tend to be relatively mild and resolve themselves of their own accord and generally fall under the diagnosis of acute stress disorder. After natural disasters, there tends to be an increase in social organization. PTSD incidence is closer to 4% (Mt. St. Helen's). Adults adapt more quickly than children. Divorce rates tend to decline in the period just after a disaster.

46. **Answer: E.** The quality of the overall environment is the main issue. The other, technical sounding, options are all indicators of community health, but are not the most important determinant. Infant mortality is one of the strongest predictors of life expectancy, but not of overall health of the community.

47. **Answer: E.** Although the others have been shown to suppress sexual desire, diazepam has not.

48. **Answer: C.** Many women report peak sexual arousal just prior to the onset of menses. Reassure the woman that her experience is normal. She needs reassurance, not problem solving or medical intervention.

49. **Answer: I.** To qualify for masochism, the sexual act must be the result of gratification that includes receiving pain in either reality or fantasy.

50. **Answer: C.** Sexual interest does not decline with age for either men or women. A prescription should not be given without an identified problem.

Learning and Behavior Modification 6

LEARNING AND BEHAVIOR

In the behaviorist model of learning and behavior modification, internal states, subjective impressions, and unconscious processes are not relevant. All that matters is the objective data, i.e., only what can be seen, observed, and measured. The behaviorist definition of learning: a relatively permanent change in behavior, not due to fatigue, drugs, or maturation.

The two main types of learning paradigms are classical (elicited) conditioning and operant (emitted) conditioning.

Classical Conditioning

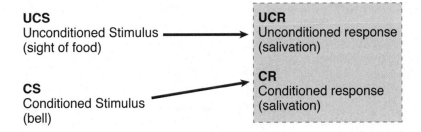

UCS
Unconditioned Stimulus
(sight of food)

UCR
Unconditioned response
(salivation)

CS
Conditioned Stimulus
(bell)

CR
Conditioned response
(salivation)

Figure 6-1. Classic (or Respondent or Pavlovian) Conditioning

1. In classical conditioning, the conditioned response is elicited by the conditioned stimulus after repeated pairings of the UCS and CS.

   a. The Pavlovian experiment paired the ringing of a bell with the bringing of food so that, eventually, the sound of the bell elicited the salivatory response, which previously occurred only with the sight of the food.

   b. Or, for example, a patient receives chemotherapy (UCS), which induces nausea (UCR). Eventually, the sights and sounds of the hospital alone (CS) elicit nausea (now a CR).

2. **A new stimulus elicits the same behavior.** Note that the triggering stimulus (CS) occurs before the response.

3. <u>Stimulus generalization</u>: the tendency for the conditioned stimulus to evoke similar responses after the response has been conditioned. If a salivation response had been conditioned to a tone of 1,000 CPS, an 800 CPS tone will elicit a similar response. Or, in the second example, generalization will have occurred if any hospital, or even meeting a physician, comes to elicit nausea from the patient.

Note

The COMLEX Requires You to Know:

- Differences between classical and operant conditioning

- Types of reinforcement

- The effects of different reinforcement schedules

- Applications of behavioral principles in clinical situations

- The behavioral substrate of depression

- The curvilinear relationship between arousal and performance

- Behavioral approaches to pain management

4. <u>Extinction</u>: after learning has occurred, removal of the pairing between the UCS and the CS results in a decreased probability that the conditioned response will be made. For example, breaking the pairing between chemotherapy and the medical setting by giving chemotherapy at home. The nausea-eliciting properties of hospitals will be extinguished.

Operant or Instrumental Conditioning

1. In operant conditioning, a new response is emitted, perhaps randomly at first, which results in a consequence.

   a. The consequence acts as reinforcement and changes the probability of the response's future occurrence.

   b. In the Skinner experiment, pressing a lever resulting in the delivery of food. After receiving food, the bar-pressing behavior increased. Because it changed behavior, the food is a reinforcing event.

2. A new response occurs to an old stimulus. Note the triggering stimulus (reinforcement) occurs after the response.

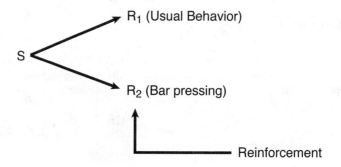

Figure 6-2. Operant or Instrumental Conditioning

3. Reinforcement is delivery of a consequence that increases the likelihood that a response will occur. A reinforcer is defined by its effects. Any stimulus is a reinforcer if it increases the probability of a response.

4. Types of reinforcers

   a. A <u>positive reinforcer</u> is a stimulus that, when applied following an operant response, strengthens the probability of that response occurring.

      i. E.g., increased pay leads to increased work from an employee

      ii. E.g., increased complaining leads to increased attention from the nursing staff

   b. A <u>negative reinforcer</u> is a stimulus that, when removed following an operant response, strengthens the probability of that response occurring.

      i. E.g., a child learns that he can stop his parents' nagging by cleaning up his room.

      ii. Aversive stimuli such as a loud noise, bright light, shock, can often be negative reinforcers

   c. Positive and negative do not imply good and bad, respectively. Rather, positive defines adding a stimulus and negative means removing a stimulus. Both positive and negative reinforcement lead to an increase in response frequency or strength.

d. <u>Punishment</u>, like negative conditioning, usually uses a noxious stimulus.

    i. However, this stimulus is imposed to weaken response.

    ii. Ordinarily, punishment should be paired with positive reinforcement for alternative behaviors.

    iii. E.g., physical punishment of a child will suppress naughty behavior, but may fade when the punishment is removed and may model aggressive physical behavior for the child.

e. <u>Extinction</u> refers to the disappearance of a response when it is no longer being reinforced.

    i. E.g., a nurse who is bombarded by constant complaints from a patient stops paying attention to the patient whenever he complains.

    ii. E.g., a child is ignored by the parents when he throws temper tantrums.

    iii. If successful, the unwanted behavior will stop.

Table 6-1. Types of Reinforcement

		Stimulus: (S)	
		Add	Remove
Behavior: (R)	**Stops**	Punishment	Extinction
	Increases	Positive reinforcement	Negative reinforcement

Note: A behavior is something that is done. A stimulus is something in sensory impression (sight, sound, smell, feeling).

5. Reinforcement schedules

a. <u>Continuous reinforcement</u>: every response is followed by a reinforcement.

    i. Results in fast learning (acquisition)

    ii. Results in fast extinction when reinforcement is stopped

b. <u>Intermittent (or partial) reinforcement</u>: not every response is reinforced

    i. Learning is slower

    ii. Response is harder to extinguish

    iii. E.g., a child throws a tantrum and the parents ignore it for long periods of time in the hope that the child will stop. They don't want to reinforce such behavior with attention. However, if their patience wears thin and, after a long spell of ignoring, they attend to the baby, they are putting the child on an intermittent reinforcement schedule and will find it harder to extinguish the tantrums.

    iv. Extinction of intermittent reinforcement often requires a change back to continuous reinforcement.

    v. Interval schedules: based on the passage of time before reinforcement is given

       • <u>Fixed interval schedule</u> reinforces the response that occurs after a fixed period of time elapses. Responses are slow in the beginning of the interval and faster immediately prior to reinforcement.

- Response pattern: on and off
- Animal or person learns to delay response until near end of time period
- E.g., cramming before an exam or working extra hard before bonus at the holidays
- <u>Variable interval schedule</u> delivers reinforcements after unpredictable time periods elapse
- Higher, steadier rate of responding
- Cannot learn when next response will be reinforced, leading to a steadier response rate
- E.g., pop quizzes or surprise bonuses at work

vi. Ratio schedules: based on the number of behaviors elicited before reinforcement is given

- <u>Fixed ratio schedule</u> delivers reinforcement after a fixed number of responses.
- Produces high response rate
- Rewards a set of behaviors rather than a single behavior, e.g., paying workers on a piecework basis.
- <u>Variable ratio schedule</u> delivers reinforcement after a changing number of responses.
- Produces the greatest resistance to extinction
- For example, in gambling, a large number of responses may be made without reward. Since any response may be the lucky one, person keeps on trying. Slot machines

Table 6-2. Reinforcement Schedules

| | | Contingency | |
		Time	Behaviors
Schedule:	Constant	Fixed interval (FI)	Fixed ratio (FR)
	Changing	Variable interval (VI)	Variable ratio (VR)

6. <u>Spontaneous recovery</u>: after extinction, the response occurs again without any further reinforcement.

7. <u>Secondary reinforcement</u>: a symbol or a token gains reinforcement value because of its association with a real reinforcer (e.g., money is not valuable in itself but because of what you can do with it).

Modeling, Observational, or Social Learning

1. Watching someone else get reinforcement is enough to change behavior
2. Follows the same principles as in operant conditioning
3. Correlating the effects of watching violence on television with committing violence "in the real world" stems from this concept.
4. Part of why group therapy works
5. Other applications: assertiveness training, social skills training, preparing children for various frightening or painful medical or surgical procedures

BEHAVIOR THERAPY AND BEHAVIOR MODIFICATION

Focus on treating symptoms directly rather than changing underlying internal conflicts.

Therapy/Modification Based on Classical Conditioning

1. Systematic desensitization—usually begins with imagining oneself in a progression of fearful situations and using relaxation strategies that compete with anxiety.
   a. Often used to treat anxiety and phobias
   b. Based on the counterconditioning or reciprocal inhibition of anxiety responses
      i. **Step 1:** Hierarchy of fear-eliciting stimuli is created, building from least to most stressful.
      ii. **Step 2:** Therapist teaches the technique of muscle relaxation, a response that is incompatible with anxiety.
      iii. **Step 3:** Patient is taught to relax in the presence, real or imagined, of each stimulus on the hierarchy from least to most stressful.
   c. When the person is relaxed in the presence of the feared stimulus, objectively, there is no more phobia.
   d. Note that this works by replacing anxiety with relaxation, an incompatible response.

2. Exposure
   a. Simple phobias can sometimes be treated by forced exposure to the feared object.
   b. Exposure maintained until fear response is extinguished
   c. E.g., fear of heights treated by having patient to ride up elevator
   d. In more extreme form, called "flooding" or "implosion" therapy

3. Aversive conditioning occurs when a stimulus that produces deviant behavior is paired with an aversive stimulus.
   a. Key properties of the original stimulus are changed
      i. E.g., Pavlov's dog being presented with spoiled meat upon ringing bell. The dog does not salivate, but instead recoils as the spoiled meat is presented.
   b. Used in the treatment of alcoholism and some forms of sexual deviance
      i. E.g., an alcoholic is given a nausea-inducing drug (disulfiram) whenever he drinks so that drinking eventually comes to elicit unpleasant rather than pleasant events; chili peppers and thumb-sucking

Therapy/Modification Based on Operant Conditioning

1. Shaping (or successive approximations)
   a. Achieves final target behavior by reinforcing successive approximations of the desired response
   b. Reinforcement is gradually modified to move behaviors from the more general to the specific responses desired.

c. E.g., an autistic boy who won't speak is first reinforced, perhaps with candy, for any utterance. From those utterances, the appropriate phonemes are selected and reinforced until the child utters the sought-after sounds. Eventually, reinforcement is contingent on his using speech correctly in the proper context.

2. Extinction

   a. Discontinuing the reinforcement that is maintaining an undesired behavior

   b. E.g., if complaining results in a patient receiving a lot of attention, stopping the attention will eventually stop the undesired behavior.

   c. E.g., instituting a "time out" with children who are acting inappropriately or test-takers who are anxious

3. Stimulus control

   a. Sometimes stimuli inadvertently acquire control over behavior. When this is true, removal of that stimulus can extinguish the response

   b. E.g., a person's eating behavior is tied to a particular stimulus, such as television watching. Reducing the time watching television should reduce the amount eaten.

   c. E.g., an insomniac is permitted in his bed only when he is so tired that he falls asleep almost at once.

4. Biofeedback (neurofeedback)

   a. Using external feedback to modify internal physiologic states

   b. Used to be thought that certain functions of the autonomic nervous system (heart rate, blood pressure, body temperature) were beyond the deliberate control of a person. We now know that both animals and humans can attain a measure of control over some of their own bodily functions through the technique of biofeedback.

      i. Often uses electronic devices to present physiologic information, e.g., heart monitor to show heart rate

   c. Biofeedback involves providing the person with information about his internal responses to stimuli and methods to control and/or modify them.

   d. Biofeedback works by means of trial-and-error learning and requires repeated practice to be effective.

   e. Uses: treatment of hypertension, migraine and muscle-contraction headaches, Raynaud syndrome, torticollis, cardiac arrhythmias, and anxiety

   f. Galvanic skin response: reduced skin conductivity = anxiety reduction

   g. Most biofeedback affects the parasympathetic system.

5. Fading

   a. Gradually removing the reinforcement without the subject discerning the difference

   b. E.g., promoting smoking cessation by reducing the nicotine content of the cigarettes gradually and "silently" over a period of time

   c. E.g., gradually replacing postoperative painkiller with a placebo

Table 6-3. Learning-Based Therapies

Based on Classical Conditioning	
Systematic desensitization	Often used to treat anxiety and phobias
	Step 1: Hierarchy of stimuli: least to most feared.
	Step 2: Technique of muscle relaxation taught.
	Step 3: Patient relaxes in presence of each stimulus on the hierarchy.
	Works by replacing anxiety with relaxation, an incompatible response
Exposure (also: flooding or implosion)	Simple phobias treated by forced exposure to the feared object. Exposure maintained until fear response is extinguished
Aversive conditioning	Properties of the original stimulus are changed to produce an aversive response. Can help reduce deviant behaviors.
Based on Operant Conditioning	
Shaping	Achieves target behavior by reinforcing successive approximations of the desired response. Reinforcement gradually modified to move behaviors from general responses to the specific responses desired.
Extinction	Discontinuing the reinforcement that is maintaining an undesired behavior. "Time out" with children or for test-anxiety.
Stimulus control	Sometimes stimuli inadvertently acquire control over behavior. When this is true, removal of that stimulus can extinguish the response. Example: an insomniac only permitted in bed when he/she is so tired that sleep comes almost at once.
Biofeedback	Using external feedback to modify internal physiologic states. Often uses electronic devices to present physiologic information, e.g., heart monitor to show heart rate
	Works by means of trial-and-error learning and requires repeated practice to be effective.
Fading	Gradually removing the reinforcement: 1. without the subject discerning the difference 2. while maintaining the desired response
	Example: Gradually replacing postoperative painkiller with a placebo

Behavioral Models of Depression

1. Learned helplessness
   a. Laboratory model of depression
   b. All normal avoidance responses are extinguished.
      i. A rat is shocked and not allowed to escape. Eventually, the rat will not take an obvious avoidance route even when it is offered.
   c. Symptoms of helplessness (in animals) include passivity, norepinepherine depletion, and difficulty learning responses that produce relief, weight, and appetite loss
   d. Characterized (in people) by an attitude of "when nothing works, why bother"
   e. Increased levels of GABA in hippocampus decrease likelihood of learned helplessness response

2. <u>Low rate of response-contingent reinforcement</u>

   a. Another explanation for depression

   b. Too little predictable positive reinforcement

   c. Person may lack the social skills necessary to elicit this positive reinforcement.

   d. Depression can be seen as a prolonged extinction schedule.

   e. Results in passivity

Special Topics

1. There is no such thing as a universal reinforcer. Reinforcement depends on the internal state of the organism.

   a. Consider how likely you are to say "thank you" to a turkey sandwich offered when you missed lunch versus just after Thanksgiving dinner

2. Curvilinear relationship between anxiety and learning

   a. Too much or too little anxiety has a disruptive effect on learning.

   b. This curvilinear relationship applies to:

      i. Anxiety and performance

      ii. Fear induction and adherence (health belief model)

      iii. Motivation and learning

      iv. Stimulus complexity and personal preferences

      v. Postsurgical recovery and anxiety

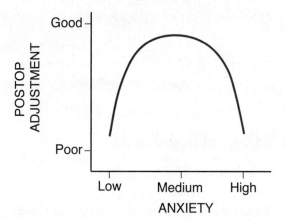

Figure 6-3. Relationship between Anxiety and Postoperative Adjustment

3. Behavioral approaches to pain management

   a. Involves no assumptions about physical or psychological origin of pain (or even if person really is in pain)

   b. Pain is a subjective state and therefore not objectively measurable.

    c. Focus is on pain behaviors (complaining, taking medications, missing work) rather than on subjective state or unconscious determinants

    d. Involves assessing changes in pain behavior and changing environmental contingencies, including medications

    e. Time contingent: takes control and administers medications at preset intervals

    f. Contrasts with hospice

        i. Pain contingent approach

        ii. Emphasizes self-control and self-administered pain medication

Review Questions

51. Psychiatric conditions must be understood as the result of biochemical imbalances and maladaptive behavioral patterns. The concept of "learned helplessness," important for the understanding of the behavioral patterns common in depressed patients, originates from animal studies in which the experimenter prevents

    (A) spontaneous recovery

    (B) extinction behavior

    (C) stimulus generalization

    (D) operant reinforcement

    (E) avoidance behavior

52. At the direction of his parents, a child has learned to pick up his toys and clean his room before he goes to bed each night. To most increase the chances that the child will continue this behavior in the future, even when the parents are not present, from this point forward reinforcement of the child should follow what type of reinforcement schedule?

    (A) Fixed ratio reinforcement

    (B) Fixed interval reinforcement

    (C) Variable ratio reinforcement

    (D) Variable interval reinforcement

    (E) Noncontingent reinforcement

53. A child's crying can be the manifestation of an innate biological response or of conditioned behavior. Operant conditioning is most likely to account for which of the following instances of crying in an 18-month-old child? Crying that

    (A) occurs spontaneously without any apparent cause

    (B) increases in intensity when the adult does not respond

    (C) occurs when the child is hungry

    (D) occurs in response to an unexpected, sudden, painful stimulus

    (E) occurs when the mother leaves the child in the care of a new babysitter

54. Two brothers have been fighting. Exasperated, the mother says to one of her sons, "Go to your room until you apologize to your brother for hitting him!" The mother's words are an example of the application of

    (A) operant conditioning

    (B) punishment

    (C) aversive conditioning

    (D) negative reinforcement

    (E) extinction

55. After repeated exposure to a nurse in a white coat followed by an injection, a child learns to cower and cry in response to anyone approaching in a white coat. The child's behavior can best be explained as an example of

   (A) shaping
   (B) instrumental conditioning
   (C) mediated reflex response arc
   (D) classic conditioning
   (E) observational learning

56. A man who has smoked two packs of cigarettes a day for the past 20 years decides to give up smoking, but is unsuccessful. When questioned by his physician, he notes that he has the most trouble refraining from smoking when he has his usual glass of bourbon every evening. Having "bourbon and a smoke" is how he relaxes at the end of the day. The physician suggests that he refrain from having his bourbon each evening and substitute an evening stroll instead. The physician's advice is based on an application of the principle of

   (A) aversive conditioning
   (B) biofeedback
   (C) systematic desensitization
   (D) fading
   (E) stimulus control

57. A 56-year-old male patient has just been diagnosed with diabetes. His physician is concerned about fostering adherence with a treatment regimen that includes regular medication and dietary changes. The patient is most likely to follow the instructions given by the physician if the conversation with the physician makes the patient

   (A) calm and collected
   (B) calm and questioning
   (C) concerned and attentive
   (D) worried and distracted
   (E) fearful and self-absorbed

Answers

51. **Answer: E.** In the animal studies, the researcher prevents the animal from getting away from the painful stimulus: avoidance is prevented.

52. **Answer: C.** Variable ratio reinforcement is most resistant to extinction. Think of gambling.

53. **Answer: B.** Operant behavior is evident when an environmental stimulus, such as eye contact or the lack of response by the adult, evokes a learned behavior. Pain response is not learned, but innate.

54. **Answer: D.** The key here is the contingency; the child gets out of his room (removal of a stimuli) when he apologizes. This removal, making a behavior more likely, is the definition of negative reinforcement. Note, the mother's words are not punishment. That would be "you have been fighting with your brother, go to your room," trying to inflict punishment to limit a behavior.

55. **Answer: D.** White coat comes to be associated with pain, just as the bell comes to be associated with the meat for Pavlov. Classic, or its synonym, respondent conditioning.

56. **Answer: E.** By avoiding the stimulus that triggers the unwanted behavior, the unwanted behavior becomes less likely. Note that this is an application of operant conditioning.

57. **Answer: C.** The Health Belief model tells us that medium levels of anxiety are best for adherence.

Defense Mechanisms 7

GENERAL ISSUES

1. Defense mechanisms are a concept born out of Freudian psychology. Recall that the Freudian psyche consists of:

   a. Id: animalistic, instinctive urges, sex, aggression, and other primary processes

   b. Ego: rational and language-based executors linking to reality

   c. Super-ego: the conscience, the moral compass insisting on socially acceptable behavior, sometimes to the point of individual deprivation begins to develop at age 5–9 (punitive).

2. Defenses are the primary tools of the ego, used to manage the internal conflicts between the primitive id and the punitive super-ego. They are the means by which the ego wards off anxiety and controls instinctive urges and unpleasant affects (emotions).

   a. All defenses are unconscious, with one exception: suppression

   b. Defenses change over time. We are only aware of our defenses in retrospect.

   c. Defenses are adaptive as well as pathologic. We all use defenses all the time. They are how we cope.

   d. Psychopathology is an issue of intensity and extent. Psychopathology = too much all at once, or for too extended a period of time. The key issue in psychopathology is the degree to which the use of defense mechanisms is disruptive of a person's ability to deal with the world around him or her. Unlike behaviorism, defenses are identified by what the person does in conjunction with his or her internal (unconscious) thought processes.

FOUR CLUSTERS OF DEFENSES (FROM LEAST MATURE TO MOST MATURE)

Narcissistic Defenses

The boundary between self and others is highly permeable. One's sense of self is very weak and vulnerable.

   a. <u>Projection</u>: person attributes his or her own wishes, desires, thoughts, or emotions to someone else. Internal states are perceived as a part of someone else or of the world in general.

      i. Examples:

         - A man who has committed adultery becomes convinced that his wife is having an affair even though there is no evidence of it.

> **Note**
>
> **The COMLEX Requires You to Know:**
>
> - How to recognize the presence of defense mechanisms and the impact they have on human behaviors and perceptions.
>
> - Special attention should be paid to the impact these defense mechanisms may have on medical practice.
>
> - Which defense mechanisms are commonly associated with specific psychiatric diagnoses.

- A girl talks about her doll as having certain feelings, which are really what the girl feels.
- A physician believes that the nursing staff is uncomfortable talking to him, when in fact, he is uncomfortable talking with them.

ii. Paranoia results from the use of projection.

b. <u>Denial</u>: not allowing reality to penetrate. Asserting that some clear feature of external reality just is not true. Used to avoid becoming aware of a painful aspect of reality

i. Examples:

- After surviving a heart attack, a patient insists on continuing his lifestyle as if nothing had happened.
- A child who is abused insists that she has been treated well.
- A woman prepares dinner for her husband expecting him to come home, even though he died a month earlier.

ii. Often the first response to bad news, such as the impending death of a loved one or oneself. Substance users are often "in denial," claiming that they are not addicted and do not have a problem in the face of clearly dysfunctional or dangerous behavior.

c. <u>Splitting</u>: people and things in the world are perceived as all bad or all good (God or the Devil). The world is pictured in extreme terms rather than a more realistic blend of good and bad qualities.

i. Examples:

- "This doctor is a miracle worker, but that doctor is totally incompetent."
- "He's just so perfect and wonderful," says a teenage girl in love.
- "No one from that family will ever amount to anything; they are all just plain no good."

ii. Borderline personality disorders use splitting and vacillate between seeing individuals in the world as all good or all bad. Prejudice and stereotypes are often the result of splitting.

Immature Defenses

Sense of self is stronger with the narcissistic defenses but the ego has areas of vulnerability.

a. <u>Blocking</u>: temporary or transient block in thinking, or an inability to remember

i. Examples:

- "Mr. Jones, you are suffering from... gee, I just can't remember what it is called."
- A student is unable to recall the fact needed to answer the exam question, although he recalls it as he walks out of the exam.
- In the middle of a conversation, a woman pauses, looks confused, and asks, "What was I just talking about?"

ii. Blocking is disruptive and can be embarrassing.

b. <u>Regression</u>: returning to an earlier stage of development. "Acting childish" or at least younger than is typical for that individual

   i. Examples:

- An older patient giggles uncontrollably or breaks down crying when told bad news.
- A husband speaks to his wife in "baby talk."
- A patient lies in bed curled up in a fetal position.

   ii. Play is regressive, i.e., a more free, simpler expression from a earlier age.

   iii. Regression is common when people are tired, ill, or uncomfortable.

   iv. Enuresis that develops in a child who previously had been continent following the birth of a new sibling is the result of regression. Similarly, when a new child is born, older children who have been weaned may demand to go back to breast-feeding.

c. <u>Somatization</u>: psychic derivatives are converted into bodily symptoms. Feelings are manifest as physical symptoms rather than psychologic distress.

   i. Examples:

- Getting a headache while taking an exam
- Feeling queasy and nauseated before asking someone out on a date
- Developing a ringing in the ears while making a presentation for Grand Rounds

   ii. Extreme forms of somatization are diagnosed as somatic symptom disorders (see section on DSM 5).

   iii. Symptoms created are physically real, not merely imagined

d. <u>Introjection</u> (Identification): features of external world or persons are taken in and made part of the self. The opposite of projection

   i. Examples:

- A resident dresses and acts like the attending physician.
- A child scolds herself out loud in the same manner that her mother scolded her the day before.
- A teenager adopts the style and mannerisms of a rock star.

   ii. When identifying with others is done consciously, it is labeled "imitation".

   iii. The superego is formed, in part, by the introjection of the same-gender parent as a resolution to the Oedipal crisis.

   iv. Introjection is why children act like their parents. "I always swore that I would treat my children differently, yet there I was saying the same things to my children that my mother always used to say to me!"

   v. Being a sports fan or a soap opera fan involves introjection.

   vi. Patients in psychotherapy gain a different (hopefully healthier) sense of self, in part, by introjecting their therapist.

Anxiety Defenses

You have a fairly strong and robust sense of self and ego. These defenses serve to address the unpleasant discomforts of anxiety.

a. <u>Displacement</u>: changing the target of an emotion or drive, while the person having the feeling remains the same

    i. Examples:

- A man who is angry at his boss pounds on his desk rather than telling his boss what he really thinks.

- An attending physician scolds a resident who later expresses his anger by yelling at a medical student.

- A married man who is sexually aroused by a woman he meets goes home and makes love to his wife.

    ii. In family therapy, one child in the family is often singled out and blamed for all the family's problems, i.e., is treated as a scapegoat by others displacing their symptoms onto this child.

    iii. Displacement often "runs downhill," i.e., from higher to lower in a power hierarchy.

    iv. Phobias are the result of displacement.

b. <u>Repression</u>: an idea or feeling is eliminated from consciousness. Note that the content may once have been known, but now has become inaccessible.

    i. Examples:

- A child who was abused by her mother and was treated for the abuse, now has no memory of any mistreatment by her mother.

- A man who survived 6 months in a concentration camp cannot recall anything about his life during that time period.

    ii. You forget, and then forget that you forgot.

    iii. Content usually not recoverable without some trauma or psychoanalysis

    iv. Differentiated from denial in that the reality was once accepted, but is now discarded

    v. One of the most basic defense mechanisms

c. <u>Isolation of affect</u>: reality is accepted, but without the expected human emotional response to that reality. Separation of an idea from the affect that accompanies it

    i. Examples:

- A child who has been beaten discusses the beatings without any display of emotions.

- A physician informs a patient of his poor prognosis in bland, matter-of-fact tones.

- A patient who has had a finger severed in an accident describes the incident to his physician without any emotional reaction.

    ii. Facts without feelings

      iii. The bland affect of schizophrenics, *la belle indifference*, that often accompanies conversion disorder is a manifestation of this defense mechanism.

  d. <u>Intellectualization</u>: affect is stripped away and replaced by an excessive use of intellectual processes. Cognition replaces affect. The intellectual content is academically, but not humanly, relevant.

      i. Examples:

- "Notice how the bone is protruding from my leg. It is interesting to contemplate the physics that allows such an event to happen."

- A physician tells a patient about his poor prognosis and talks a great deal about the technical aspects by which the prognosis was derived.

- A boy who is about to ask a girl out on a date for the first time talks with his friend about the importance of mating rituals for the long-term survival of the species and the mechanisms by which societies arrange for these rituals.

- Intellect in place of emotion

      ii. Physicians who are too concerned with the technical aspects of the profession and not enough with the patient may well be using this defense mechanism.

      iii. In obsessive–compulsive anxiety disorder, rumination can result from this defense mechanism.

  e. <u>Acting out</u>: massive emotional or behavioral outburst to cover up underlying feeling or idea. Strong action or emotions to cover up unacceptable emotions. Note: The real emotion is covered, not expressed.

      i. Examples:

- Temper tantrum is thrown by an abandoned child to cover the depression he really feels

- "Whistling in the dark" hides the real underlying fear.

- For adolescents, substance-related disorder, overeating, or getting into fights are "strong" actions that coverup underlying feelings of vulnerability.

      ii. Differentiated from displacement in that the emotion is covered up, not redirected

      iii. Common in borderline and antisocial personality disorders

  f. <u>Rationalization</u>: rational explanations are used to justify attitudes, beliefs, or behaviors that are unacceptable.

      i. Examples:

- "Yes, I believe killing is wrong, but I killed him because he really deserved it."

- A man who is unfaithful to his wife tells himself that this liaison will actually make him appreciate his wife more.

- A young single woman tells herself that engaging in oral sex with a married man is not the same thing as having a "sexual relationship" with him.

      ii. Look for the "string of reasons"

      iii. Note that this is not a reasoned action, but a search for reasons to allow an unacceptable action already selected.

  iv. Used to relieve guilt and shame

  v. Often accompanies obsessive–compulsive behavior

g. <u>Reaction formation</u>: an unacceptable impulse is transformed into its opposite. A global reversal in which love is expressed as hate, for example

  i. Examples:

  - A student who always wanted to be a physician expresses relief and says, "This is the best news I've ever heard," after not being accepted into medical school.

  - A teenage boy intrigued by "dirty pictures" organizes an antiporno-graphy campaign.

  - Two coworkers fight all the time because they are actually very attracted to each other.

  ii. Excessive overreaction can often be a sign of reaction formation. As if the person is trying to convince self, or anyone else, that the original feeling or impulse did not exist. From Shakespeare: "The lady doth protest too much, methinks."

  iii. Found in many anxiety disorders

h. <u>Undoing</u>: acting out the reverse of unacceptable behavior. Repairs or fixes the impulse

  i. Examples:

  - A man who is sexually aroused by woman he meets immediately leaves and buys his wife flowers.

  - Superstitions such as "knock on wood" after wishing someone well

  - A man repeatedly checks the burners on the stove to make sure that they are turned off before leaving the house.

  ii. Many religions offer a type of institutionally sanctioned undoing: the penance after confession or making the sign of the cross to ward off anxiety.

  iii. Obsessive–compulsive behavior (e.g., repeated handwashing) is undoing.

i. <u>Passive-aggressive</u>: nonperformance or poor performance after setting up the expectation of performance. Regarded as a passive (indirect) expression of hostility

  i. Examples:

  - "I could give you a good example of this, but I'm not going to."

  - A student agrees to share class notes but goes home without sharing them.

  - A physician ignores and does not answer the direct questions of a patient whom he finds annoying.

  ii. The feelings of hostility are unconscious, and the person using the defense is generally unaware of them.

  iii. If you consciously set someone up, it is not a defense, but simply being mean.

  iv. Often used by borderline personality disorders and young children

j. <u>Dissociation</u>: separates self from one's experience. Third-person rather than first- person experience. The facts of the events are accepted, but the self is protected from the full impact of the experience.

    i. Examples:

- A woman who was raped reports that it was as if she was floating on the ceiling watching it happen.
- The survivor of an automobile accident tells of the feeling that everything happened in slow motion.
- A child who was sexually abused recalls only the bad man who came to her in her dreams.

    ii. Increasingly common in clinical settings

    iii. In extreme forms, this becomes a dissociative disorder, e.g., fugue states, amnesia, identity (multiple personality) disorder (see section on DSM 5).

Mature Defenses

These defenses distort reality less than the other defenses and are thus considered more mature

a. <u>Humor</u>: permits the overt expression of feelings and thoughts without personal discomfort

    i. Examples:

- A man laughs when told he is going to be fired.
- A student smiles when he realizes that a particularly intimidating professor looks like a penguin.
- A terminally ill cancer patient makes fun of his condition.

    ii. Laughter covers the pain and anxiety.

    iii. We laugh the easiest at the things that make us most anxious.

b. <u>Sublimation</u>: impulse-gratification is achieved by channeling the unacceptable or unattainable impulse into a socially acceptable direction. The unacceptable/unattainable impulse becomes the motive force for social benefit.

    i. Examples:

- Dante wrote the *Inferno* as an outlet for his adoration of the woman Beatrice.
- An executive who is attracted to a female associate becomes her mentor and advisor.
- A patient with exhibitionist fantasies becomes a stripper.

    ii. Much art and literature spring from sublimation.

    iii. Considered by some to be the most mature defense mechanism

c. <u>Suppression</u>: conscious decision to postpone attention to an impulse or conflict. Conscious setup and unconscious follow-through. The suppressed content temporarily resides in the unconscious.

    i. Examples:

- A student decides to forget about a pending exam to go out and have a good time for an evening.
- A woman who is afraid of heights ignores the drop of the cliff to appreciate the beautiful vista.
- A terminally ill cancer patient puts aside his anxiety and enjoys a family gathering.

ii. Unlike repression, suppressed content is recalled with the right cue or stimulus.

iii. Forget, but remember that you forgot

TRANSFERENCE

The patient unconsciously transfers thoughts and feelings about a parent or significant other person onto his physician. This is not a defense mechanism. Can be positive (cause you to unaccountably like someone) or negative (cause you to unaccountably dislike someone)

1. Easily established in cases of physical illness, because the patient often undergoes a psychologic regression
2. Not necessarily related to the length of time the patient has known physician
3. Note that for a learning theorist, transference is just another instance of stimulus generalization.
4. Countertransference is transference from the physician to the patient.

Table 7-1. Common Freudian Defense Mechanisms

Defense Mechanism	Short Definition	Important Associations
Projection	Seeing the inside in the outside	Paranoid behavior
Denial	Saying it is not so	Substance-related disorders, reaction to death
Splitting	The world composed of polar opposites	Borderline personality; good vs evil
Blocking	Transient inability to remember	Momentary lapse
Regression	Returning to an earlier stage of development	Enuresis, primitive behaviors
Somatization	Physical symptoms for psychological reasons	Somatic symptom disorders
Introjection	The outside becomes inside	Superego, being like parents
Displacement	Source stays the same, target changes	Redirected emotion, phobias, scapegoat
Repression	Forgetting so it is nonretrievable	Forget and forget
Isolation of affect	Facts without feeling	Blunted affect, *la belle indifference*
Intellectualization	Affect replaced by academic content	Academic, not human, reaction
Acting out	Affect covered up by excessive action or sensation	Substance-related disorders, fighting, gambling
Rationalization	Why the unacceptable is OK in this instance	Justification, string of reasons
Reaction formation	Unacceptable transformed into its opposite	Manifesting the opposite, feel love but show hate, "Girls have cooties"
Undoing	Action to symbolically reverse the unacceptable	Fixing or repairing, obsessive–compulsive behaviors
Passive-aggression	Passive nonperformance after promise	Unconscious, indirect hostility
Dissociation	Separating self from one's own experience	Fugue, depersonalization, amnesia, multiple personality
Humor	A pleasant release from anxiety	Laughter hides the pain
Sublimation	Unacceptable impulse into acceptable channel	Art, literature, mentoring
Suppression	Forgetting but it is retrievable	Forget and remember

Review Questions

58. "No, I don't remember, and I don't want to remember," cries a man asked to recall a painful episode from his childhood. The defense mechanism most closely suggested by this man's words and behavior is

    (A) projection
    (B) denial
    (C) intellectualization
    (D) dissociation
    (E) repression

59. A woman finds herself in a town some distance from her home, without any recollection of how she got there. The defense mechanism that most likely accounts for this scenario is

    (A) repression
    (B) suppression
    (C) dissociation
    (D) reaction formation
    (E) denial

60. When asked about his impending heart operation, the patient recounts the procedures in detail. He seems remarkably well versed and, upon questioning, admits that he has been "reading everything I can get my hands on" about it. He discusses the details for hours, yet shows no emotional reaction to the impending events. The defense mechanism that most likely accounts for this scenario is

    (A) rationalization
    (B) repression
    (C) regression
    (D) isolation
    (E) intellectualization

61. A woman with no previous history of promiscuity suddenly begins to take on sexual partners of both sexes, one right after the other. The record shows that her new pattern of sexual behavior started soon after the death of a child to whom she was very close. Yet, there is no indication of a period of mourning. The woman's behavior suggests the defense mechanism of

    (A) isolation
    (B) suppression
    (C) denial
    (D) acting out
    (E) undoing

62. A 32-year-old Irish male appears at the clinic complaining of "a slight pain" on his left side. Upon examination, he is found to have two broken ribs. When informed of this, the man insists that it cannot be that serious and asks only for some medication for the pain. This is best characterized as the defense mechanism of

    (A) displacement
    (B) denial
    (C) depression
    (D) isolation
    (E) reaction formation

63. A father, who has lost his daughter as the result of a traffic accident involving a drunk driver, organizes a local chapter of a national group campaigning to stop the sale of liquor to minors and to legislate mandatory jail time for anyone convicted of drunk driving. "If I can't have my girl back, at least I can make sure it doesn't happen to some other father," he says. The defense mechanism that most likely accounts for this behavior is

    (A) acting out
    (B) suppression
    (C) reaction formation
    (D) displacement
    (E) sublimation

64. A 64-year-old male factory worker is hospitalized after barely surviving a serious myocardial infarction. His life was saved by the administration of emergency balloon angioplasty. The following day his primary care physician visits the patient's hospital room. Much to his surprise, he finds the patient, who never did much exercise before, on the floor doing push-ups and saying, "Time to get in shape, doc!" The patient's word and behavior in this instance are most likely the result of the defense mechanism of

    (A) denial
    (B) dissociation
    (C) acting out
    (D) undoing
    (E) reaction formation

65. Bob is an avid sports fan who runs 5 miles everyday for fitness and relaxation, and frequently plays touch football with others in this neighborhood. One day after he had had an argument with his wife, Bob got into a fistfight during a football game and had to be restrained by his teammates. The defense mechanism that most likely accounts for Bob's behavior is

    (A) acting out

    (B) denial

    (C) displacement

    (D) dissociation

    (E) intellectualization

    (F) introjection

    (G) isolation

    (H) passive–aggressive

    (I) projection

    (J) rationalization

    (K) reaction formation

    (L) regression

    (M) repression

    (N) splitting

Answers

58. **Answer: E.** Repression is forgetting, and forgetting that you forgot. It is enduring and motivated by unconscious desires. Repression is one of the most basic defense mechanisms.

59. **Answer: C.** Amnesia with travel is the classic definition of psychogenic fugue state, the result of dissociation as a defense mechanism.

60. **Answer: E.** Rather than responding with the expected level of apprehension and anxiety, the patient spends his time reading and cognitive activity. Anxiety is replaced by cognitive activity: intellectualization.

61. **Answer: D.** Rather than showing the expected grief reactions, the woman embarks on a new course of behavior. This behavior masks the underlying, unexpressed feeling and constitutes acting out.

62. **Answer: B.** The patient responds to the reality of broken ribs by saying that it is not so. This bald-faced negation of objective facts is denial.

63. **Answer: E.** The father gets gratification from the impulse to save his daughter by helping others. The behavior is not simply redirected as with displacement, but targeted directly to the issue of concern to the benefit of others.

64. **Answer: D.** The patient is doing action to fix or make up for his heart condition. This behaviorally focused reversal is what undoing is all about.

65. **Answer: C.** The anger Bob feels toward his wife is redirected into a fight with someone else. Bob is still angry, but the recipient of the anger changes from his wife to another.

Psychologic Health and Testing 8

PSYCHOLOGIC HEALTH AND PHYSICAL HEALTH

1. Type A behavior pattern (or the Coronary Prone Behavior Pattern)

    a. A cluster of behavioral traits that has been associated with increased prevalence and incidence of coronary heart disease

    b. The extreme Type A person is engaged in a chronic struggle to obtain an unlimited number of things from his environment in the shortest possible period of time.

    c. Traits: impatient, competitive, preoccupied with deadlines, and highly involved with their jobs

    d. Recent data suggest that how people handle hostility is the key component of Type A behavior. People who get hostile and angry at everyday slights are more at risk.

    e. One major prospective study has shown that the Type A behavior pattern is associated with a twofold increase in incidence of coronary heart disease, even after controlling for the major risk factors (systolic blood pressure, cigarette smoking, cholesterol).

    f. Following a first heart attack, Type As who survived had a lower chance of a second attack than did Type Bs.

PSYCHOLOGIC ADJUSTMENT AND PHYSICAL HEALTH

1. A study of physically healthy men (Harvard sophomores between 1942 and 1944) followed for nearly 40 years showed that mentally healthy individuals do not deteriorate in physical health as quickly as do those in poor mental health. Chronic anxiety, depression, and emotional maladjustment predict negative health events later in life.

2. Stressful life events: Holmes and Rahe scale used to quantify stressful life events

    a. On this scale, different life events contribute different weightings to the total score.

    b. The death of a spouse is weighed as the most stressful event

    c. The correlation between stressful life events and developing illness is a small but significant positive correlation between +0.30 and +0.40.

3. Why individuals react differently to the same objective stressors

    a. The individual's appraisal of the meaning of the stressor

    b. Hardy personality type: clear sense of values, goals, and capabilities; an unshakable sense of the meaningfulness of life; and a strong sense of control over one's own fate

    c. Social support

        i. Belief is more important than objective support.

        ii. Having one significant person to turn to is key.

Note
The COMLEX Requires You to Know:

- Type A behavior pattern, how stress impacts physical health, and what intelligence is and the basic tests for measuring it

- The difference between objective and projective tests and common examples of each

- Commonly used neuropsychologic tests

- Computing and understanding the IQ

   iii. Women use support more effectively than do men.

   iv. Presence of a familiar person lowers blood pressure in a person under stress.

   v. Widows and widowers have higher rates of heart attacks in the year just after a spouse dies.

4. Physiologic changes in response to stress

 a. Key stress response pathway: hypothalamic-pituitary-adrenal axis

 b. Cortisol levels rise then fall within 24 hours after stressor.

 c. Secondary spike in cortisol levels 48 to 72 hours after stressor

INTELLIGENCE QUOTIENT (IQ)

1. Definition: a general estimate of the functional capacities of the person

2. 70% inherited, recent studies suggest most from mother

3. IQ is not an absolute score but a comparison among people.

4. Distribution mean: 100; standard deviation: 15

Table 8-1. Distribution of IQ Scores in the General Population

Range	Label	Distribution
Less than 69	Intellectual disability	About 2.5% of the population
70 to 79	Borderline	
80 to 89	Low average	
90 to 109	Average	About 50% of the population
110 to 119	High average	
120 to 129	Superior	
over 130	Very superior	About 2.5% of the population

5. Scaling intelligence: calculating an intelligence quotient

 a. Mental age method

  i. Mental age (MA) = median test score for a given age

  ii. Chronological age (CA) = actual age of the person taking the test

  iii. Formula: (MA/CA) $\times$ 100 = IQ score

  iv. Example: A 10-year-old child got a test score of 25. If 25 is the median score of 13-year-olds, then MA = 13, CA = 10, and (13/10) $\times$ 100 = 130

  v. Note that as CA goes up, if MA stays constant, IQ goes down.

 b. Deviation from norms method

  i. For each age range (cohort), take a sample of the IQ test scores.

  ii. The mean is 100 and the standard deviation is 15.

  iii. If a child age 10 scores a 25 on the test, find the table for age 10 and look up a score of 25 to see what IQ level the score corresponds to

 c. Error margin for both mental age method and deviation from norms method is ±5 points.

6. IQ facts

    a. IQ is highly correlated with education and is an excellent predictor of academic achievement.

    b. Mental illness is distributed across all ranges of intelligence, although measured IQ may be lower when assessed because of interference of symptoms.

    c. Autistic children tend to be of below-average intelligence, with 80% having IQs less than 70.

    d. Longitudinal tests for intelligence show:

        i. Very little decline in the elderly

        ii. Verbal ability holds up best

        iii. Perceptual and motor tests show some decline

    e. IQ is very stable from age 5 onward.

    f. Increased exposure to verbal behavior early in life leads to a higher IQ.

    g. IQ tests contain elements of cultural bias, asking about words and objects more familiar in some cultures than in others.

7. Commonly used IQ tests

    a. Wechsler Adult Intelligence Scale, Revised (WAIS-R) is for adults, aged 17 and older.

    b. Wechsler Intelligence Scale for Children, Revised (WISC-R) is for children aged 6 to 17.

    c. Wechsler Preschool and Primary Scale of Intelligence (WPPSI) is for children aged 4 to 6.

    d. Stanford-Binet Scale was the first formal IQ test (1905) and is used for children aged 2 to 18. Today, it is most useful with children younger than 6, the impaired, or the very bright.

PERSONALITY TESTS

1. <u>Objective tests</u>: simple stimuli (usually questions), restricted range of responses possible (select between choices given), scored mechanistically using scoring key; no clinical experience required to score. There are two types of objective personality tests:

    a. Criterion referenced

        i. Results are given meaning by comparing them with a preset standard.

        ii. E.g., COMLEX-USA Level 1

        iii. "Every student who scores above 75% will pass."

    b. Norm referenced

        i. Results are given meaning by comparing them with a normative group.

        ii. Classic example: Minnesota Multiphasic Personality Inventory (MMPI) revised 1989

            • >550 statements to which respondent answers true or false

            • Most widely used (and misused) personality test. Serves as criterion for newly developed tests

            • Yields 10 primary clinical dimensions and 3 validity scales

2. <u>Projective tests</u>: ambiguous stimuli; wide range of responses possible, scored by experienced clinician using consensual standards

   a. Meaning of responses found by clinical correlation between collected cases of responses and personal characteristics, psychopathologies

   b. Classic examples:

      i. Rorschach Inkblot Test

         ● Patients are asked to look at an inkblot and report what they see.

      ii. Thematic Aperception Test (TAT)

         ● Patients are asked to tell a story about what is going on in the pictures.

      iii. Sentence Completion Test

         ● Patient is asked to complete a set of sentence stems with the first thing that comes to mind

      iv. Projective drawings

         ● Patient is given a sheet of paper and asked to draw a house, a tree, a person, a family, or some other subject

NEUROPSYCHOLOGIC TESTS

1. Halstead-Reitan Battery

   a. Tests for presence and localization of brain dysfunction

   b. Consists of five basic tests: category test, tactual performance test, rhythm test, speech sounds perception test, finger oscillation test. These are combined to provide an impairment index.

2. Luria Nebraska Battery

   a. Tests level of impairment and functioning

   b. Subscales: motor, rhythm, tactile, visual–spatial, receptive speech, expressive speech, writing, reading, arithmetic, amnestic, intellectual, right and left hemisphere function

3. Bender Visual Motor Gestalt Test

   a. Screens for brain dysfunction

   b. Nine designs are presented to the patient and copied by him. The patient is then asked to recall as many designs as he or she can

4. Benton Visual Retention Test

   a. Spatial construction, drawing task

   b. 10 designs that the patient copies as presented or from memory

5. Wechsler Memory Scale

   a. Assess memory impairment

   b. Subcomponents: recall of current and past information, orientation, attention, concentration, memory for story details, memory designs, and learning

   c. Yields a memory quotient

Human Development 9

DEVELOPMENTAL MILESTONES

General Patterns in Human Development

1. Development occurs along multiple lines: physical, cognitive, intellectual, and social.

2. We tend to chart development for each of these lines in terms of milestones, i.e., skills achieved by a certain age. Milestones are simply normative markers at median ages. Some children develop slower and some faster. The ages for the milestones are therefore only approximate and should not be taken as dogma.

3. Although children generally progress along the lines of development together, they often may not. Thus, a child may match the milestones for cognitive development but show slower growth in the social area.

Infants

1. Recent research has changed our past assumptions about the capabilities of infants. Evidenced at birth:
   a. Reaching and grasping behavior
   b. Ability to imitate facial expressions
   c. Ability to synchronize their limb movements with speech of others (coupling or entrainment)
   d. Attachment behaviors, such as crying and clinging

2. Newborn preferences
   a. Large, bright objects with lots of contrast
   b. Moving objects
   c. Curves versus lines
   d. Complex versus simple designs
   e. Evidence of a preference for facial stimuli

3. The fact that a neonate will demonstrate defensive movements if an object looms toward his or her face suggests the ability to perceive a three-dimensional world.

4. Recent research also suggests that the neonatal nervous system gives special attention to language versus nonlanguage stimuli.
   a. Left-brain–evoked potentials are larger than right-brain–evoked potentials to language stimuli (but not to nonlanguage stimuli).
   b. Neonates can discriminate between language and nonlanguage stimuli.
   c. Infants do not learn language but learn to use the language capacity they are born with (Broca's area).

Note

The COMLEX Requires You to Know:

- Capacities and preferences of infants

- Basic developmental patterns, including reproducing shapes and learning movements

- Common ages corresponding to physical milestones

- The basic issues in personality development

- How social capacities change with age

- The sequence of cognitive development

- How language skills develop with age

- Characteristic patterns of play at given ages

- How to discipline children

- Coping with attachment and loss

- Differentiating grief and depression and children's conceptions of death and illness

- Dealing with abuse

5. At just 1 week old, the infant responds differently to the smell of the mother compared with the father.

6. Smiling

   a. The smile develops from an innate reflex present at birth (endogenous smile).

   b. An infant shows exogenous smiling in response to a face at 8 weeks.

   c. A preferential social smile, e.g., to the mother's rather than another's face, appears about 12 to 16 weeks.

7. Physical development

   a. Hands and feet are the first parts of the body to reach adult size.

   b. Motor development follows set patterns:

      i. Grasp precedes release

      ii. Palm up maneuvers occur before palm down maneuvers

      iii. Proximal to distal progression

      iv. Ulnar to radial progression

   c. Capacity to copy shapes follows in alphabetical order:

      i. Circle, cross, rectangle, square, triangle

      ii. The exception is a "diamond," which can generally not be reproduced until age 7.

   d. First words (10 months), then first birthday, then first steps (13 months)

Figure Copied		Approximate Age
○	Circle	3
+	Cross	4
▭	Rectangle	4½
□	Square	5
△	Triangle	6
◇	Diamond	7

Figure 9-1. Figures Copied and Approximate Ages

8. Key developmental issues

   a. Brain-growth spurt: "critical period" of great vulnerability to environmental influence

      i. Extending from last trimester of pregnancy through first 14 postnatal months

      ii. Size of cortical cells and complexity of cell interconnections undergo their most rapid increase. Brain adapts structure to match environmental stimulation.

   b. Earliest memories, roughly ages 2–4

   c. Stranger anxiety: distress in the presence of unfamiliar people

      i. It appears at 6 months, reaches its peak at 8 months, disappears after 12 months

      ii. Can occur even when child is held by parent

   d. Separation anxiety: distress of infant following separation from a caretaker

      i. Appears at 8–12 months

      ii. Begins to disappear at 20–24 months

      iii. Continued separation, especially prior to 12 months, leads to withdrawal and risk of anaclitic depression

      iv. School phobia (Separation Anxiety Disorder) is failure to resolve separation anxiety. Treatment focuses on child's interaction with parents, not on activities in school

   e. Imprinting: an interesting facet of attachment behavior in animals

      i. Some animals (geese, ducks, quail) will follow the first object they see after birth.

      ii. May even run to it, rather than to the mother, when frightened

      iii. Does *not* apply to humans

Table 9-1. Child Development Milestones

Age	Physical and Motor Developments	Social Developments	Cognitive Developments (Piaget)	Language Developments
1st year of life	• Puts everything in mouth • Sits with support (4 mo) • Stands with help (8 mo) • Crawls, fear of falling (9 mo) • Pincer grasp (10 mo) • Follows objects to midline (4 wk) • One-handed approach/grasp of toy • Feet in mouth (5 mo) • Bang and rattle stage • Changes hands with toy (6 mo)	• Parental figure central • Issues of trust are key • Stranger anxiety (7 mo) • Play is solitary and exploratory • Pat-a-cake, peek-a boo (10 mo)	• Sensation/movement • Schemas • Assimilation and accommodation	• Laughs aloud (4 mo) • Repetitive responding (8 mo) • "ma-ma, da-da" (10 mo)
Age 1	• Walks alone (13 mo) • Climbs stairs alone (18 mo) • Emergence of hand preference (18 mo) • Kicks ball, throws ball • Pats pictures in book • Stacks three cubes (18 mo)	• Separation anxiety (12 mo) • Dependency on parental figure (rapproachment) • Onlooker play	• Achieves object permanence	• Great variation in timing of language development • Uses 10 words
Age 2	• High activity level • Walks backwards • Can turn doorknob, unscrew jar lid • Scribbles with crayon • Stacks six cubes (24 mo) • Stands on tiptoes (30 mo) • Able to aim thrown ball	• Selfish and self-centered • Imitates mannerisms and activities • May be aggressive • Recognizes self in mirror • "No" is favorite word • Parallel play	• A world of objects • Can use symbols • Transition objects • Strong egocentrism • Concrete use of objects	• Use of pronouns • Parents understand most • Telegraphic sentences • Two-word sentences • Uses 250 words • Identifies body parts by pointing
Age 3	• Rides tricycle • Stacks 9 cubes (36 mo.) • Alternates feet going up stairs • Bowel and bladder control (toilet training) • Draws recognizable figures • Catches ball with arms • Cuts paper with scissors • Unbuttons buttons	• Fixed gender identity • Sex-specific play • Understands "taking turns" • Knows sex and full name		• Complete sentences • Uses 900 words • Understands 4× that • Strangers can understand • Recognizes common objects in pictures • Can answer, "Tell me what we wear on our feet?" "Which block is bigger?"

(continued)

Table 9-1. Child Development Milestones *(continued)*

Age	Physical and Motor Developments	Social Developments	Cognitive Developments (Piaget)	Language Developments
Age 4	• Alternates feet going down stairs • Hops on one foot • Grooms self (brushes teeth) • Counts fingers on hand	• Imitation of adult roles • Curiosity about sex (playing doctor) • Nightmares and monster fears • Imaginary friends	• Points to and counts three objects • Repeats four digits • Names colors	• Can tell stories • Uses prepositions • Uses plurals • Compound sentences
Age 5	• Complete sphincter control • Brain at 75% of adult weight • Draws recognizable man with head, body, and limbs • Dresses and undresses self • Catches ball with two hands	• Conformity to peers important • Romantic feeling for others • Oedipal phase	• Counts 10 objects correctly	• Asks the meaning of words • Abstract words elusive
Ages 6 to 12	• Boys heavier than girls • Permanent teeth (11 y) • Refined motor skills • Rides bicycle • Prints letters • Gains athletic skill • Coordination increases	• "Rules of the Game" are key • Organized sport possible • Being team member focal for many • Separation of the sexes • Sexual feelings not apparent • Demonstrating competence is key	• Abstract from objects • Law of conservation acheived • Adherence to logic • Seriation • No hypotheticals • Mnemonic strategies • Personal sense of right and wrong	• Shift from egocentric to social speech • Incomplete sentences decline • Vocabulary expands geometrically (50,000 words by age 12)
Age 12 + (adolescence)	• Adolescent "growth spurt" (girls before boys) • Onset of sexual maturity (10+ y) • Development of primary and secondary sexual characteristics	• Identity is critical issue • Conformity most important (11–12 y) • Organized sports diminish for many • Cross-gender relationships	• Abstract from abstractions • Systematic problem-solving strategies • Can handle hypotheticals • Deals with past, present, future	• Adopts personal speech patterns • Communication becomes focus of relationships

Table 9-2. Tanner stages (pubic hair)

Look for	Median ages
1. No hair	≤ 10 years
2. Small amount, downy	10 to 11 years
3. Hair coarse and curly	11 to 13 years
4. Adult-like but not on thigh	13 to 14 years
5. Extends to medial thigh	> 14 years

APPLYING CHILD-DEVELOPMENT PRINCIPLES

Discipline of Children

    a. Be sure discipline is developmentally age-appropriate. Abstract, cognitive reasonings mean little to a child younger than 6 years.

    b. If trying to stop a young child from hitting another, don't expect the child to understand how the other feels.

    c. Best application of discipline would be "time out."

    d. Punishment by hitting the child is too confusing; you are doing exactly what you are telling the child not to do.

    e. Discipline should be clearly connected (in time and space) to behavior to be modified.

Teenagers

    a. Identity formation is the key issue. Issues of independence and self-definition predominate.

    b. The teenage years may be stressful but are not generally filled with the type of traumas often portrayed in the popular press.

    c. Teenagers' values reflect those of their parents.

    d. Rebellion is manifested as minor disagreements regarding hair, music, dress, friends.

    e. Rebellion is most likely in early teenage years.

    f. Sexual experimentation with opposite- and same-sex partners is common.

Attachment and Loss

    a. In childhood

        i. Bowlby postulates three phases of response to prolonged separation of children aged 7 months to 5 years
- Protest: crying, alarm, aggression
- Despair: hopes of regaining loved one fades
- Detachment: feelings of yearning and anger are repressed

        ii. Psychologic upset is more easily reversed in stages of protest or despair than after detachment has set in.

        iii. Because separation has behavioral consequences, pediatric hospitalization must take it into account through provision of parental contact (e.g., rooming-in practices, flexible visiting hours, assurances that mother will be present when child awakes from surgery).

    b. In adults

        i. Adults who are bereaved or are mourning the loss of a loved one also go through a series of phases.

        ii. Initial phase (protest, acute disbelief)
- Lasts several weeks
- Weeping
- Hostility and protest

iii. Intermediate phase (grief, disorganization)
- 3 weeks to 1 year
- Sadness, yearning, somatic symptoms
- Obsessional review, searching for deceased
- May believe they see or hear deceased
- Confronting reality

iv. Recovery (or reorganization) phase
- Reinvestment of energies and interests
- Begins second year after death, memories fade in intensity

Table 9-3. Normal Grief versus Depression

Normal Grief	Depression
Normal up to 1 year	After 1 year, sooner if symptoms severe
Crying, decreased libido, weight loss, insomnia	Same but more severe
Longing, wish to see loved one, may think they hear or see loved one in a crowd (illusion)	Abnormal overidentification, personality change
Loss of other	Loss of self
Suicidal ideation is rare	Suicidal ideation is common
Self-limited, usually less than 6 months	Symptoms do not stop (may persist for years)
Antidepressants not helpful	Antidepressants helpful

Dealing with Dying Patients

a. Stages of adjustment (Kubler-Ross)
   i. Denial
   ii. Anger
   iii. Bargaining
   iv. Depression
   v. Acceptance

b. People move back and forth through the stages. Not everyone passes through all stages or reaches adequate adjustment.

c. Similar stages for dealing with loss or separation

d. Rules for dealing with the dying:
   i. Tell the patient everything.
   ii. Do not give false hope.
   iii. Allow person to talk about feelings.
   iv. Keep involved in activities.
   v. Avoid social isolation.

Children's Conceptions of Illness and Death

a. Children do not see the real world, do not live in the same world that we do.

  i. They have a limited cognitive repertoire; their thinking is concrete and egocentric.

  ii. When they become ill, they may interpret this as a punishment and may have misconceptions about what is wrong with them.

b. Children from birth to 5 years old really have no conception of death as an irreversible process.

c. More than death, the preschool child is more likely to fear:

  i. Separation from parents

  ii. Punishment

  iii. Mutilation (Freud's castration anxiety)

d. Only after age 8 or 9 is there understanding of the universality, inevitability, and irreversibility of death.

Facts about the Elderly and Aging

a. U.S. population aged 65 or older:

  i. 4% in 1960

  ii. 11.2% in 1980

  iii. 13% in 2010

b. Fastest growing age cohort is persons older than 85.

c. The elderly account for more than one-third of all health care expenditures.

d. Roughly 70% of men older than 75 are married, but only 22% of women.

e. 13% of the elderly are below the poverty line.

  i. This is the same rate as the rate for the total population.

  ii. The rate is two times greater for Hispanics and three times greater for blacks.

f. Only 5 to 10% of those older than 65 have moderate or severe dementia.

  a. Older than 85, the rate is 25%.

  b. 50% of dementia cases are due to Alzheimer.

g. With the exception of cognitive impairment, the elderly have a *lower* incidence of all psychiatric disorders compared with younger adults.

h. The elderly in the United States are generally not isolated or lonely, but may not receive the same respect as in other cultures.

  i. 80% have children and most have frequent contact with them.

  ii. The family is still the major social support system for the elderly in times of illness.

  iii. Institutionalization is undertaken only as a last resort.

i. 85% of the elderly have at least one chronic illness.

  i. 50% have some limitation to their activities.

  ii. Only 5% are homebound.

j. Among noninstitutionalized, 60% call their health excellent or good, 20% fair.

k. Suicide rates per 100,000:

Suicide Rates* Among Persons Age ≥65, by Race/Ethnicity and Sex, United States, 2005–2009

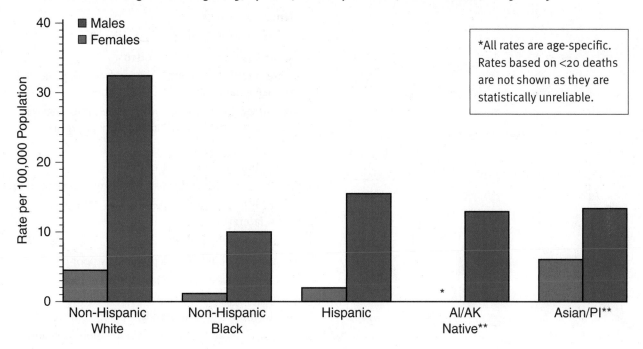

*All rates are age-specific. Rates based on <20 deaths are not shown as they are statistically unreliable.

** AI/AK Native: American Indian/Alaskan Native, PI: Pacific Islander

Content source: CDC

During 2005–2009, the highest suicide rates for males age ≥65 were among the Non-Hispanic Whites (32.37 suicides per 100,000), and for females age ≥65 were among the Asian/Pacific Islanders (6.01 suicides per 100,000).

l. Currently about 2 million, or about 6%, of the elderly population are institutionalized.

m. One in 10 persons aged 75 or older is in a nursing home; for 85 and older, the ratio is 1 in 5.

n. Preventive occupational therapy (OT) programs offer clear advantages over "just keeping busy" to reduce decline in mental and physical health in the elderly.

o. Best predictor of nursing home admissions: falls and fall related injuries. Exercise improves balance and reduces risk of falls in the elderly. Also, "safe proof" the home.

ABUSE

Child Abuse

i. More than 6,000 children are killed by parents or caretakers each year in the United States.

ii. More than 3 million annually are reported abused, 50% of these are confirmed by investigation.

iii. Likely that many abuse cases unreported

iv. Defining abuse

- Tissue damage
- Neglect
- Sexual exploitation
- Mental cruelty

v. Mandatory reportable offense up to age 18

- Failure to do so is criminal offense.
- If case is reported in error, the physician is protected from legal liability.
- Remember your duty to protect the child (separate from the parents), as well as the duty to report.

vi. Clinical signs:

- Broken bones in first year of life
- Sexually transmitted disease (STD) in young children
- 92% of injuries are soft tissue injuries (bruises, burns, lacerations).
- 5% have no physical signs.
- Nonaccidental burns have a particularly poor prognosis.
    - They are associated with death or foster home placement.
    - If burn is on arms and hands, it was likely an accident.
    - If burn is on arms but not hands, it is more likely abuse.
- Shaken baby syndrome: look for broken blood vessels in eyes

vii. Children at risk for abuse are

- Younger than 1 year of age
- Stepchildren
- Premature children
- Very active
- "Defective" children

viii. Parents likely themselves to have been abused, and/or perceive child as ungrateful and as cause of their problems

ix. Be careful not to mistake benign cultural practices such as "coining" or "moxibustion" as child abuse

- These and other folk medicine practices should usually be accepted.
- Key is whether practice causes enduring pain or long-term damage to child
- Treat female circumcision as abuse
- Look for an opening to discuss with parents how they treated child prior to seeing the physician

x. Children who are abused are more likely to:

- Be aggressive in the classroom
- Perceive others as hostile
- View aggression as a good way to solve problems
- Have abnormally high rate of withdrawal (girls)
- Be unpopular with school peers and other children; the friends they do have tend to be younger.

Child Sexual Abuse

    i. 150,000 to 200,000 cases of sexual abuse per year

    ii. 50% of sexual abuse cases are within the family.

    iii. 60% of victims are female.

    iv. Most victims are aged 9 to 12 years.

    v. 25% of victims younger than 8 years

    vi. Most likely source: uncles and older siblings, although stepfathers are also more likely

    vii. In general, males more likely to be sources

    viii. Risk factors:

- Single-parent families
- Marital conflict
- History of physical abuse
- Social isolation

    ix. More than 25% of adult women report being sexually abused as a child (defined as sex experience before age 18 with a person 5 years older).

- 50% by family members
- 50% told no one

    x. Sexually abused women are more likely to:

- Have more sexual partners
- Have 3–4 times more learning disabilities
- Have 2 times more pelvic pain and inflammation
- Be overweight (slight increased risk)

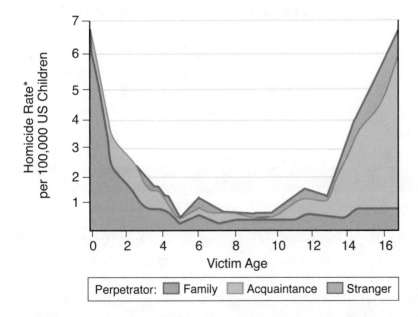

Figure 9-2. Relationship of Child Homicide Victims to Perpetrators

Domestic Partner Abuse

    i. An estimated 4 to 6 million women are beaten each year.

    ii. Each year, 1,500 women are killed by their abusers.

iii. Not mandatory reportable offense. If confronted with a case, give the victim information about local shelters and counseling.

iv. Number of attacks has held steady since mid-1970s.

v. Domestic violence is the #1 cause of injury to American women (for men, traffic accidents and other unintentional injuries are #1).

vi. Occurs in all racial and religious backgrounds, and across all SES groups

vii. More frequent in families with drug abuse, especially alcoholism

viii. If one attack occurs, more are likely.

ix. Male more likely abuser if:

- Considers wife his belonging
- He is jealous or possessive.
- There are verbal assaults to his self-esteem.

x. Female more likely abused if:

- Grew up in a violent home (about 50%)
- Married at a young age
- Perceives self as unable to function alone (dependent)
- Abused spouses tend to blame themselves for the abuse, identification with the aggressor.
- Pregnant, last trimester (highest risk)

Elder Abuse

i. Elder abuse is a mandatory reportable offense.

ii. Prevalence rate 5 to 10%

iii. Includes physical, psychological, financial, or neglect

iv. Neglect is the most common type (50% of all reported cases).

v. Caretaker is the most likely source of abuse; spouses are often caretakers.

Table 9-4. Types of Abuse and Important Issues

	Child Abuse	Elder Abuse	Domestic Abuse
Annual cases	Over 2 million	5 to 10% in population	Over 4 million
Most common type	Physical battery/neglect	Neglect	Physical battery
Likely gender of victim	Before age 5: female After age 5: male	63% Female	Female
Likely gender of perpetrator	Female	Male or Female	Male
Mandatory reportable?	Yes	Yes	No
Physician's response	Protect and report	Protect and report	Counseling and information

Review Questions

66. An 8-year-old girl attains a score of 35 on a standard intelligence test. Included in the test-scoring packet is a table showing median test scores for specific ages. An extract from the table is presented below:

Age	Median Score
4	15
5	18
6	22
7	25
8	29
9	32
10	35
11	40
12	45

Based on this table, the most likely IQ for this 8-year-old girl is

(A) 85

(B) 100

(C) 110

(D) 125

(E) 140

67. A psychiatric researcher develops an observational test to assess the level impulse control of found bipolar patients. As a part of the test development strategy, the results of this observational test are compared with patients' scores on a standard paper-and-pencil test that also assesses impulse control. If the observational test has a high correlation with the paper-and-pencil test, the researcher would be most likely to regard this as evidence for

(A) construct validity

(B) test-retest reliability

(C) predictive validity

(D) split-half reliability

(E) convergent validity

68. A 55-year-old executive makes a habit of doing several things at once. He always seems to be in a hurry and frequently worries that there are just not enough hours in the day to get things done. He is impatient with his subordinates and often gets angry with them when they do not perform to his standards or get their work to him on time. The pattern of behavior displayed by this man suggests that in the next 10 years he is most at risk for developing

(A) a gastric ulcer

(B) prostate cancer

(C) respiratory difficulties

(D) mental health problems

(E) an acute myocardial event

69. A 5-year-old child is referred to a mental health practitioner for evaluation. The practitioner wants to gain insight into the conscious and unconscious preoccupations of the child. To accomplish this objective, the practitioner is most likely to make use of

   (A) Luria Nebraska Battery
   (B) Halsted-Reitan Battery
   (C) Minnesota Multiphasic Personality Inventory
   (D) Projective Drawing Test
   (E) Rorschach test
   (F) Wechsler Intelligence Scale for Children

70. A 3-year-old boy talks when his parents are talking in spite of being repeatedly told not to do so. His parents become frustrated with his behavior and ask his physician about the reason for this behavior pattern. The physician should advise the parents that this tendency of children to test the extremes of behavior that their parents will tolerate

   (A) is indicative of later maladjustment
   (B) persists with partial parental reinforcement
   (C) results from the action of classic conditioning
   (D) can be resolved by a clear, reasoned explanation to the child
   (E) is more commonly observed in boys than girls

71. A 5-month-old and a 12-month-old infant observe their mothers leaving the room. Which one will most likely begin to cry?

   (A) The 5-month-old
   (B) The 12-month-old
   (C) Both will cry
   (D) Neither will cry

72. A young child is able to walk when held by one hand and speaks in strings of unrecognizable words. When placed in a room with other children, the child stays close to his mother but plays by himself. Based on these observations, in the next six to eight months the child is most likely to learn to

   (A) ride a tricycle
   (B) stand on his tiptoes
   (C) draw a circle
   (D) build a tower of three blocks
   (E) play peek-a-boo

73. A child is observed walking down the stairs using alternating feet, can throw and catch a ball, states her gender accurately, and is able to correctly name the colors of presented objects. Based on this evidence, which of the following geometric shapes did the child most recently learn to draw?

    (A) Cross
    (B) Diamond
    (C) Square
    (D) Triangle
    (E) Circle

74. Conformity with peers is a core characteristic of a number of normative developmental stages. In general, conformity of children to the norms of their peer groups is *most* intense at a time of development that also features

    (A) toilet training
    (B) use of transition objects
    (C) focal attachment to the caretaker
    (D) beginning of formal schooling
    (E) puberty

75. Studies of infants in wartime and natural disasters have revealed a number of characteristic changes in the expected developmental sequence. In comparison with those undergoing normal development, infants who experience severe psychosocial deprivation are more likely to display

    (A) separation anxiety
    (B) infantile symbiosis
    (C) anxiety with strangers
    (D) delayed language development
    (E) rapprochement

76. Although much of human behavior is learned, infants are born with certain capacities. Which of the following important behavioral skills are present in most infants at birth?

    (A) Following objects to midline
    (B) Laughing aloud
    (C) Putting feet into mouth
    (D) Reaching and grasping
    (E) Recognition of the mother

77. A 4-year-old girl is brought by her mother to see the local pediatrician. The mother insists that the girl be given a complete physical exam. The physical exam turns up nothing abnormal. The mother insists that something must be wrong with the girl because she spends hours playing by herself and talking with a "friend" that no one else can see. In addition, two to three times a week the girl wakes up screaming from nightmares and is convinced that there is some sort of "monster" in her closet that is going to eat her as she sleeps. The physician's next action should be to

   (A) ask the mother about any recent trauma or changes in the girl's life

   (B) reassure the mother that the girl is displaying normal behavior for her age

   (C) re-examine the girl for signs of sexual abuse

   (D) schedule the girl for psychiatric evaluation

   (E) send the girl for a neurologic consultation

78. An 8-year-old girl is brought to the emergency department by her grandmother, who reports that she found the girl sitting in her apartment, dirty and disheveled, during a heat wave. The girl reports that she had not eaten in 2 days or seen her mother in the past 24 hours. Physical examination shows the girl to be severely dehydrated and lethargic in her responses to physical stimuli. At this point, the physician's next step would be to

   (A) ask the girl if she would like to stay in the hospital for a while

   (B) contact the local child welfare agency

   (C) contact the police and report the girl's mother for neglect

   (D) initiate IV fluids for the child

   (E) obtain permission from the grandmother to begin treatment for the child

   (F) try to contact the girl's mother

79. A 67-year-old woman visits her physician 4 months after the death of her husband. She reports that she has difficulty sleeping and often finds herself crying at the "smallest things." The physician notices that she has lost weight and seems to avoid eye contact when interviewed. With some embarrassment, she confesses that she came to see the physician after thinking that she saw her husband across the street in a crowd, an experience that left her confused and shaken. At this point, the physician's best response would be to

   (A) ask her if she has much interest in sex lately

   (B) ask her to talk about her relationship with her husband prior to his death

   (C) detain her for observation as a suicide precaution

   (D) explain to her that she has an adjustment disorder

   (E) schedule her for a psychiatric evaluation

   (F) tell her that these are normal reactions and that adjustment takes time

   (G) write her a prescription for antidepressants

Answers

66. **Answer: D.** Use the mental age method. $(MA/CA) \times 100 = IQ$. A score of 35 is median for a 10-year-old. Therefore, $(10/8) \times 100 = 125$.

67. **Answer: E.** Reliability means consistency. Validity means detecting truth. When two similar tests produce the same result, we have a confirmation of truth called convergent validity.

68. **Answer: E.** The question presents an example of Type A behavior pattern. People who display this behavior pattern are more than twice as likely to experience a heart attack.

69. **Answer: D.** The limited verbal skills of the child make this the best choice. Note that the Wechsler is an IQ test that does not give the information sought. The Halsted-Reitan and the Luria Nebraska are batteries that assess and localize brain dysfunction.

70. **Answer: B.** Children will always learn by testing. This is normal behavior and not indicative of maladjustment. However, it persists, like any behavior, if the parents reinforce it, however, unintentionally.

71. **Answer: B.** The key issue here is the timing of separation anxiety. It begins between 8 to 12 months of age and continues for most of the second year of life. The 5-month-old is too young. The 12-month-old is in the right age range.

72. **Answer: D.** The child described is about 1 year of age. Stacking three blocks is expected by about 18 months of age. The child should already know peek-a-boo, standing on tiptoes is achieved at about 30 months of age, riding tricycle and drawing a circle are skills learned at about three years of age.

73. **Answer: A.** The child described is about 4 years of age and has most recently learned to draw a cross. Circle is 3 years of age. Square is 5 years of age. The other options are for age 6 and up.

74. **Answer: E.** Conformity is most intense between the ages of 11 and 13, although it is also important during ages 4 to 6.

75. **Answer: D.** All of these listed are part of normal development with the exception of delayed language development. Infantile symbiosis is part of the early attachment relationship between mother and child. Rapprochement occurs as the child is learning separation from the parents.

76. **Answer: D.** Following objects to midline is 4 weeks, feet in mouth and laughing aloud about 4 to 5 months. It takes the infant about a week after birth before it can recognize the mother.

77. **Answer: B.** Imaginary friends and nightmares are common in children of this age. They represent normal developmental patterns and are NOT indicative of abuse, trauma, or more deep-seated psychological problems.

78. **Answer: D.** This victim of child neglect requires essential medical intervention. Care for the patient's needs first, and then worry about contacting the appropriate child welfare agency.

79. **Answer: F.** The question portrays a woman in normal grief, both by description and time frame. She needs reassurance that her reactions, including "seeing" her husband, are a part of a normal grief process.

Sleep and Sleep Disorders 10

SLEEP ARCHITECTURE

Sleep consists of two distinct states: NREM and REM.

NREM: Non–rapid Eye Movement Sleep

a. Divided into 4 stages on the basis of EEG criteria

b. Alternates with REM sleep throughout the sleep period and is characterized by:

    i. Slowing of the EEG rhythms

    ii. Higher muscle tone

    iii. Absence of eye movements

    iv. Absence of "thoughtlike" mental activity

c. Is an idling brain in a movable body.

REM: Rapid Eye Movement Sleep

a. Characterized by:

    i. An aroused EEG pattern

    ii. Sexual arousal

    iii. Saccadic eye movements

    iv. Elaborate visual imagery (dreaming)

    v. Associated with pons

b. Is an awake brain in a paralyzed body.

Note

The COMLEX Requires You to Know:

- Sleep architecture, including how to read sleep diagrams and EEG tracings

- Developmental changes in sleep patterns, including sleep for infants and the elderly

- The effects of sleep deprivation

- Diagnosis and treatment of sleep disorders

- Clinical correlates of sleep patterns with psychiatric conditions and pharmacology

- The biochemistry of sleep

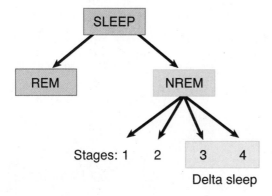

Figure 10-1. Types of Sleep

Biologic Rhythms

1. The sleep-wake cycle itself is a circadian rhythm, i.e., an endogenous cyclic change occurs in an organism with a periodicity of roughly 24 hours.
2. The cycle is regulated by the superchiasmatic nucleus (SCN).
3. The REM cycle, which is approximately 90 minutes, is an example of an ultradian rhythm, occurring with a periodicity of less than 24 hours.

Sleep Facts

1. Most of NREM Stages 3 and 4 (the deepest sleep levels) occur during the first half of the night.
2. Stages 3 and 4 together are referred to as delta sleep or slow-wave sleep.
3. Most REM sleep occurs during the last half of the night. REM sleep gets progressively longer as the night goes on.
4. The average adult spends most sleep time in Stage 2, least in Stage 1. Adults most commonly wake out of REM or Stage 2 sleep.
5. Duration of delta sleep is 65% inherited.

Latency

1. Sleep latency: period between awake until sleep onset. Insomniacs have long sleep latencies. Typically, 5–15 minutes.
2. REM latency: period between falling asleep until first REM. In the average adult, REM latency is 90 minutes.

```
              SL              RL
            ‿‿‿‿          ‿‿‿‿
Awake ——————— Sleep ——————— REM
```

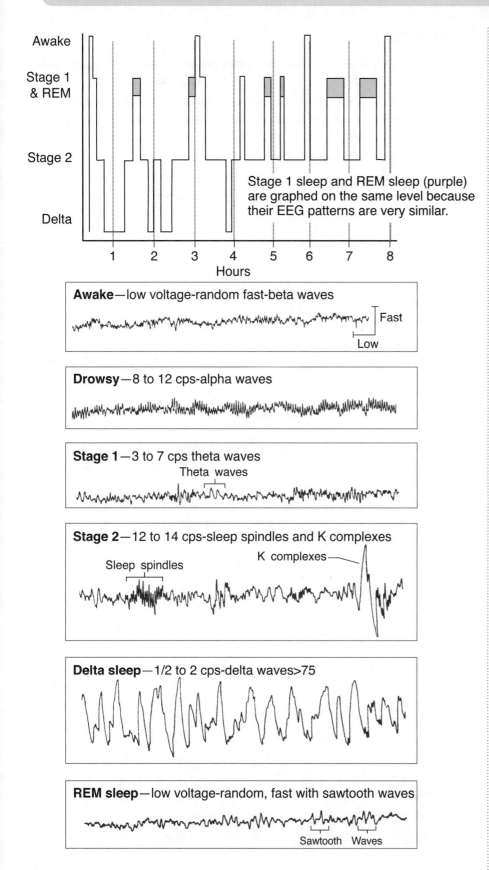

Stage 1 sleep and REM sleep (purple) are graphed on the same level because their EEG patterns are very similar.

Awake—low voltage-random fast-beta waves

Fast
Low

Drowsy—8 to 12 cps-alpha waves

Stage 1—3 to 7 cps theta waves

Theta waves

Stage 2—12 to 14 cps-sleep spindles and K complexes

Sleep spindles

K complexes

Delta sleep—1/2 to 2 cps-delta waves>75

REM sleep—low voltage-random, fast with sawtooth waves

Sawtooth Waves

Figure 10-2. Sleep Architecture Diagram Showing Stages of Sleep in Sequence

Sleep Deprivation

1. The cerebral cortex shows the greatest effects of sleep deprivation but has the capacity to cope with one night's sleep loss.

2. The rest of the body seems relatively unaffected by sleep deprivation. Physical restitution of the body comes from the immobility that is a by-product of sleep, not from sleep itself.

3. Only about one-third of lost sleep is made up.
   a. 80% of lost Stage 4 is recovered.
   b. About one-half of the missing REM is recovered.

4. If getting 5 hours of sleep or less per night, person functions at level of someone legally drunk!

5. The longer the prior period of wakefulness, the more Stage 4 sleep increases during the first part of the night and the more REM declines.

6. Short sleepers lose the latter part of REM sleep.

7. In sleep-deprived individuals, the following occurs:
   a. Lymphocyte levels decline
   b. Cortisol levels rise
   c. Blood pressure rises
   d. Glucose tolerance is reduced
   e. Greater amygdala activation
   f. Lower prefrontal cortical activity
   g. Increased negative mood

8. REM sleep appears to increase somewhat in both children and adults after learning, especially the learning of complex material, in the previous waking period.
   a. REM sleep is essential to get the most out of studying. It is when most long-term memories are consolidated by the hippocampus.

9. REM deprivation
   a. Does not impede the performance of simple tasks
   b. Interferes with the performance of more complex tasks
   c. Makes it more difficult to learn complex tasks
   d. Decreases attention to details but not the capacity to deal with crisis situations

10. Delta sleep increases after exercise and seems to be the result of raised cerebral temperature.

Table 10-1. Changes in First 3 Hours of Sleep

Human growth hormone (HGH)	Increase
Prolactin	Increase
Dopamine	*Decrease*
Serotonin	Increase
Thyroid-stimulating hormone (TSH)	*Decrease*

11. Melatonin is not related to sleeping, but rather to feelings of sleepiness:
   a. Produced in the pineal gland and directly in the retinas of the eyes
   b. Sensitive to light via a pathway from the eyes

   c. Release is inhibited by daylight, and, at nighttime, levels rise dramatically

   d. Likely mechanism by which light and dark regulate circadian rhythm

   e. Responsible for "jet lag"

   f. Responsible for seasonal affective disorder (SAD)

   g. Adjust melatonin with bright light therapy, *not* pills

DEVELOPMENTAL ASPECTS OF SLEEP

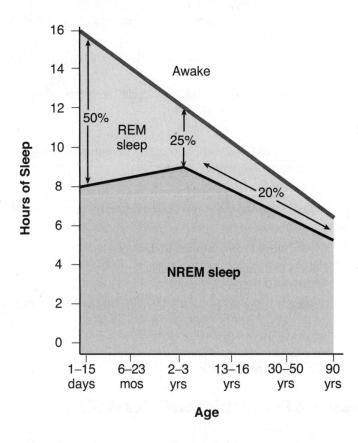

Figure 10-3. Changes in Daily Sleep Over the Life Cycle

1. Sleep develops during childhood and adolescence into adult patterns.

Age	Total Sleep Time/24 Hours
Neonate	16–18 hours
1 y	12 hours
10 y	10 hours
13–16 y	8 hours

Age	Number of Sleep Periods/24 Hours
Neonate	6–9
1–2 y	2–3
5–10 y	1

2. Infants

   a. Premature infants do not demonstrate a discernible sleep-wake cycle.

   b. EEG demonstrates adultlike rhythms of sleep and wakefulness by about 1 year.

   c. Neonatal sleep cycle: starts at 30 to 40 minutes, gradually lengthens to 90 minutes by teens

   d. Mismatch of infant and adult cycles produces "sleep fragmentation" for new parents.

3. Adults

   a. Initial REM cycle: approximately 90 minutes. Subsequent cycles across the evening are shorter.

   b. REM: 20% of sleep time

   c. Total sleep time/24-hour period decreases gradually with age.

4. Elderly

   a. Total sleep time continues to decline.

   b. REM percentage remains constant (20%) up to around 80 years of age, then declines further.

   c. Stage 4, then Stage 3 NREM (delta sleep) vanish. Elderly often complain that they don't feel as rested as they used to feel.

BIOCHEMISTRY OF SLEEP

Chemical and Psychiatric Correlates of Sleep

1. Dopamine

   a. Any pharmacology that increases dopamine increases wakefulness.

   b. Dopamine blockers (e.g., antipsychotics) increase sleep somewhat.

2. Benzodiazepines

   a. Limited decrease in REM and Stage 4 sleep, much less than previously thought

   b. Little rebound effect

   c. Chronic use increases sleep latency.

3. Alcohol consumption

   a. Moderate

      i. Early sleep onset

      ii. Increased wakefulness during the second half of the night

   b. Intoxication

      i. Decreases REM

      ii. REM rebound (with nightmares) during withdrawal

4. Barbiturates

    a. Decreases REM

    b. REM rebound, including nightmares, follows stoppage of chronic use.

5. Major depression

    a. Increases REM

    b. Decreases REM latency (45 rather than 90 minutes)

    c. Decreases Stages 4 and 3 sleep

    d. Increased sleep in multiple periods over 24 hours

    e. Early morning waking

    f. Diurnal improvement

    g. Sleep deprivation gives 60% remission from symptoms

    h. People who characteristically get a lot of REM are more susceptible to onset of depression

Neurotransmitters Associated with Sleep: "SANDman"

1. **S**erotonin: helps initiate sleep

2. **A**cetylcholine (ACh): higher during REM sleep (associated with erections in men)

3. **N**orepinephrine (NE): lower during REM sleep

    a. Ratio of ACh and NE is the biochemical trigger for REM sleep.

    b. NE pathway begins in the pons, which regulates REM sleep.

4. **D**opamine: produces arousal and wakefulness. Rises with waking

SLEEP DISORDERS

Narcolepsy

A condition characterized by the brain's inability to control sleep-wake cycle.

1. The narcoleptic tetrad:

    a. Sleep attacks and excessive daytime sleepiness (EDS)

    b. Cataplexy (pathognomonic sign)

    c. Hypnagogic hallucinations (hypnopompic can occur, but not pathognomonic)

        i. Hypnagogic: while falling asleep

        ii. Hypnopompic: while waking up

    d. Sleep paralysis

2. Narcolepsy is a disorder of REM sleep: onset of REM within 10 minutes.

3. Linked to deficiency in hypocretin when cataplexy is present. Loss of hypocretin results in an inability to regulate sleep.

4. Treatment

    a. Modafinil or psychostimulants for excessive daytime sleepiness

        i. inhibits DA re-uptake

        ii. activates glutamate; inhibits GABA

    b. Antidepressants (TCA, SNRI)

    c. Gamma hydroxybutyrate (GHB) to reduce daytime sleepiness and cataplexy

Sleep Apnea

1. Types:
    a. Obstructive (upper airway) sleep apnea
        i. Middle-aged
        ii. Overweight
        iii. Rasping snoring
    b. Central (diaphragmatic) sleep apnea
        i. Elderly
        ii. Overweight
        iii. Cheyne-Stokes (60-second hyperventilation, followed by apnea)
    c. Mixed sleep apnea

2. Clinical presentation and features:
    a. High risk of sudden death during sleep, development of severe nocturnal hypoxemia, pulmonary and systemic hypertension (with elevated diastolic pressure)
    b. Nocturnal cardiac arrhythmias (potentially life-threatening)
    c. Bradycardia, then tachycardia
    d. Males outnumber females by 8 to 1
    e. EDS and insomnia often reported
    f. Heavy snoring with frequent pauses
    g. Kicking, punching of sleeping partner
    h. Obesity is often part of the clinical picture, but not always
    i. Short sleep duration, frequent waking, insomnia, decreased Stage 1, decreased delta and REM

3. Treatment:
    a. Weight loss (if applicable)
    b. Behavioral conditioning to change sleep position
    c. Continuous positive airway pressure (CPAP). Most likely medical intervention
    d. For severe obstructive and mixed apnea: tonsillectomy or tracheostomy

Sudden Infant Death Syndrome (SIDS): Unexplained Death in Children Age <1

1. 3,000 deaths annually
2. 50% reduction in incidence if baby placed on back, rather than on stomach
3. Avoid overstuffed toys and pillows
4. Rate is two to three times higher in families where someone smokes
5. 5-HT levels 26% below normal
6. Fetal exposure to maternal smoking also strong risk factor

Insomnia

1. Possible causes:
    a. Secondary to hypnotic medication abuse
        i. Development of tolerance to sedative hypnotics is common and leads to escalating doses
        ii. Sleep architecture becomes disrupted and sleep fragmentation occurs.
    b. Emotional problems, especially anxiety, depression, mania
    c. Conditioned poor sleep: sleep cycle is so disrupted that habit of sleep is lost
    d. Withdrawal from drugs or alcohol
2. When working up an insomniac, examine for medical explanations such as apnea and drug use (prescription or illicit), as well as psychiatric factors such as depression, anxiety, and schizophrenia
3. 50% of insomnia in sleep labs is due to psychological factors.
4. Insomniacs may have GABA levels 30% lower than normal.
5. Treatment:
    a. Sleep hygiene
    b. Behavior therapy still is best (most effective).
        i. Muscle relaxation
        ii. Stimulus control
    c. Drugs
        i. Action on GABA receptors
            • Zaleplon
            • Zolpidem
            • Eszopiclone
        ii. Ramelteon
            • Melatonin receptor agonist (MT1, MT2)
            • Low chance of dependence
            • No hangover or rebound

Night Terrors versus Nightmares

Table 10-2. Differences Between Night Terrors and Nightmares

	Night Terrors	Nightmares
Sleep stage	Stage 4 (delta sleep)	REM
Physiologic arousal	Extreme	Elevated
Recall upon waking	No	Yes
Waking time anxiety	Yes, usually unidentified	Yes, often unidentified
Other issues	Runs in families	Common from ages 3 to 7
	More common in boys	If chronic, likelihood of serious pathology
	Can be a precursor to temporal lobe epilepsy	Desensitization behavior therapy provides marked improvement

Note

Recent research suggests that getting an extra 30 to 40 minutes of sleep a night greatly reduces both nightmares and night terrors.

Somnambulism (Sleep-walking)

1. First third of the night
2. Stage 4 sleep (Delta)
3. If wakened, the person is confused and disoriented.
4. Treat with benzodiazepines

Enuresis (Bed-wetting)

1. Most seen in Stages 3 and 4 sleep, but can occur in all stages.
2. Boys twice as likely as girls. At age 5, 7% of boys, 3% of girls
3. Boys cease wetting later.
4. Often history with same-sex parent
5. Common after change or new sibling born. Defense mechanism of regression
6. Treat with desmopressin, imipramine or bell pad technique.

Bruxism (Teeth-grinding)

1. Stage 2 sleep
2. Prevention is to use oral device to prevent teeth grinding

Physician-Patient Relationship

11

GENERAL RULES

Theme: The physician-patient relationship is a potent healing partnership based on trust. In the setting of a productive alliance there are tremendous opportunities for clinical interventions that can significantly improve the patient's health and quality of life. The key is what the ideal physician should do.

Note

The COMLEX Requires You to Know:

- This section lays out a set of rules that seek to orient students as to what constitutes the best answer on the COMLEX. Apply these rules to answer presented questions on the exam.

- Note that a number of these rules are different than current medical practice.

Rule #1: Patient is number one; always place the interests of the patient first.

    a. Choose the patient's comfort and safety over yours or anyone else's.

    b. The goal is to serve the patient, not to worry about legal protection for the physician.

    c. Make it a point to ask about and know the patient's wishes.

Rule #2: Nothing should be between you and patient

    a. Get rid of tables and computers. If you must have a table, pick the smallest one.

    b. Ask family members to leave the room. If patient says that he or she wants them to stay, then that is okay.

Rule #3: Tell the patient everything, even if he or she does not ask.

    a. Answer any question that is asked.

    b. Respond to the emotional as well as the factual content of questions.

    c. Patient should know what you know and as soon as you know it.

    d. Do not force a patient to hear bad news if he does not want it at that moment, but do try to discuss it with him or her as soon as possible.

    e. If you have only partial information, say that it is partial and tell what you know.

    f. We tell them so they tell us. Make reciprocity the norm.

    g. Information should flow through the patient to the family, not the reverse.

Rule #4: Work on long-term relationships with patients, not just short-term problems.

    a. Each encounter is an opportunity to develop a better relationship.

    b. Make eye contact.

    c. Defined touch: tell him or her what you are doing.

    d. Talk to patient, not colleagues: patient is always the focus.

    e. Arrange seating for comfortable, close communication.

    f. Both patient and physician should both be sitting at the same eye level if at all possible.

Rule #5: Listening is better than talking.

    a. Be an "information sponge." You know what matters, but they don't

    b. Getting the patient to talk is generally better than having the physician talk.

    c. Take time to listen to the patient before you, even if other patients or colleagues are waiting.

    d. Ask what the patient knows before explaining.

    e. End encounter by asking, "Is there anything else?"

    f. Listen without interrupting

    g. Allow silences while patients search for words

Rule #6: Negotiate rather than order.

    a. Treatment choices are the result of agreement, not commands by the physician.

    b. Remember, the patient makes medical decisions from the choices provided by the physician.

    c. Relationship and agreement support adherence.

Rule #7: Solve the problem presented

    a. Look for a "solution," not the "answer."

    b. Stay in the room; do not leave.

    c. Change your plan to deal with new information when it is presented.

    d. Don't assume that the patient likes or trusts you.

    e. Treat difficult or suspicious patients in a friendly, open manner.

Rule #8: Admit to the patient when you make a mistake.

    a. Everything is your responsibility.

    b. Take responsibility. Don't blame it on the nursing staff or on a medical student.

    c. Admit the mistake even if it was corrected and the patient is fine.

Rule #9: Never "pass off" your patient to someone else.

    a. Refer to psychiatrist or other specialist when beyond your expertise (but usually not the case).

    b. Refer only for ophthalmology or related subspecialties.

    c. You provide instruction in aspects of care, e.g., nutrition, use of medications.

Rule #10: Express empathy, then give control: "I'm sorry, what would you like to do?"

    a. Important when faced with a patient who is grieving or is angry.

    b. Important when faced with angry or upset family members.

    c. Acknowledge and legitimize feelings

Rule #11: Agree on problem before moving to solution.

    a. Discuss diagnosis fully before moving to treatment options

    b. Ask what patient knows about diagnosis before explaining it

    c. Tell the patient your perceptions and conclusions about the condition before moving to treatment recommendations.

    d. Informed consent requires the patient to fully understand what is wrong.

    e. Offering a correct treatment before the patient understands his or her condition is wrong.

Rule #12: Be sure you understand what the patient is talking about before intervening.

    a. Patients may present problems with much emotion without clearly presenting what they are upset about.

    b. Seek information before acting.

    c. When presented with a problem, get some details before offering a solution.

    d. Begin with open-ended questions, then move to closed-ended questions.

Rule #13: Patients do not get to select inappropriate treatments.

    a. Patients select treatments, but only from presented, appropriate choices.

    b. If a patient asks for an inappropriate medication that he heard advertised, explain why it is not indicated

    c. Make conversations positive. Talk about options that are available; don't just say no to a patient's request.

Rule #14: Best answers serve multiple goals.

    a. Think broadly about everything you want to achieve.

    b. Consider both short- and long-term goals.

    c. Best answers deal with patients' health issues, while supporting relationships and acting ethically

Rule # 15: Never lie.

    a. There is no such thing as a "white lie."

    b. Do not lie to patients, their families, or insurance companies.

    c. Do not deceive to protect a colleague.

Rule #16: Accept the health beliefs of patients.

    a. Be accepting of benign folk medicine practices. Expect them. Diagnoses need to be explained in the way patients can understand, even if not technically precise.

    b. Offer to explain things to family members for the patients.

Rule #17: Accept patients' religious beliefs and participate if possible.

    a. Your goal is to make the patient comfortable. Religion is a source of comfort to many.

    b. A growing body of research suggests that patients who pray and are prayed for have better outcomes.

    c. Ask about a patient's religions beliefs if you are not sure (but not as a prelude to passing off to the chaplain!).

d. Of course, you are not expected to do anything against your own religious or moral beliefs, or anything which risks patient's health.

Rule #18: Anything that increases communication is good.

a. Take the time to talk with patients, even if others are waiting.

b. Ask "why?"

c. Ask about the patient beyond the disease: job, family, children, etc.

d. Be available. Take calls. Answer emails.

Rule #19: Be an advocate for the patient.

a. Work to get the patient what he or she needs.

b. Never refuse to treat a patient because he or she cannot pay.

Rule #20: The key is not so much what you do, but how you do it.

a. Focus on the process, not just goals; focus on means, not just ends.

b. Do the right thing, the right way.

c. The right choices are those that are humane and sensitive, and put the interests of the patient first.

d. Treat family members with courtesy and tact, but the wishes and interests of the patient come first.

MISCELLANEOUS PHYSICIAN-PATIENT RELATIONSHIP TOPICS

Types of Questions and Statements

a. Open-ended question: allows broad range for answer

b. Closed-ended question: limits answer, e.g., yes or no

c. Leading question: suggests or indicates preferred answer

d. Confrontation: brings to the patient's attention some aspect of appearance or demeanor

e. Facilitation: gets the patient to continue a thought, talk more, "tell me about that..."

f. Redirection: puts question back to the patient

g. Direct question: seeks information directly. Avoid judgmental terms.

Components of the Sick Role

a. Exempt from normal responsibilities

b. Not to blame for illness

c. Obligated to get well

d. Obligated to seek competent help

e. Note: The sick role generally does not apply to chronic illness or very minor illnesses.

The Significance of a Good Relationship with the Patient

a. The key is not the amount of time spent with a patient, but what is done during that time.

b. Lack of rapport is the chief reason that terminally ill patients reject medical advice, or why patients change physicians or miss appointments.

c. Failure of patient to cooperate, or even to keep appointments, should be seen as the result of physician insensitivity or seeming indifference.

d. An early Scandinavian study found a significant increase in sudden deaths on a coronary care unit during or immediately following ward rounds. The formality of rounds and the imposing authority that physicians project onto patients may have raised patient anxiety to dangerous levels.

e. The amount of information that surgical candidates receive about their upcoming operation and about the postsurgical pain affects outcome.

    i. Patients given more information about what to anticipate and what they can do about it were ready for discharge 2.7 days earlier than were controls.

    ii. They also requested 50% less morphine.

f. A good rapport:

    i. Fosters adherence to treatment regimens

    ii. Is positively associated with a reduction of malpractice suits

Fostering Patient Adherence with Treatment Recommendations

a. It is not enough for a physician to provide information and treatment and leave adherence to the patient. Rather, the physician must present information in ways that will optimize patient adherence.

b. Patients are less compliant when limited information has been exchanged and when there is dissatisfaction with the interview. A consistent complaint is that insufficient medical information was made available to the patient (or to the parents). Fewer positive statements made by the physician and less sought-after information offered by the physician results in less patient compliance.

c. For best adherence:

    i. Attend to the amount of information

    ii. Explain its complexity

    iii. Note the patient's affective state

    iv. Explain why this particular treatment is being recommended

    v. Stress the threat to health of nonadherence

    vi. Stress the effectiveness of the prescribed regimen

    vii. Give instructions both orally and in writing

    viii. Arrange for periodic follow-up

    ix. Ask patient to do less

d. Research has shown that physicians cannot tell which of their patients do and do not adhere. They assume that more of their patients are adhering than actually are.

e. When a patient does fail to adhere, do not blame the patient.

f. If the patient is nonadherent, check for these problems:

    i. Patient dissatisfaction with the physician

    ii. Misunderstanding of instructions

    iii. Interference by family

    iv. Inability to afford medications

g. The health belief model:

    i. Adherence is a function of perceived threat.

    ii. Moderate fear level is best for adherence. Recall curvilinear relationship between fear and adherence.

    iii. Perceived threat is a function of:

       ● Perceived seriousness

       ● Perceived susceptibility

    iv. External barriers, such as finances or lack of access to care, can prevent adherence even if perceived threat is sufficient.

Review Questions

80. Psychiatric diagnoses and exogenous pharmacology have long been associated with specific changes in sleep patterns. Based on current sleep laboratory data, decreases in rapid eye movement sleep would most likely occur in a patient who has been

    (A) abusing alcohol
    (B) taking L-tryptophan purchased at a health food store
    (C) diagnosed with a major affective disorder
    (D) taking lithium carbonate
    (E) diagnosed with a generalized anxiety disorder

81. A 35-year-old woman complains that she has trouble sleeping at night. Her physician prescribes a course of benzodiazapines to deal with this problem. As he hands her the prescription, he should also caution her that prolonged use of this class of medications to induce sleep will most likely result in the appearance of what side effect?

    (A) Sleep apnea syndrome
    (B) Depressed mood
    (C) Insomnia
    (D) Nocturnal enuresis
    (E) Somnambulism

82. At about the same time that children are toilet trained, their sleep patterns are characterized by

    (A) about 50% of time in REM
    (B) two to three sleep periods throughout the day
    (C) about 15 hours of total sleep time per day
    (D) achievement of the 90-minute sleep cycle
    (E) initiation of Stage 4 sleep

83. K-complexes are characteristic of a stage of sleep also distinguished by

    (A) delta waves
    (B) theta waves
    (C) sawtooth waves
    (D) alpha waves
    (E) sleep spindles

84. In a typical 30-year-old adult, the first three hours of sleep each night are accompanied by a measurable increase in

    (A) corticosteroids
    (B) output of human growth hormone
    (C) dopamine
    (D) thyroid-stimulating hormone
    (E) norepinephrine

85. A measurable increase in delta stage sleep is often observed following

    (A) alcohol intoxication
    (B) ingestion of melatonin
    (C) medication with imipramine
    (D) onset of major depression
    (E) physical exercise

86. A 45-year-old male presents to his physician complaining of fatigue. He reports difficulty going to sleep each night, waking up multiple times each night, and headache upon awaking in the morning. His wife has started sleeping on the couch because of his loud snoring and thrashing during the night. Physical exam shows the patient to be 40 pounds overweight and hypertensive. Based on this preliminary information, the physician suspects that the most likely underlying cause of the patient's reported problems is

    (A) bruxism
    (B) central apnea
    (C) insomnia
    (D) narcolepsy
    (E) nightmares
    (F) night terrors
    (G) obstructive apnea
    (H) restless legs syndrome

87. A 35-year-old woman goes to see a gynecologist for her first visit on a hot August day. The physician walks into the examination room to find the woman still fully dressed, fidgeting in her chair, and looking around the examination room nervously. The physician introduces himself and shakes the patient's hand. The patient's hand is sweating and clammy. At this point, what should the physician say next?

    (A) "Boy, it sure is hot out today."
    (B) "Don't worry. I have been doing this for years."
    (C) "Is something wrong?"
    (D) "I need you to get undressed so we can get started."
    (E) "Let me tell you about my credentials and training."
    (F) "So what brings you in here today?"
    (G) "This is our first meeting. Tell me a little bit about yourself."
    (H) "You need to relax. I won't hurt you."
    (I) "You seem a little nervous. That's normal at this point."

88. Following an annual physical exam, a 43-year-old woman asks her physician for a prescription to cope with anxiety. When the physician points out that she has no symptoms and has never mentioned the need before, the woman confesses that the prescription is for her husband who works during normal office hours and is unable to come to see the doctor. The physician's best response would be

    (A) give her the prescription, but ask that her husband schedule an appointment as soon as possible

    (B) give her the prescription, but instruct her that she should give her husband the medication only if he really needs it

    (C) give her a referral for her husband to a local psychiatrist

    (D) offer to write her husband a prescription if he will call and talk with you on the phone

    (E) offer to write her husband the prescription after he comes in for a scheduled appointment

    (F) refuse to write the prescription

    (G) tell her that you will see her husband outside of normal office hours and evaluate the need for the prescription

89. A 68-year-old woman, referred by a health management organization (HMO), complains angrily to her physician about how long she had to wait before he was able to see her. The physician's best response would be

    (A) "I'll speak to the receptionist."

    (B) "I'm very sorry you had to wait so long. How can we do better in the future?"

    (C) "It will never happen again."

    (D) "Please understand my staff is very busy."

    (E) "Things just take longer with these HMOs."

    (F) "Well, you are here now. What can I do for you?"

    (G) "Would you like to come back on another day?"

90. A mother takes her 2-year-old boy who is suffering from severe diarrhea to see the pediatrician. Stool samples reveal the presence of *Campylobactor jejuni*. At this point, what is the next action the physician should take?

    (A) Describe to the boy's mother the dangers inherent in severe diarrhea in a child of this age

    (B) Describe the medical problem to the boy in simple, easy-to-understand language

    (C) Explain to the boy's mother the nature of the problem and the important features of the pathogen involved

    (D) Instruct the boy's mother to give the boy fluids and schedule a follow-up appointment in 1 week

    (E) Provide the boy's mother with a prescription for the appropriate antibiotic

    (F) Refer the boy to an infectious disease specialist

91. A 56-year-old male executive complains to his physician that he has been having trouble sleeping for the past several months. His insomnia has become disruptive to both his professional and personal life. He mentions that a friend of his was given a prescription for benzodiazapines by his physician for a similar problem, and asks you to give him the same medication to "make this go away." The physician's best response would be to

    (A) assess his current level of alcohol intake
    (B) ask him about any recent stressors in his life
    (C) inquire about the specifics of the insomnia
    (D) give him some free samples of the medication he requests so he can try it out
    (E) provide him with the prescription he requests
    (F) instruct him to get more physical exercise
    (G) refer him to a local psychiatrist for evaluation and counseling

92. A 24-year-old woman is scheduled for delivery by Cesarean section after her unborn child is determined to be wedged in a breech position. Prior to the surgery, the woman asks the physician to pray with her, and to carry a "charm," a dried animal tongue, with him as he performs the procedure. The physician is not religious and is taken aback by the request. He comes to you and asks your advice as to what he should do. Your best advice would be to tell him to

    (A) advise the patient that her beliefs are not in keeping with modern medical practice
    (B) go along with the patient's request by praying with her and carrying the charm
    (C) politely explain to the patient that he does not share her religious beliefs
    (D) pray with her and tell her he will carry the charm, but leave it outside the operating theater for sanitary reasons
    (E) schedule an appointment for the patient with the appropriate hospital chaplain
    (F) stand in the room as she prays, but decline to carry the charm
    (G) suggest to the patient that she might be more comfortable with another physician performing the procedure

Answers

80. **Answer: A.** Alcohol abuse suppresses REM sleep. REM sleep increases for major depression. L-tryptophan decreases sleep latency. Lithium carbonate should increase REM as it allows the manic patient to get more sleep. Anxiety by itself has no demonstrated effect on REM.

81. **Answer: C.** Although often given to help patients to go to sleep, paradoxically, one of the side effects of sedative hypnotic medication is insomnia with long-term use.

82. **Answer: B.** By age 2 to 3 years, about 25% of the child's sleep time is spent in REM sleep. This sleep is characterized by several sleep periods totaling about 11 (less than 15) hours of sleep in each 24-hour period. Stage 4 sleep is present at birth. The 90-minute sleep cycle is achieved only during the teenage years.

83. **Answer: E.** Stage 2 sleep is characterized by sleep spindles and K-complexes. Delta waves go with Stages 3 and 4. Theta waves are Stage 1. Sawtooth waves appear in REM.

84. **Answer: B.** Human growth hormone and serotonin levels rise during the first three hours of sleep.

85. **Answer: E.** The increased cerebral temperature that results from exercise is associated with increased delta sleep.

86. **Answer: G.** These symptoms suggest sleep apnea. The age of the patient and the loud snoring indicate obstructive apnea.

87. **Answer: G.** Take time to find out a little bit about the patient. Rule #5 tells us that getting the patient to talk is the best approach.

88. **Answer: G.** Do not give a prescription before evaluating the patient. If your office hours are an impediment for the patient, see him outside of normal office hours. (Rule #14 and Rule #1)

89. **Answer: B.** Faced with an irate patient the rule is: express empathy, then give control. (Rule #10)

90. **Answer: C.** Before discussing treatment, be sure that the patient understands the problem. Discuss the disease before discussing treatment. (Rule #11)

91. **Answer: C.** Get the details about the patient's condition before proceeding to treatment. Of course you will not give medication just because the patient asks for it. You must be sure that it is needed.

92. **Answer: B.** Rule #17. Participating in the patient's religion is associated with better patient outcomes.

Diagnostic and Statistical Manual (DSM 5)

12

DISORDERS USUALLY DIAGNOSED IN CHILDHOOD

Intellectual Disability

    a. Fetal alcohol syndrome (FAS) most common known cause

    b. Down and fragile-X syndromes most common genetic causes

Table 12-1. Intellectual Disability

Level	IQ	Functioning
Mild	70–50	Self-supporting with some guidance. 85% of intellectually disabled. Two times as many are male. Usually diagnosed first year in school.
Moderate	49–35	Benefits from vocational training, but needs supervision. Sheltered workshops.
Severe	34–20	Vocational training not helpful, can learn to communicate, basic self-care habits.
Profound	Below 20	Needs highly structured environment, constant nursing care, and supervision.

Autism Spectrum Disorders

    a. Formerly pervasive development disorders

    b. Usually diagnosed before the age of 3

    c. Clinical signs

        i. Problems with reciprocal social interaction, decreased repetoire of activities and interests

        ii. Abnormal or delayed language development, impairment in verbal and nonverbal communication

        iii. No separation anxiety

        iv. Oblivious to external world

        v. Fails to assume anticipatory posture, shrinks from touch

        vi. Pronoun reversal

        vii. Preference for inanimate objects

        viii. Stereotyped behavior and interests

    d. Male:female ratio = 4:1

    e. Linked to chromosome #15, #11

    f. Occurs in 1 of every 150 births

Note

The COMLEX Requires You to Know:

- Recognize and offer differential diagnosis of Axis I and Axis II diagnoses, including common treatment interventions.

- Special attention should be paid to:

  Mental retardation, eating disorders, and stress disorders

  Biological markers and behavior patterns for schizophrenia and affective disorders

  Differential diagnosis and the preferred treatments for anxiety disorders

  Differential diagnosis for somatoform disorders

  The differential diagnosis of personality disorders

Note

Definitions

- **Anhedonia:** can't experience or even imagine any pleasant emotion
- **Clang associations:** illogical connections by rhythm or puns
- **Delusions:** false beliefs not shared by culture
- **Echolalia:** repeating in answer many of same words as in question
- **Echopraxia:** imitations of movements or gestures
- **Flight of ideas:** topics strung together
- **Hallucinations:** sensory impression, no stimuli
- **Illusions:** misperception of real stimuli
- **Loose associations:** jump from one topic to the next
- **Mannerisms,** e.g., grimacing
- **Mutism:** no speech
- **Neologisms:** new expressions
- **Perseveration:** responding to all questions the same way
- **Poverty of speech:** sparse and slow speech
- **Pressured speech:** abundant and accelerated speech
- **Verbigeration:** senseless repetition of same words or phrases

g. Monozygotic concordance greater than dizygotic concordance

h. 80% have IQs below 70.

i. Potential causes

    i. Association with prenatal and perinatal injury, e.g., rubella in first trimester

    ii. 2x more likely if mother had asthma, allergies, or psoriasis while pregnant

j. Differential diagnosis

    i. Rett's—g > b, hand wringing, microcephaly

    ii. Autism spectrum disorder without language impairment (formerly Asperger's)—language is normal, IQ is normal, higher level of functioning

k. Treatment: behavioral techniques (shaping), risperidone reduces agitation/aggression

Attention deficit hyperactivity disorder (ADHD)

a. Problems with inattention, impulsivity, hyperactivity

b. Male-to-female ratio is 10:1.

c. Associated with lower dopamine levels

d. Treatment: methylphenidate, dextroamphetamine, atomoxetine

SCHIZOPHRENIA

General Overview

a. Criteria

    i. Bizarre delusions

    ii. Auditory hallucinations (in 75%)

    iii. Blunted affect

    iv. Loose associations

    v. Deficiency in reality testing, distorted perception; impaired functioning overall

    vi. Disturbances in behavior and form and content of language and thought

    vii. > 6 months in duration

b. Differential

    i. <u>Schizophreniform</u>: if symptoms <6 months

    ii. <u>Brief psychotic disorder</u> if symptoms >1 day and <30 days

c. Epidemiology

    i. Onset: male, age 15–24; female, age 25–34

    ii. Prevalence: 1% of population cross-culturally; however, less chronic and severe in developing countries than in developed countries

    iii. Downward drift to low SES

    iv. 50% of patients attempt suicide, 10% succeed

    v. Over 50% of schizophrenics do not live with their families, nor are they institutionalized

d. Genetic contribution

    i. Rates for monozygotic twins reared apart = rates for MZ twins raised together (47%)

    ii. Dizygotic concordance: 13%

    iii. If two schizophrenic parents: 40% incidence

    iv. If one parent or one sibling: 12%

    v. Heritability index: $(MZ - DZ)/(100 - DZ)$ = proportion of conditions due to genetic factors

    vi. Risk in biologic relatives 10 times general population (i.e., 10%)

Clinical Presentation

a. Severity

    i. DSM-5 does not include subtypes of schizophrenia. Rather, current severity is documented from a low of 0 to a high of 4 for the following 5 symptoms:

- delusions
- hallucinations
- disorganized speech
- abnormal psychomotor activity
- negative symptoms

b. Paranoid symptoms

    i. Delusions of persecution or grandeur

    ii. Often accompanied by hallucinations (voices)

c. Catatonic symptoms

    i. Complete stupor or may have pronounced decrease in spontaneous movements

- May be mute
- Often negativism, echopraxia, automatic obedience
- Rigidity of posture; can be left standing or sitting in awkward positions for long periods of time

    ii. Alternatively, can be excited and evidence extreme motor agitation

- Incoherent and often violent or destructive
- In their excitement, can hurt themselves, or collapse in exhaustion
- Repetitious, stereotyped behaviors

Important Terms

a. Positive symptoms (Type I)

    i. What schizophrenic persons have that normals do not, e.g., delusions, hallucinations, bizarre behavior

    ii. Associated with dopamine receptors

b. Negative symptoms (Type II)

    i. What normals have that schizophrenics do not, e.g., flat affect, motor retardation, apathy, mutism

    ii. Associated with muscarinic receptors

Predictors for Good Prognosis

a. Paranoid symptoms

b. Late onset (female)

c. Quick onset

d. Positive symptoms

e. No family history of schizophrenia

f. Family history of mood disorder

g. Absence of structural brain abnormalities

Neurochemical Issues

a. The <u>dopamine hypothesis</u> is based on:

   i. The effectiveness of neuroleptic medications in ameliorating the symptoms of schizophrenia

   ii. The correlation of clinical efficacy with drug potency in dopamine receptor antagonists

   iii. Findings of increased dopamine receptor sensitivity in postmortem studies

   iv. Positron emission tomographic (PET) scan studies of schizophrenic patients compared with controls

b. <u>Role of serotonin</u> (5-HT)

   i. Genes involved in serotoninergic neurotransmission are implicated on the pathogenesis of schizophrenia.

   ii. LSD affects serotonin and can produce a psychotic-like state.

   iii. Newer antipsychotics (e.g., clozapine) have high affinity for serotonin receptors.

   iv. Serotonin rises when dopamine falls in some areas of the brain.

c. <u>Role of glutamate</u>

   i. Major neurotransmitter in pathways key to schizophrenic symptoms

   ii. N-methyl-D-aspartate (NMDA) receptors

     • Regulates brain development and controls apoptosis

     • Phencyclidine and ketamine block the NMDA channel: these can create positive and negative psychotic symptoms identical to schizophrenia

     • Drugs which indirectly enhance NMDA receptor function can reduce negative symptoms and improve cognitive function.

   iii. 2-(aminomethyl)phenylacetic acid (AMPA) receptors

     • Abnormally sparse in temporal lobes of schizophrenics

     • Ampakines selectively enhance transmission and improve memory in patients

Attention and Information Processing Deficits

a. Smooth pursuit eye movement (SPEM)

    i. The capacity of the eye to follow a slow-moving target is impaired in schizophrenic patients.

    ii. Although normals perform this task without error, up to 80% of schizophrenic patients and half of their relatives show saccadic eye movement and deficits at this tracking task.

b. Prefrontal cortical (PFC) impairment

    i. Faced with a cognitive task, increased activity is found in the prefrontal cortex of normal individuals.

    ii. Schizophrenics show decreased physiologic activity in prefrontal lobes when faced with these tasks.

    iii. Impaired performance on the Wisconsin Card Sort (WCST), a test sensitive to prefrontal dysfunction

    iv. Clinical profile has similarities with patients with frontal lobe injury (e.g., cognitive inflexibility, problem-solving difficulties, and apathy).

Brain Structural and Anatomic Abnormalities

a. Cortical abnormalities

    i. Larger ventricle size and ventricular brain ratios (VBRs)

    ii. Cortical atrophy

    iii. Smaller frontal lobes

    iv. Atrophy of temporal lobes

    v. Association with specific clinical and cognitive correlates, including deficit symptoms, cognitive impairment, and poor outcome

        • Correlation between ventricle size, type, and prognosis of illness

        • More dilation with negative symptoms

        • However, dilated ventricles also reported among patients having unipolar, bipolar, and schizoaffective disorders (sensitive, but not specific indicator)

b. Subtle anomalies in limbic structures

    i. Limbic system seen as the site of the primary pathology for schizophrenia

    ii. Changes in hippocampus, parahippocampal gyrus, entorhinal cortex, amygdala, cingulate gyrus

        • Smaller volume of left hippocampus and amygdala

        • Also found in high-risk, nonsymptomatic patients

Long-term Course

    a. Antipsychotic medications reduce acute (positive) symptoms in 75% versus 25% with placebo

    b. Relapse rates

        i. 40% in 2 years if on medication

        ii. 80% in 2 years if off medication

    c. Prognosis

        i. 33% of patients lead normal lives.

        ii. 33% of patients experience symptoms but function in society.

        iii. 33% of patients require frequent hospitalizations

DEPRESSIVE DISORDERS AND BIPOLAR AND RELATED DISORDERS (MOOD DISORDERS)

Depression and elation are normal human emotions. Disorder is when it gets too long-term or too extreme.

Table 12-3. Mood Disorders

	Mild	**Severe**
Stable	Persistent Depressive Disorder	Major depression
Alternating	Cyclothymia	Bipolar (manic-depression)

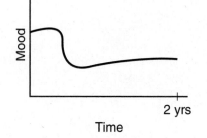

Basic Subtypes

Persistent Depressive Disorder

        i. Chronic (at least 2 years)

        ii. Depressed mood on most days for greater than 2 years

        iii. Patient is functional, but at a suboptimal level

        iv. Not severe enough for hospitalization

        v. Lifetime prevalence 5%

Cyclothymia

        i. Alternating states between depressed moods and hypomania

        ii. > 2 years

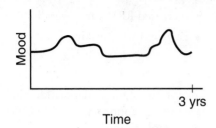

Depression with Seasonal Pattern (seasonal affective disorder)

 i. Depressive symptoms during months with short or long days

 ii. May be related to abnormal melatonin metabolism

 iii. Treat with bright light therapy (not melatonin tablets)

Major depressive disorder

 i. Symptoms for at least 2 weeks

 ii. Must represent a change from previous functioning

 iii. May be associated with:

- Anhedonia
- No motivation
- Feelings of worthlessness
- Decreased concentration
- Weight loss or gain
- Depressed mood
- Recurrent thoughts
- Insomnia or hypersomnia
- Psychomotor agitation or retardation
- Somatic complaints
- Delusions or hallucinations (if mood congruent)
- Loss of sex drive

 iv. Suicide:

- 60% of depressed patients have suicidal ideation.
- 15% of depressed patients die by suicide.

 v. Decreases in most hormones

 vi. Neurochemical changes

- Decreased norepinephrine
- Decreased serotonin
- Decreased dopamine
- Metabolites of these also decreased

 vii. Sleep correlates

- Increased REM in first half of sleep
- Decreased REM latency
- Decreased Stage 4 sleep

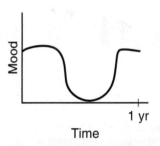

- Increased REM time overall
- Early morning waking

Bipolar disorder

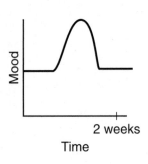

Mood / Time / 2 weeks

i. Symptoms of major depression plus symptoms of mania: a period of abnormal and persistent elevated, expansive, or irritable mood

ii. Alternates between depression and mania

iii. Subtypes
- Bipolar I: mania and major depression
- Bipolar II: major depression plus hypomanic episodes

iv. Manic symptoms
- Increased self-esteem or grandiosity
- Low frustration tolerance
- Decreased need for sleep
- Flight of ideas
- Excessive involvement in activities
- Weight loss and anorexia
- Erratic and uninhibited behavior
- Increased libido

v. Neurochemical changes
- Increased norepinephrine (NE)
- Increased serotonin

vi. Sleep correlates
- Multiple awakenings
- Markedly decreased sleep time

vii. Most genetic of all psychiatric disorders

Table 12-4. Epidemiology of Mood Disorders

	Depression	Bipolar
Point prevalence	Men: 2 to 3%, women: 5 to 9%	Men and women less than 1%
Gender differences	Women 2× men (stress of childbirth, hormonal effects, abused as children)	Rates are effectively equal
Lifetime prevalence	Men 10%, women 20%	Men and women 1%
Onset	Mean age 40	Mean age 30
SES	Low SES more likely	Higher SES more likely
Relationships	More prevalent among those with no close relationships, separation, divorce	More prevalent among single and divorced (causal?)
Family history	Higher risk if parents depressed or alcoholic; increased risk if parental loss before age 11	Higher risk if parent has bipolar

EATING DISORDERS

Bulimia Nervosa

a. Compulsive, rapid ingestion of food followed by compensatory behavior such as self-induced vomiting, use of laxatives, or exercise: binge and purge. If there is no compensatory behavior, the diagnosis is binge-eating disorder rather than bulimia.

b. Roughly 4% females and 0.5% males; 5 to 10% of women experience it at some point during their lives.

c. Clinical signs:

    i. Scars on back of hand

    ii. Esophageal tears

    iii. Enlarged parotid gland

    iv. Minimal public eating

d. Personality: outgoing and impulsive

e. Often associated with girls who previously were obese

f. Low baseline serotonin concentrations (repeated binges raise serotonin)

g. One-third have drug or alcohol problem.

h. Treatment: SSRIs, insight, and group therapy

Anorexia Nervosa

a. Self-imposed dietary limitations, significant weight loss (15% to 20% below ideal body weight); self starvation (BMI<17.5)

b. Fear of gaining weight

c. "Feel fat" even when very thin (body image disturbance)

d. Appearance of lanugo (baby-fine hair)

e. Prevalence

    i. 0.5% of population, 2% of adolescent females

    ii. Ages 10 to 30 (85% between 13 and 20); uncommon in women older than 40

    iii. 95% female

f. Mortality: 5 to 18%

g. Predisposing factors

    i. Family dynamics linked to relationship with the father; harsh mother

    ii. Mother with history, 50% of susceptibility inherited

    iii. 50% of anorexics also binge and purge

h. Treatment

    i. Usually resistant to treatment (denial of illness)

    ii. Full treatment: stabilizing weight, then family and individual therapy

    iii. Pharmacologic treatment: antidepressants (to cause weight gain)

Table 12-5. Eating Disorders

	Anorexia Nervosa	Bulimia Nervosa
Gender	W > M	W > M
Age	Mid-teenage years	Late adolescence/early adulthood
SES	Not specific to high	Not specific to high
Weight	>15% below ideal body weight	Varies, usually nl. or >nl.
Neurotransmitters	Serotonin/norepinephrine?	Serotonin/norepinephrine?
Binge/purge	Yes	Yes
Laxative/diuretics	Yes	Yes
Sexual adjustment	Poor	Good
Medical complications	• Amenorrhea • Lanugo • High mortality • Dental cavities • Electrolyte imbalances	• Electrolyte imbalances • Dental cavities • Callous on hands/fingers • Enlarged parotid and salivary glands • Cardiac abnormalities

ANXIETY DISORDERS

1. Most common psychiatric disorders in women of all ages. For men, substance-related disorders are most common.

Types of Anxiety Disorders

Generalized anxiety disorder

   i. Symptoms exhibited more days than not over a 6-month period (worry about things they do not need to worry about).

   ii. Symptoms

- Motor tension (fidgety, jumpy)
- Autonomic hyperactivity (heart pounding, sweating, chest pains), hyperventilation
- Apprehension (fear, worry, rumination), difficulty concentrating
- Vigilance and scanning (impatient, hyperactive, distracted)
- Fatigue and sleep disturbances common, especially insomnia and restlessness
- Treat with SSRI or buspirone

Panic disorder

   i. Three attacks in 3-week period and worry about more

   ii. No clear circumscribed stimulus; phobic-level reaction, without a phobic object

iii. Abrupt onset of symptoms, peak within 10 minutes

iv. Symptoms of a panic attack

- Great apprehension and fear
- Palpitations, trembling, sweating
- Fear of dying or going crazy
- Hyperventilation, "air hunger"
- Sense of unreality

v. Epidemiology

- Young women
- 1.5% of population has disorder; 4% lifetime prevalence
- 10 to 14% of cardiology patients have panic attacks
- Patients with allergies are 2× more likely to have attacks.
- Premenstrual period: heightened vulnerability

vi. Can induce panic attacks by hyperventilation, carbon dioxide, yohimbine, sodium lactate, epinephrine (panicogens)

vii. Treatment

- Alprazolam, clonazepam, lorazepam
- SSRI
- Carbon dioxide (for hyperventilation)

viii. Relapse is common; keep on medication for 6 to 12 months

Phobias

i. General

- Prevalence: 4% men, 9% women
- Public speaking is the #1 phobia.

ii. <u>Specific phobias:</u> fear of specific object, e.g., spiders, snakes

- Anxiety when faced with identifiable object
- Phobic object avoided
- Fear must be persistent and disabling
- Treat with behavioral modification (systematic desensitization, exposure, flooding)

iii. <u>Social anxiety disorder:</u> fear of feeling or being embarrassed or humiliated

- Leads to dysfunctional circumspect behavior, e.g., inability to urinate in public washrooms, go to restaurants, and speak in public
- Prevalence: 1% of general population
- May accompany avoidant personality disorder
- Treat with SSRI
- <u>Discrete performance anxiety</u> (stage fright): atenolol or propranolol (beta blocker)

OBSESSIVE–COMPULSIVE DISORDER AND RELATED DISORDERS

Obsessive–Compulsive Disorder

    i. <u>Obsession:</u> thoughts which are repetitive, intrusive, and senseless

    ii. <u>Compulsion:</u> act which controls the thought, time consuming

    iii. Common defenses: undoing, reaction formation

    iv. Epidemiology
- 1.5% have disorder, 3% lifetime prevalence
- 50% remain unmarried
- Males = females
- Major depression among 70% over lifetime

    v. Increased frontal lobe metabolism

    vi. Increased activity in the caudate nucleus

    vii. Treatment
- SSRIs

Hoarding Disorder

Characterized by persistent difficulty with parting of one's possessions regardless of their value. This typically leads to changes in functioning.

Treatment is SSRIs.

Body Dysmorphic Disorder

    i. Believes body part is abnormal, misshapen, or defective

    ii. Sees self as ugly or horrific when normal in appearance

    iii. Preoccupation disrupts day-to-day life

    iv. Not accounted for by other disorder (e.g., anorexia nervosa)

    v. May seek multiple plastic surgeries or other extreme interventions

TRAUMA AND STRESS-RELATED DISORDERS

1. Manifestations:
   a. Re-experience of the event as recurrent dreams or recollections (flashbacks)
   b. Avoidance of associated stimuli
   c. Diminished responsiveness to external world
   d. Sleep disruption or excess
   e. Irritability, loss of control, impulsivity
   f. Headaches, inability to concentrate
2. Symptoms must be exhibited for >1 month; if less, diagnose as acute stress disorder

3. Following psychologically stressful event outside the range of normal human experience

    a. Most commonly, serious threat to life, family, children, home, or community

    b. Common reaction to rape war, earthquakes, etc.

4. Often long latency period, e.g., abused as child, manifest symptoms as an adult

5. Quicker onset correlates with better prognosis

6. Increased vulnerability if:

    a. Prior emotional variability; excessive autonomic reactions is a predictor of occurrence

7. Adults recover quicker; very young and very old have harder time coping

8. Prevalence: 0.5% in men, 1.2% in women

9. Sleep changes: increase in REM latency; decrease in amount of REM and Stage 4 sleep

10. Increased, sustained activity in amygdala

11. Increased levels of norepinephrine and epinephrine

12. Decreased cortisol levels

13. Co-occurrence with other psychiatric disorders common

14. Treatment: group therapy to facilitate working through normal reactions blocked by disorder. SSRIs can improve patients' functional level.

SOMATIC SYMPTOM DISORDERS, FACTITIOUS DISORDER, AND MALINGERING

Somatic Symptom Disorders

Somatic symptom disorder

    i. ≥1 somatic symptoms distressing enough to cause changes in level of functioning, as well as excessive and disproportionate thoughts, feelings, and behavior regarding those symptoms.

    ii. Must be present >6 months

    iii. Onset age <30

    iv. Symptoms can occur over a period of years

    v. More common in females than in males (20 to 1)

Conversion disorder (functional neurological symptom disorders)

    i. Stressor followed by ≥1 symptoms

    ii. Usually skeletal, muscular, sensory, or a peripheral non-autonomic system, e.g., paralysis of hand, loss of sight

    iii. Look for *la belle indifference*

Illness anxiety disorder

    i. Unrealistic interpretation of physical signs as abnormal

    ii. Preoccupation with illness or fear of illness when none present

iii. Preoccupation persists in spite of reassurance

iv. At least 6 months duration

Somatic symptom disorder with predominant pain

i. Severe, prolonged pain

ii. No cause found

iii. Pain disrupts day-to-day life

iv. Rule out depression

v. Look for secondary gain

Table 12-6. Somatic Symptom Disorders Versus Factitious Disorders and Malingering

	Somatic Symptom	Factitious	Malingering
Symptom production	Unconscious	Intentional	Intentional
Motivation	Unconscious	Unconscious	Intentional

Factitious Disorder

a. Some conscious, some unconscious

i. Intentional illness production

ii. Unconscious motivation, therefore, a compulsion

iii. Patients aware of manufacturing their symptoms but unaware of why they go to such lengths

iv. Both primary and secondary gain

v. Types:
- Imposed on self
- Imposed on others (inducing symptoms in others e.g., a mother producing symptoms in her child)

vi. Factitious disorders require treatment; foster relationship and look for motive

Malingering

a. Everything conscious

i. Intentional symptom production for gain

ii. Conscious motivation

iii. Symptoms purely for secondary gain, e.g., to avoid a court date, military induction, or school

ADJUSTMENT DISORDER

1. Residual category, use *only* if no other diagnosis applies

2. Criteria:

a. Presence of identifiable stressor and symptoms must occur within 3 months of onset

b. Symptoms last <6 months after end of stressor

    c. Symptoms are clinically significant, with significant social, occupational, and/or academic impairment

    d. <u>Cannot</u> be a grief response

    e. Cannot meet criteria for other disorder

DISSOCIATIVE DISORDERS

1. Use the defense mechanism of dissociation where you split off a group of activities or thoughts from the main part of consciousness

2. Typically due to traumatic events

3. Fugue

    a. Sudden unexpected travel

    b. Inability to recall one's past

    c. Confusion of identity or new identity

4. Subtypes (fugue state may appear with all subtypes)

    a. Amnesia: inability to recall important personal information

    b. Dissociative identity disorder (multiple personality)

        i. Presence of two or more distinct identities

        ii. Will have lapses in memory

    c. Depersonalization disorder

        i. Recurrent experiences of being detached from or outside of one's body—"out of body experiences"

        ii. Reality testing stays intact

        iii. Causes significant impairment

PERSONALITY DISORDERS

1. General characteristics

    a. Inflexible, inability to adapt

    b. One way of responding

    c. Lifelong

    d. All areas of life are affected

    e. Maladaptive patterns of behavior

    f. Ego-syntonic

Cluster A: Odd or Eccentric

Higher prevalence in (a) biologic relatives of schizophrenics, and (b) males

Paranoid

        i. Long-standing suspiciousness or mistrust of others: a base line of mistrust

        ii. Preoccupied with issues of trust

        iii. Reluctant to confide in others

        iv. Reads hidden meaning into comments or events

        v. Carries grudges

    vi. Differentiate from:

- Paranoid schizophrenic has hallucinations and formal thought disorders; paranoid personality disorder does not
- Delusional disorder, paranoid type has fixed, focal delusions; paranoid personality disorder does not

Schizoid

    i. Lifelong pattern of social withdrawal, and they like it that way

    ii. Seen by others as eccentric, isolated, withdrawn

    iii. Restricted emotional expression

Schizotypal

    i. Very odd, strange, weird

    ii. Magical thinking (including ESP and telepathy), ideas of reference, illusions

    iii. Social anxiety (paranoid)

    iv. Suspiciousness

    v. Lack of close friends

    vi. Incongruous affect

    vii. Odd speech, social isolation

    viii. May have short-lived psychotic episodes

Cluster B: Dramatic and Emotional

Histrionic

    i. Colorful, dramatic, extroverted

    ii. Inability to maintain long-lasting relationships

    iii. Attention-seeking, constantly wanting the spotlight

    iv. Seductive behavior

Narcissistic

    i. Grandiose sense of self-importance

    ii. Preoccupation with fantasies of unlimited wealth, power, love

    iii. Demands constant attention

    iv. Fragile self-esteem, prone to depression

    v. Criticism met with indifference or rage

    vi. Genuine surprise and anger when others don't do as they want

    vii. Can be charismatic

Borderline

    i. Females two times more than males

    ii. Very unstable affect, behavior, self-image

    iii. In constant state of crisis, chaos

    iv. Self-detrimental impulsivity: promiscuity, gambling, overeating, substance-related disorders

    v. Unstable but intense interpersonal relationships: very dependent and hostile, love/hate

    vi. Great problems with being alone

    vii. Self-injurious behavior

    viii. History of sexual abuse

    ix. Common defenses: splitting, passive–aggressive

    x. Particularly incapable of tolerating anxiety

    xi. Often coupled with mood disorder

    xii. 5% commit suicide

Antisocial

    i. 3% males, 1% females

    ii. Continual criminal acts

    iii. Inability to conform to social norms: truancy, delinquency, theft, running away

    iv. Can't hold job, no enduring attachments, reckless, aggressive

    v. Onset before age 15; if younger than 18, diagnose as conduct disorder

Cluster C: Anxious and Fearful

Behaviors associated with fear and anxiety

Avoidant

    i. Extreme sensitivity to rejection

    ii. Sees self as socially inept

    iii. Excessive shyness, high anxiety levels

    iv. Social isolation, but an intense, internal desire for affection and acceptance

    v. Wants the world to change, to be nicer, more accepting

    vi. Tends to stay in same job, same life situation, same relationships

Obsessive–compulsive

    i. Orderliness, inflexible, perfectionist

    ii. More common in males, firstborn, harsh discipline upbringing

    iii. Loves lists, rules, order

    iv. Unable to discard worn-out objects

    v. Doesn't want change

    vi. Excessively stubborn

    vii. Lacks sense of humor

    viii. Wants to keep routine

ix. Differentiate from obsessive–compulsive anxiety disorder. The anxiety disorder has obsessions and compulsions that are focal and acquired. Personality disorders are lifelong and pervasive.

Dependent

i. Gets others to assume responsibility

ii. Subordinates own needs to others

iii. Can't express disagreement

iv. Great fear of having to care for self

v. May be linked to abusive spouse

Table 12-7. Personality Disorders

	Definition	Epidemiology	Associated Defenses
Paranoid	Attributes involvement motives to others, suspicious	1. Men > women 2. Increased incidence in families with schizophrenia	Projection
Schizoid	Isolated lifestyle, has no longing for others, "loner"	1. Men > women 2. Increased incidence in families with schizophrenia	
Schizotypal	Weird, eccentric behavior, thought, speech	1. Prevalence is 3% 2. Men > women	
Histrionic	Excessive emotion and attention seeking	1. Women > men 2. Underdiagnosed in men	
Narcissistic	Grandiose, overconcerned with issues of self-esteem	Common	
Borderline	Instability of mood, self-image, and relationships	1. Women > men 2. Increased mood disorders in families	Splitting
Antisocial	Does not recognize the rights of others	Prevalence: 3% in men; 1% in women	Superego lacunae
Avoidant	Shy or timid, fears rejection	1. Common 2. Possible deforming illness	
Dependent	Dependent, submissive	1. Common 2. Women > men	
Obsessive-compulsive	Perfectionistic and inflexible, orderly, rigid	1. Men > women 2. Increased concordance in identical twins	1. Undoing 2. Reaction formation

Review Questions

93. A 6-year-old boy was referred by his first grade teacher for evaluation after she noticed that he had trouble keeping up with the other children in his class. After psychologic testing and an evaluation interview, the boy's IQ is assessed at 62. Based on this information, when he is an adult the boy most likely will

    (A) find work in a sheltered workshop setting

    (B) have difficulty with basic reading and math skills

    (C) lead a normal life with no special support required

    (D) require custodial care

    (E) need guidance for important life decisions

94. A 45-year-old woman presents to her primary care physician complaining of fatigue and headaches. Over the past month, she reports that she has had trouble sleeping, difficulty concentrating, and episodes of crying for no reason. In addition, she says that she feels sad and worthless. The neurologic pathway most likely implicated as the source of these symptoms is the

    (A) meso-limbic-cortico pathway

    (B) locus ceruleus pathway

    (C) nigrostriatal pathway

    (D) nucleus accumbens pathway

    (E) glycolytic pathway

95. A 42-year-old woman has always been extremely neat and conscientious, skills she makes good use of as the executive secretary to the president of a large corporation. Something of a perfectionist, she often stays long after normal working hours to check on the punctuation and spelling of letters that she prepared during the day. Although her work is impeccable, she has few close relationships with others. Her boss referred her for counseling after she repeatedly got into fights with her coworkers. "They just don't take the job to heart," she says disapprovingly about them. "All they seem to want to do is joke around all day." The most likely preliminary diagnosis for this patient is

    (A) obsessive–compulsive personality disorder

    (B) paranoid personality disorder

    (C) schizoid personality disorder

    (D) hysterical personality disorder

    (E) antisocial personality disorder

    (F) narcissistic personality disorder

    (G) borderline personality disorder

    (H) dependent personality disorder

    (I) avoidant personality disorder

    (J) schizotypal personality disorder

96. A 22-year-old male patient refuses to provide answers to standard questions during an initial history and physical exam, including address and telephone number. When asked the reason for the refusal, he says he doesn't see why the physician needs such irrelevant information and eyes the physician suspiciously. When pressed further, he asks angrily, "Look, are you going to treat me or do I have to get my lawyer?" This behavior is most consistent with a diagnosis of

(A) obsessive–compulsive personality disorder

(B) paranoid personality disorder

(C) schizoid personality disorder

(D) hysterical personality disorder

(E) antisocial personality disorder

(F) narcissistic personality disorder

(G) borderline personality disorder

(H) dependent personality disorder

(I) avoidant personality disorder

(J) schizotypal personality disorder

97. A patient's past medical history indicates numerous admissions to a local public hospital, mostly during the winter months. On each occasion, he has been brought to the hospital after passing out in a public location. His appearance is disheveled and his clothes are torn. He complains that the cold makes him dizzy and asks the physician, with tears in his eyes, to "please help him get better." Neurologic examination is unable to uncover any underlying cause for his reported symptoms. The most likely preliminary diagnosis for this patient would be

(A) dysthymia

(B) somatic symptom disorder

(C) delusional disorder

(D) factitious disorder

(E) malingering

98. A man awakens to find a bright sunny day. As he dresses, he makes sure to put on a yellow shirt to ensure that it will stay sunny all day. This behavior can best be described as

(A) delusion

(B) hallucination

(C) idea of reference

(D) magical thinking

(E) illusion

99. Glenn has been a model patient on the ward for more than 2 years. He is never in any trouble. Whatever he is told to do he does. He sits quietly for hours, rarely talking, and hardly moving, except to ape the movements of those who pass by him. The most likely diagnosis for Glenn is

    (A) schizophreniform disorder
    (B) schizoid personality disorder
    (C) brief psychotic disorder
    (D) schizotypal personality disorder
    (E) schizophrenia, catatonic specifier

100. According to twin studies, the strongest evidence of a genetic cause is for

    (A) schizophrenia
    (B) bipolar disorder
    (C) unipolar depression
    (D) antisocial personality disorder
    (E) alcoholism

101. A patient suffering from paranoid schizophrenia has been on his medication for a full year. During this time, his positive symptoms have abated and he shows no signs of relapse. If he continues to be adherent with his medication, his chance of relapse over the coming years is most likely to be

    (A) 80%
    (B) 50%
    (C) 40%
    (D) 30%
    (E) 10%

102. A 22-year-old intellectually disabled male lives on his own but works in a sheltered workshop setting. He has an active social life and is well liked by his peers. He meets weekly with a counselor who helps him handle his money and provides advice about some life decisions. Based on this information, this man will most likely be considered as having what level of intellectual disability?

    (A) Below average
    (B) Mild
    (C) Moderate
    (D) Severe
    (E) Profound

103. A 38-year-old woman is brought by her husband to see her primary care physician. The husband reports that she is getting hard to live with. Physical exam reveals rapid heartbeat and profuse sweating. In conversation, the woman has a hard time focusing and gets up from her chair repeatedly. After some time, she reports that she is tired and has had difficulty sleeping for "what seems like a year, now." She attributes this difficulty sleeping to her tendency to worry about her children and confides that she checks on them 10 to 20 times a night. When questioned about friends, she states that she just doesn't see them much any more. Based on this preliminary information, the most likely diagnosis for this woman would be

    (A) agoraphobia
    (B) generalized anxiety disorder
    (C) social anxiety disorder
    (D) obsessive–compulsive disorder
    (E) panic disorder

104. A 42-year-old man who makes his living as a computer programmer and works out of his own home is referred by his employer for evaluation. He is reluctant to venture out to meet with other people, and rarely has people in to visit. When selected for a company-wide award, he refuses to have his picture taken for the company newsletter. During an assessment interview, he averts his face and asks the examiner to "stop looking at me." Although he is average in appearance, he is convinced that his face is ugly and misshapen and says that he stays away from people so they "won't have to look at me." The most likely diagnosis for this man would be

    (A) agoraphobia
    (B) body dysmorphic disorder
    (C) factitious disorder
    (D) obsessive–compulsive disorder
    (E) social anxiety disorder
    (F) somatic symptom disorder

105. A young woman of unknown age is brought by the police to the local emergency department for evaluation after they found her wandering in a local park. The woman carries no purse and no identification. Physical exam shows no abnormalities. When questioned, the woman is pleasant and attentive, making eye contact and answering each question as it is asked. She is unable to state her name or any details about her life, except that the name Phoenix seems familiar, although she is not sure why. The police in Phoenix, Arizona, are contacted and find a missing persons report matching the patient's description. Based on this information, the most likely diagnosis for this patient is

    (A) adjustment disorder
    (B) amnesia
    (C) conversion disorder
    (D) depersonalization disorder
    (E) dissociative identity disorder
    (F) factitious disorder
    (G) dissociative amnesia with fugue

106. For 3 weeks following an automobile accident where she watched her child die, a 28-year-old woman reports difficulty sleeping, headaches, and an inability to concentrate. Her family reports that she suffers from nightmares and violent emotional outbursts when awake. Since the accident, she refuses to either drive or ride in a car. The symptoms presented here are most consistent with a diagnosis of

    (A) adjustment disorder
    (B) post-traumatic stress disorder
    (C) acute stress disorder
    (D) dysthymia
    (E) major depression
    (F) normal grief

107. A 28-year-old white male presents at a local clinic complaining of severe abdominal pain. He reports tenderness during palpation, dizziness, and difficulty concentrating. Review of the medical record shows that this is the fourth time in the past year that the patient has appeared for medical attention. On each previous occasion, no identifiable medical problem could be uncovered. When confronted with this history, the patient confesses that he manufactures his symptoms before coming to the clinic. He says that he knows this is wrong, but he cannot stop himself from doing this. Based on the information, the most likely diagnosis for this patient would be

    (A) somatic symptom disorder
    (B) conversion disorder
    (C) illness anxiety disorder
    (D) factitious disorder
    (E) malingering

Answers

93. **Answer: E.** The tested IQ suggests mild intellectual disability. These individuals live their own lives and make their own decisions, but often need assistance at some of life's important transitions points. Note that they are legally competent.

94. **Answer: B.** Starting in the retrolateral part of the pons, this is the major pathway for norepinepherine. Mesolimbic and nigrostriatal pathways are associated with dopamine and therefore, schizophrenia.

95. **Answer: A.** Focusing on details, loving routine, having a sense that there is only one right way to do things, lack of humor, and few close relationships suggests an obsessive–compulsive personality disorder.

96. **Answer: B.** General suspiciousness and mistrust suggests a paranoid personality disorder.

97. **Answer: E.** The timing during the winter months and the public venue for the passing out are all suggestive of the secondary gain of malingering.

98. **Answer: D.** The yellow shirt influences the sunny day. This is an example of magical thinking.

99. **Answer: E.** Glenn is an example of schizophrenia with catatonic specifier.

100. **Answer: B.** The Heritability Index tells us that about 62% of bipolar disorder is due to inheritance. This is greater than schizophrenia (40%) and the other options.

101. **Answer: E.** If patients are compliant with medication and make it past the first year without relapse, the chance of relapse is a low 10%.

102. **Answer: C.** Moderate intellectual disability (IQ 49 to 35). He is able to take care of some of his own affairs, but needs weekly help with finances and works in a sheltered workshop.

103. **Answer: B.** The symptoms and timeframe are consistent with a diagnosis of generalized anxiety disorder. Although some features of other disorders are present, they do not match criteria.

104. **Answer: B.** The central issue is the negative appraisal of his own appearance. All other symptoms arise from this.

105. **Answer: G.** One of the dissociative disorders defined as sudden travel and inability to recall one's past or confusion about one's identity.

106. **Answer: C.** Avoidance of associated stimuli and nightmares after an identified traumatic event are the criteria for PTSD. But the timeframe, 3 weeks, makes acute stress disorder the better answer.

107. **Answer: D.** Factitious disorders are characterized by conscious symptom production and unconscious motivation. Somatic symptom disorder, conversion disorder, and illness anxiety disorder are all subtypes of somatic symptom disorders. Malingering is a conscious symptom production and there is clear, conscious secondary gain.

TOURETTE'S DISORDER

1. Definition: multiple motor and vocal tics
    a. Tics occur many times every day or intermittently for >1 year.
    b. Tics can be simple (rapid, repetitive contractions) or complex (appear as more ritualistic and purposeful).
    c. Simple tics appear first.
2. Characteristics
    a. Prevalence is 0.5–1 per 1,000.
    b. Mean age of onset is 7 (onset must be age <18).
    c. Male to female ratio is 3:1.
    d. Evidence of genetic transmission: ~50% concordance in monozygotic twins
    e. Associated with increased levels of dopamine
    f. Associated with ADHD and OCD.
    g. Treatment: haloperidol, pimozide, or clonidine

DELIRIUM VERSUS NEUROCOGNITIVE DISORDER

1. <u>Delirium:</u> acute onset, impaired cognitive functioning, fluctuating and brief, reversible
2. <u>Neurocognitive Disorder:</u> loss of cognitive abilities, impaired social functioning, loss of memory, personality change; only 15% reversible; may be progressive or static

Note

The COMLEX Requires You to Know:

- The signs and symptoms of common organic conditions.

- Special emphasis should be placed on differential diagnosis among related disorders and between organic disorders and psychiatric disorders.

Table 13-1. Delirium versus Neurocognitive Disorder

	Delirium	Neurocognitive Disorder
History	Acute, identifiable date	Chronic, cannot be dated
Onset	Rapid	Insidious
Duration	Days to weeks	Months to years
Course	Fluctuating	Chronically progressive
Level of consciousness	Fluctuating	Normal
Orientation	Impaired periodically	Disorientation to time → place → person
Memory	Recent markedly impaired	Recent impaired then remote
Perception	Visual hallucinations	Hallucinations, sundowning

(continued)

Table 13-1. Delirium versus Neurocognitive Disorder (continued)

	Delirium	Neurocognitive Disorder
Sleep	Disrupted sleep-wake cycle	Less sleep disruption
Reversibility	Reversible	Most not reversible
Physiologic changes	Prominent	Minimal
Attention span	Very short	Not reduced

Neurocognitive Disorders

1. <u>Epidemiology</u>
   a. 5% of population older than 65
   b. 20% older than 80
   c. 15% of neurocognitive disorders are reversible.
2. <u>Primary degenerative neurocognitive disorder of the Alzheimer type (DAT)</u>
   a. Ten warning signs of Alzheimer disease
      i. Memory loss that affects job skills
      ii. Difficulty performing familiar tasks
      iii. Problems with language
      iv. Disorientation to time and place
      v. Poor judgment
      vi. Problems with abstract thought
      vii. Misplacing things
      viii. Changes in mood or behavior
      ix. Changes in personality
      x. Loss of initiative
   b. Epidemiology
      i. Most common, represents 65% of neurocognitive disorders in patients age >65
      ii. Prevalence increases with age
      iii. Women greater than men
      iv. Family history confers greater risk
      v. Less risk for higher educated
      vi. Linked to chromosomes 1 and 14 (mutations), 19 (apolipoprotein E), 21 (linked to Down syndrome)
   c. Etiology
      i. Unknown
      ii. Theories: maternal age at birth, deficiency of brain choline, autoimmune disorders, viral etiology, familial
   d. Gross pathology
      i. Diffuse atrophy of the brain on CT or MRI
      ii. Flattened cortical sulci

    iii. Enlarged cerebral ventricles

    iv. Deficient blood flow in parietal lobes correlated with cognitive decline

    v. Reduction in choline acetyl transferase

    vi. Reduced metabolism in temporal and parietal lobes

  e. Microscopic pathology

    i. Accumulation of amyloid beta-peptides (protein fragment)

    ii. Senile plaques

    iii. Neurofibrillary tangles

    iv. Granulovascular degeneration of the neurons

    v. Anatomic changes: to amygdala, hippocampus, cortex, basal forebrain

  f. Treatment

    i. Supportive

    ii. Symptomatic

    iii. Reduce environmental changes

    iv. Reduce hypertension and LDL cholesterol levels

    v. Donepezil hydrochloride, rivastigmine, galantamine, memantine

3. <u>Vascular neurocognitive disorder</u>

  a. Definition: decremental or patchy deterioration in cognitive functioning due to severe cerebrovascular disease

  b. Epidemiology

    i. Most prevalent between ages 60 and 70

    ii. Appears earlier than does DAT

    iii. Men > women

    iv. Hypertension is predisposing factor

    v. 15% of all neurocognitive disorders in the elderly

    vi. Can often find some lateralizing neurologic signs

  c. Etiology

    i. Vascular disease is present.

    ii. Affects small- and medium-sized cerebral vessels that infarct and produce parenchymal lesions over wide areas of the brain

  d. Treatment

    i. Treatment of underlying condition (hypertension, diabetes mellitus, hyperlipidemia)

    ii. General measures for neurocognitive disorder

Table 13-2. Neurocognitive Disorder, Alzheimer Type versus Vascular Neurocognitive Disorder

Neurocognitive Disorder, Alzheimer Type	Vascular Neurocognitive disorder
General deterioration	Patchy deterioration
More in women	More in men
Later onset	Earlier onset
Most common, 65% of neurocognitive disorders	Less common, 15% of neurocognitive disorders
Etiology unknown	Etiology features hypertension
Progressive onset	Quick onset
No lateral signs	Lateralizing neurologic signs

4. Frontal/Temporal disease
   a. Affects frontal and temporal lobes
   b. Very rare
   c. Similar picture to neurocognitive disorder, Alzheimer type (DAT)
   d. Prominent frontal lobe symptoms (personality change)
   e. Reactive gliosis in frontal/temporal lobes
   f. CT or MRI sometimes shows frontal lobe involvement but definitive diagnosis is only at autopsy

5. Prion disease
   a. Neurocognitive disorder caused by prion (no DNA or RNA)
   b. Rapidly progressive
   c. Generally onset between ages 40 and 50
   d. Initially, vague somatic complaints and unspecified anxiety, followed by ataxia, choreoathetosis, and dysarthria
   e. Fatal in 2 years (usually sooner)
   f. CT demonstrates atrophy in cortex/cerebellum
   g. No treatment

6. Huntington chorea
   a. Autosomal dominant
   b. Defect in chromosome 4
   c. Males = females
   d. Basal ganglia and caudate atrophy
   e. Choreoathetoid movements, neurocognitive disorder, psychosis
   f. Onset between ages 30 and 40
   g. Progressive deterioration
   h. Neurocognitive disorder, later with psychosis progressing to infantile state

     i. Death in 15–20 years

     j. Suicide is common.

7. <u>Parkinson's disease</u>

    a. Decreased dopamine in substantia nigra

    b. Annual prevalence is 200 in 100,000

    c. Symptoms

        i. Bradykinesia

       ii. Resting tremor

      iii. Pill-rolling tremor

      iv. Masklike facies

       v. Cogwheel rigidity

      vi. Shuffling gait

    d. 40% to 80% develop neurocognitive disorder

    e. Depression is common; treat with antidepressants or electroconvulsive therapy (ECT)

    f. Treatment: L-dopa or deprenyl

8. <u>Wilson disease</u>

    a. Defect in chromosome 13

    b. Ceruloplasmin deficiency

    c. Abnormal copper metabolism

    d. Kaiser-Fleischer rings

9. <u>Normal pressure hydrocephalus</u>

    a. Symptom triad of:

        i. Neurocognitive disorder

       ii. Urinary incontinence

      iii. Gait apraxia (magnetic gait)

    b. Increased ventricles on CT

    c. Normal pressure on lumbar puncture

    d. Treat with shunt

10. <u>HIV-related neurocognitive disorder</u>

    a. Caused by chronic HIV encephalitis and myelitis

        i. Two-thirds have insidious onset, one-third has florid onset

       ii. 70 to 95% of patients with AIDS have HIV-related neurocognitive disorder before death.

    b. Clinically consists of the following:

        i. Cognitive symptoms: forgetfulness, loss of concentration, confusion

       ii. Behavioral symptoms: apathy, withdrawal, dysphoric mood, organic psychosis

      iii. Motor symptoms: loss of balance, leg weakness, poor handwriting

    c. Average survival from onset to death is 4.2 months

d. Early signs of HIV-related neurocognitive disorder: dysphoric mood, apathy, social withdrawal

e. Often misdiagnosed at first as depression

f. HIV levels in the spinal fluid are good predictors of onset

HEMISPHERIC DOMINANCE

1. <u>Left hemisphere</u>

    a. Language

    b. Dominant in 97% of population, 60 to 70% in left-handed persons

    c. Calculation-type problem solving

    d. Stroke damage to left is more likely to lead to depression

    e. Larger in size than is the right side and processes information faster

2. <u>Right hemisphere</u>

    a. Perception, artistic, visual–spatial

    b. Activated for intuition-type problem solving

    c. Stroke damage to right is more likely to lead to apathy and indifference

APHASIAS

Broca (nonfluent)

a. Lesion of frontal lobe (Brodmann area 44)

b. Comprehension unimpaired

c. Speech production is telegraphic and ungrammatical.

d. Often accompanied by depressive symptoms

e. "I movies" instead of "I went to the movies"

f. Trouble repeating statements

g. Muscle weakness on the right side

Wernicke (fluent)

a. Lesions of superior temporal gyrus (Brodmann area 22)

b. Comprehension impaired

c. Speech is fluent but incoherent.

d. Trouble repeating statements

e. Verbal paraphasias (substituting one word for another, or making up word)

f. No muscle weakness

g. Resembles formal thought disorder

h. Mania-like, rapid speech hyperactivity

Note

- Apraxia: loss of ability to learn or to carry out specific movements, e.g., unable to flip a coin when asked to do so

- Agnosia: failure to recognize sensory stimuli, e.g., visual agnosia, unable to recognize object when shown but able to recognize when touched

- Alexia: acquired disorder of reading ability; often accompanied by aphasia. Distinguish from dyslexia (developmental reading problem)

- Agraphia: acquired inability to write

Conduction (fluent)

    a. Lesion in the parietal lobe or arcuate fasciculus

    b. Connection between Broca and Wernicke areas broken

    c. Words comprehended correctly but cannot be passed on for speech or writing

    d. Trouble repeating statements

    e. Naming always impaired

Global (nonfluent)

    a. Wide lesions in the presylvian speech area

    b. Both Broca and Wernicke areas damaged

    c. Labored telegraphic speech with poor comprehension

    d. Trouble repeating statements

    e. Naming severly impaired

Transcortical

    a. Lesion in the prefrontal cortex

    b. Capacity to repeat statements is unimpaired

    c. Patient cannot speak spontaneously

BRAIN AND BEHAVIOR

Original Drawing	Patient's Drawing	Name	Localization
	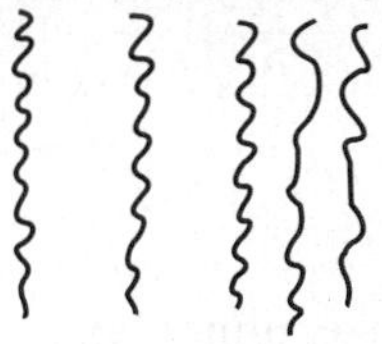	Perseveration	Frontal lobe
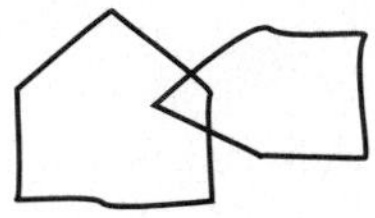		Constructional apraxia	Nondominant (right) parietal lobe
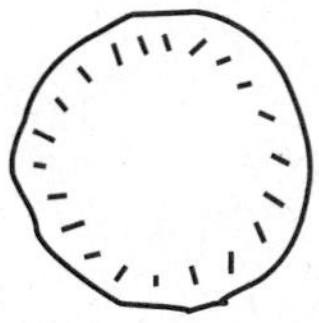		Hemineglect/ hemi-inattention	Right parietal lobe (usually non-dominant)

Figure 13-1. Dysfunctions on Common Neurologic Exams

Frontal Cortex: Global Orientation

a. Key functions

    i. Speech

    ii. Critical to personality

    iii. Abstract thought

    iv. Memory and higher-order mental functions

    v. Capacity to initiate and stop tasks

    vi. Concentration

b. Lesions of dorsal prefrontal cortex

    i. Apathy

    ii. Decreased drive, initiative

    iii. Poor grooming

    iv. Decreased attention

    v. Poor ability to think abstractly

    vi. Broca aphasia (if in dominant hemisphere)

c. Lesions of orbitomedial frontal cortex

    i. Withdrawal

    ii. Fearfulness

    iii. Explosive mood

    iv. Loss of inhibitions

    v. Violent outbursts

Temporal Cortex

a. Functions

    i. Language

    ii. Memory

    iii. Emotion

b. Lesions stem from stroke, tumor, and trauma; herpes virus CNS infections often affect temporal cortex

c. Bilateral lesions: neurocognitive disorder

d. Lesions of the rostal (front) left temporal lobe: deficits in recall or learning of proper names

e. Lesions of dominant lobe:

    i. Euphoria

    ii. Auditory hallucinations

    iii. Delusions

    iv. Thought disorders

    v. Poor verbal comprehension (Wernicke)

f. Lesions of nondominant lobe:

    i. Dysphoria

    ii. Irritability

    iii. Decreased visual and musical ability

Parietal Cortex

    a. Key function: intellectual processing of sensory information

        i. Left: verbal processing (dominant)

        ii. Right: visual–spatial processing (nondominant)

    b. Lesions of dominant lobe: Gerstmann syndrome

        i. Agraphia

        ii. Acalculia

        iii. Finger agnosia

        iv. Right-left disorientation

        v. Dysfunctions in this area account for aproportion of learning disabilities

    c. Lesions of nondominant lobe:

        i. Denial of illness (anosognosia)

        ii. Construction apraxia (difficulty outlining objects)

        iii. Neglect of the opposite side (e.g., not washing or dressing opposite side of body)

Occipital Cortex

    a. Key functions

        i. Visual input

        ii. Recall of objects, scenes, and distances; PET scans show activity in this area during recall of visual images

    b. Destruction: cortical blindness

    c. Bilateral occlusion of posterior cerebral arteries: Anton syndrome

        i. Cortical blindness

        ii. Denial of blindness

Limbic System

    a. Consists of hippocampus, hypothalamus, anterior thalamus, cingulate gyrus, amygdala

    b. Associated cortical areas can suppress external displays of internal states

    c. Key functions

        i. Motivation

        ii. Memory

        iii. Emotions (mediation between cortex and lower centers)

        iv. Reflex arc for conditioned responses

        v. Violent behaviors

        vi. Sociosexual behaviors

    d. Associated dysfunctions

        i. Apathy

        ii. Aggression

        iii. Vegetative-endocrine disturbances

        iv. Memory problems and learning new material

e. <u>Hypothalamus</u>

    i. Implicated in involuntary internal responses that accompany emotional strategy

    ii. Regulation of some physiologic responses

- Increased heart and respiration
- Elevation of blood pressure and diversion of blood to skeletal muscles when angry
- Regulation of endocrine balance
- Control of eating (hunger/thirst centers)
- Regulation of body temperature
- Regulation of sleep-wake cycle

    iii. Dysfunctions

- Destruction of ventromedial hypothalamus: hyperphagia and obesity
- Destruction of lateral hypothalamus: anorexia and starvation

f. <u>Thalamus</u>

    i. Critical to pain perception

    ii. Dysfunctions lead to impaired memory and arousal

g. <u>Reticular activating system (RAS)</u>

    i. Motivation

    ii. Arousal

    iii. Wakefulness

h. <u>Hippocampus:</u> critical for memory and new learning

Table 13-3. Lesions and Memory

Lesion	Short-Term Memory	Long-Term Memory	New Learning
Medial temporal lobe	Spared	Spared	Impaired
Hippocampus	Spared	Impaired	Impaired

i. <u>Amygdala</u>

    i. Dorsomedial portion of temporal lobe

    ii. Connection with corpus striatum

    iii. Direct link between limbic system and motor system

    iv. Critical role in emotional memory and rudimentary learning

    v. The "unconscious mind"?

    vi. <u>Klüver-Bucy syndrome</u>

- Removal of the amygdala
- Tame
- No fear of natural enemies
- Hyperactive sexually
- High rage threshold
- "Make love, not war"

vii. <u>Korsakoff syndrome</u>
- Amnesia resulting from chronic thiamin deficiency
- Associated with alcoholism
- Neuronal damage in the thalamus
- Once neuronal damage in the thalamus, not treatable with thiamin

Basal Ganglia

a. Functions: initiation and control of movement, implicated in depression and neurocognitive disorder
b. Dysfunctions (see Neurocognitive Disorder section)
   i. Parkinson disease
   ii. Huntington chorea
   iii. Wilson disease
   iv. Fahr disease
   - Rare hereditary disorder
   - Calcification of the basal ganglia
   - Onset at age 30
   - Neurocognitive disorder at age 50
   - Resembles negative symptom schizophrenia

Pons

a. Start of NE pathway
b. Important for REM sleep
c. Anomolies here linked to autism

Cerebellum

a. Key for balance
b. Skill-based memory
c. Facilitates verbal recall
d. Implicated in some learning disabilities

BRIEF REVIEW OF NEUROTRANSMITTERS

Acetylcholine (ACh)

1. Neurotransmitter at nerve-muscle connections for all voluntary muscles of the body
2. Also many of the involuntary (autonomic) nervous system synapses
3. Despite long history, the exact role of ACh in the brain unclear
4. Cholinergic neurons concentrated in the RAS and basal forebrain
5. Significant role in Alzheimer disease
6. Neurocognitive disorder in general associated with decreased ACh concentrations in amygdala, hippocampus, and temporal neocortex

7. Associated with erections in males

8. Muscarinic and nicotinic receptors

9. In the corpus striatum, ACh circuits are in equilibrium with dopamine neurons.

Norepinephrine (NE)

1. One of the catecholamine neurotransmitters

2. Transmitter of the sympathetic nerves of the autonomic nervous system, which mediate emergency response

    a. Acceleration of the heart

    b. Dilatation of the bronchi

    c. Elevation of blood pressure

3. Implicated in altering attention, perception, and mood

4. Key pathway: locus ceruleus in upper pons

5. Implicated in monoamine hypothesis of affective disorders:

    a. Depletion of NE leads to depression

    b. Excess of NE (and serotonin) leads to mania

    c. Based on two observations:

        i. Reserpine depletes NE and causes depression.

        ii. Antidepressant drugs block NE re-uptake, thus increasing the amount of NE available postsynaptically.

6. Receptors:

    a. Alpha-1: sympathetic (vasoconstriction)

    b. Alpha-2: on cell bodies of presynaptic neurons, inhibit NE release

    c. Beta-1: excitatory for heart, lungs, brain

    d. Beta-2: excitatory for vasodilatation and bronchodilatation

Dopamine

1. The other catecholamine neurotransmitter

2. Synthesized from the amino acid tyrosine

3. D_2 receptors most important

4. D_1 and D_5 stimulate G-protein and increase cAMP and excitation

5. D_2, D_3, and D_4 inhibit G-protein and decrease cAMP and excitation

6. Three pathways of known psychiatric importance:

    a. Nigrostriatal pathway

        ● Blockade leads to tremors, muscle rigidity, bradykinesia

    b. Meso-limbic-cortico pathway

        ● Blockade leads to reduction of psychotic symptoms

    c. Tuberoinfundibular system

        ● Blockade leads to increases in prolactin (Dop = PIF)

Serotonin (5-hydroxytryptamine, 5-HT)

1. The transmitter of a discrete group of neurons that all have cell bodies located in the raphe nuclei of the brain stem

2. Changes in the activity of serotonin neurons are related to the actions of psychedelic drugs.

3. Involved in the therapeutic mechanism of action of antidepressant treatments (most are 5-HT re-uptake inhibitors; a few new ones are 5-HT agonists)

4. Has inhibitory influence; linked to impulse control

5. Low 5-HT = low impulse control

6. Has role in regulation of mood, sleep, sexual activity, aggression, anxiety, motor activity, cognitive function, appetite, circadian rhythms, neuroendocrine function, and body temperature

Glutamic Acid

1. One of the major amino acids in general metabolism and protein synthesis, also a neurotransmitter

2. Stimulates neurons to fire; principal excitatory neurotransmitter in the brain

3. The neurotransmitter of the major neuronal pathway that connects the cerebral cortex and the corpus striatum

4. Also the transmitter of the granule cells, which are the most numerous neurons in the cerebellum

5. Evidence that glutamic acid is the principal neurotransmitter of the visual pathway

6. May have a role in producing schizophrenic symptoms

7. Reason for PCP symptoms (antagonist of NMDA glutamate receptors)

8. Glutamate agonists produce seizures in animal studies

Enkephalins

1. Composed of two peptides, each containing five amino acids

2. Normally occurring substances that act on opiate receptors, mimicking the effects of opiates

3. Neurons are localized to areas of the brain that regulate functions influenced by opiate drugs.

Substance P

1. Peptide containing 11 amino acids

2. A major transmitter of sensory neurons that convey pain sensation from the periphery, especially the skin, into the spinal cord

3. Also found in numerous brain regions

4. Opiates relieve pain in part by blocking the release of substance P.

5. New class of antidepressant medications being tested to work on substance P

Gamma Amino-butyric Acid (GABA)

1. One of the amino-acid transmitters in the brain
2. Occurs almost exclusively in the brain
3. Reduces the firing of neurons; principle inhibitory neurotransmitter in the brain
4. The transmitter present at 25 to 40% of all synapses in the brain
5. Quantitatively, the predominant transmitter in the brain
6. Associated with anxiety, cannabis, benzodiazepines

Psychopharmacology 14

ANTIPSYCHOTICS (NEUROLEPTICS)

General Issues

1. Treatment concerns
   a. Most common cause of relapse is nonadherence
   b. Most common reason for failure of treatment is inadequate dosage
   c. Worse behavioral symptoms on antipsychotics, check for undiagnosed organic condition

2. Common uses
   a. Psychotic symptoms: hallucinations, alterations of affect, ideas of reference, delusions, etc.
   b. Tourette's: haloperidol, pimozide, clonidine, risperidone
   c. Movement disorders: Tourette, Huntington, and hemiballism (flailing movements)
   d. Nausea and vomiting
   f. Intractable hiccups
   f. Pruritus

3. Mechanisms of action
   a. Dopamine blockage at postsynaptic receptors
   b. Alpha-adrenergic blockade; therefore, hypotensive effect
   c. Anticholinergic action by blocking the muscarinic receptors
   d. Blocks both NE re-uptake and serotonin and histamine receptors

4. Adverse effects
   a. Neurologic effects
      i. Anticholinergic effects: very common, effects additive if given with other anticholinergic agents; blocks parasympathetic receptors
         - Dry mouth
         - Blurry vision
         - Constipation
         - Urinary retention
         - Delirium
         - Memory aid: "blind as a bat, dry as a bone, red as a beet, mad as a hatter"
         - Especially frequent in the elderly

Note

Extrapyramidal reactions:

- Choreiform: jerky movements

- Athetoid: slow, continuous movements

- Rhythmic: stereotypical movements

ii. <u>CNS effects</u>: from antagonism of H1 receptors
- Weight gain
- Sedation very common
- Impaired memory

iii. <u>Extrapyramidal (EP) reactions</u>: due to decreased dopamine; appear in one-half of all patients in first few months
- Treat with benztropine, trihexyphenidyl, diphenhydramine

Table 14-1. Extrapyramidal Reactions to Antipsychotic Medications

Side Effects	Peak
Dystonic reactions (jerky movements, trouble speaking)	1 week (younger are more at risk)
Akinesia	2 weeks
Rigidity	3 weeks
Tremors	6 weeks
Akathisia	10 weeks
Pisa and Rabbit syndromes	18+ weeks

iv. <u>Tardive dyskinesia (TD)</u>
- Rarely before 3 to 6 months, 1 month if older than 60
- Signs: tongue protrusion, tremors and spasms of the neck, body, and limbs
- Persists after medications are terminated (5 to 10% remit); incapacitating in 5% of cases
- Cause: supersensitivity of postsynaptic dopamine receptors
- Predisposing factors include older patients, long treatment, smoking, diabetes mellitus
- Symptoms do not occur during sleep
- Suppressed by voluntary movements for short time (versus cerebellar disease tremor, which worsens with intentional movement)
- Stress and movements in other body parts aggravates
- No treatment, focus on prevention: pimozide or loxapine has less chance of inducing TD, clozapine not associated with TD at all

b. Non-neurologic effects

i. <u>Cardiovascular effects</u>: orthostatic hypotension (do not use epinephrine, lowers blood pressure further)

ii. <u>Particular taste</u> (also dental cavities)

iii. <u>Vomiting common</u> with long-term use, especially among smokers

  iv. <u>Sexual effects</u>: prolactin elevated
   - Men: decreased libido, inhibition of ejaculation, retrograde ejaculation
   - Women: breast enlargement and lactation, changes in libido
  v. <u>Altered bodily response to temperature</u>

Table 14-2. Potency of Antipsychotic Medications

Potency	Extrapyramidal Symptoms	Anticholinergic Effects
High (haloperidol)	High	Low
Low (chlorpromazine)	Low	High

Table 14-3. Typical versus Atypical Antipsychotics

Typical	Atypical
Dopamine	Dopamine and serotonin
Treats mostly positive symptoms	Treats positive and negative symptoms
More side effects	Fewer side effects

Typical Anti-Psychotics

Haloperidol (Typical) and Fluphenazine (Typical)

  i. Short- and long-acting preparations
  ii. Still used frequently

Thioridazine (Typical)

  i. Retinitis pigmentosa
  ii. Retrograde ejaculation

Atypical Anti-Psychotics

Clozapine (Atypical)

  i. Weak reaction on D2 receptors
  ii. High affinity for serotonin receptors
  iii. Affects negative and positive symptoms
  iv. Side effects: agranulocytosis (more common in Jews) (<1%) and seizures (14% of doses >600 mg)
  v. Less incidence of EP, TD, prolactin, or sexual effects

Risperidone (Atypical)

  i. Affects positive and negative symptoms, thought disorders
  ii. Side effects: dizziness, fatigue, dry mouth, tachycardia, hypotension
  iii. Raises prolactin levels, EP effects, highest risk of movement disorders

Olanzapine (Atypical)

    i. Affects positive and negative symptoms, thought disorders

    ii. Highest incidence of diabetes, ↑weight, ↑chol, etc.

Quetiapine (Atypical)

    i. D2 and 5-HT2 antagonist

    ii. Also affects H1 and alpha-1 receptors

    iii. For schizophrenia and bipolar

    iv. Side effects: somnolence, dizziness, dry mouth, weight gain

    v. Lowest risk of movement side effects

Aripiprazole (Atypical)

    i. Partial agonist on D2 and 5-HT1 receptors. Antagonist at 5-HT2 receptor.

    ii. Side effects: akathisia, headache, tiredness, nausea

    iii. Also used for bipolar and adjunt therapy for depression

    iv. Partial dopamine against at low doses

Ziprasidone (Atypical)

    i. High affinity for DA, 5-HT, alpha-adrenergic, and histamine receptors

    ii. Some inhibition of 5-HT reuptake

    iii. For acute agitation of psychoses, acute mania

    iv. Intramuscular injection

    v. Prolongs QT interval

ANTIDEPRESSANTS

General Issues

Common uses

    a. Depression

    b. Anxiety

    c. Chronic pain, with and without depression

Cyclic antidepressants

    a. Action: blocking of re-uptake of serotonin and norepinephrine, blocking of alpha-1 adrenergic receptors, and muscarinic receptors.

    b. Pharmacokinetics

        i. Fat soluble

        ii. Metabolized by the liver and excreted by the kidneys

        iii. Requires reaching plasma levels for imipramine, nortriptyline, desipramine, and amitriptyline for efficacy

    c. Adverse effects

        i. Anticholinergic effects (see Antipsychotics section)

      ii. <u>CNS effects</u>
- Drowsiness
- Insomnia and agitation
- Disorientation and confusion
- Headache
- Fine tremor

     iii. <u>Cardiovascular</u>: from antagonism of alpha-1 adrenore-ceptors and inhibition of 5-HT reuptake
- Most common in elderly
- Tachycardia
- Orthostatic hypotension: managed by sodium chloride tablets, caffeine, support hose, or biofeedback
- Lethal in overdose due to cardiac complications

     iv. <u>Sexual</u>
- Men: impotence, testicular swelling
- Women: anorgasmia and breast enlargement (treat with cyproheptadine)

      v. <u>Metabolic</u>: changes in blood sugar levels

e. <u>Cautions</u>

      i. Effective in only 70% of depressed patients

     ii. Not for patients with respiratory difficulties; dries up bronchial secretions

    iii. May lower seizure threshold

    iv. May impair driving

     v. Potentiates effects of alcohol

    vi. Manic episode induced in 50% of bipolars

   vii. Avoid during first trimester

  viii. Baby gets 1% of mother's dose in breast milk

f. Withdrawal

      i. After prolonged use, should be gradual

     ii. Akathisia, dyskinesia, anxiety, sweating, dizziness, vomiting, cholinergic rebound, depression rebound

Selective serotonin re-uptake inhibitors (SSRI)

a. Most widely used antidepressants

b. No effect on NE or dopamine, very selective blockage of re-uptake of serotonin

c. Fewest adverse effects of any antidepressants currently available, also the largest selling

d. Adverse effects:

      i. <u>Anorgasmia and delayed orgasm</u> in 15 to 20% of patients

     ii. <u>Serotonin syndrome</u>
- Associated with: high doses, MAOI and SSRI combo, MAOI and synthetic narcotic combo
- Symptoms: general restlessness, sweating, insomnia, nausea, diarrhea, cramps, delirium

- Treatment: remove causative agent, stop SSRIs, give cyproheptadine

  e. Drugs from this class

      i. Fluoxetine: longest half-life

      ii. Sertraline

      iii. Paroxetine

      iv. Fluvoxamine: approved for OCD

      v. Citalopram

      vi. Escitalopram

Monoamine oxidase inhibitors (MAOIs)

  a. Mechanism of action

      i. Inhibits MAO, an enzyme that metabolizes serotonin, epinephrine, and NE

      ii. For best effect, reduce MAO activity by 80%

  b. Adverse effects

      i. MAOI + TYRAMINE = HYPERTENSIVE CRISIS

      - Problem foods: cheese, dried fish, sauerkraut, sausage, chocolate, avocados

      - Safe foods: cottage cheese, some wines

      - Signs: occipital headache, stiff neck, nausea and vomiting, chest pain, dilated pupils, nosebleed, elevated blood pressure

      - Treatment: stop medication, give phentolamine (alpha-blockage) or chlorpromazine (antipsychotic with hypotensive effects)

Electroconvulsive Therapy (ECT)

Common uses

  a. Depression (80%)

  b. Schizoaffective disorder (10%)

  c. Bipolar disorder

Mechanism of action

  a. Electricity is passed from the frontal cortex to the striatum.

  b. 90% show some immediate improvement

  c. Usually requires 5 to 10 treatments

  d. Only relative contraindication is increased cranial pressure (e.g., tumor)

Side effects

  a. Memory loss and headache common, returns to normal in several weeks

  b. Serious complications <1:1,000

Other issues

    a. Although not usually first-line treatment, should be considered for:

        i. Highly suicidal patients

        ii. Depressed pregnant patients

    b. Improvement associated with large increase in slow wave (delta) activity in the prefrontal area; greater increase = greater recovery

Drugs to Highlight

Trazodone

    a. 5-HT receptor antagonist, alpha-1 blocker

    b. Almost no anticholinergic adverse effects

    c. Sedating, but effective at improving sleep quality, does not decrease Stage 4 sleep

    d. May lead to priapism; therefore, sometimes used to treat erectile dysfunction

Mirtazapine

    a. Stimulates NE and 5-HT release

    b. Blocks 5-HT2 and 5-HT3 receptors

    c. Side effects: somnolence (60%), increased appetite, weight gain

Bupropion

    a. Weak inhibitor of dopamine, modest effect on NE, no effect on 5-HT reuptake

    b. No anticholinergic effect

    c. Little cardiac depressant effect

    d. Increased risk of seizures

    e. Less sexual effects or weight gain

    f. Side effects: appetite suppressant, agitation, insomnia

    g. Approved for smoking cessation

Venlafaxine

    a. Inhibits reuptake of NE and 5-HT, mild dopamine effect (SNRI)

    b. Side effects: sweating, nausea, constipation, anorexia, vomiting, somnolence, tremor, impotence

Duloxetine

    a. Targets 5-HT and NE receptors (SNRI)

    b. Side effects: nausea, dry mouth, dizziness, constipation, decreased appetite, increased blood pressure

    c. Approved for depression and neuropathic pain

MOOD STABILIZERS

Lithium

a. For long-term control and prophylaxis of bipolar disorder, migraine cluster headaches, chronic aggression; combined with tricyclics for resistant depression

b. Works for 70% of cases

c. Hypothesized mechanism: blocks inositol-1-phosphate (second messenger)

d. Pharmacokinetics:

   i. Quickly absorbed from the gastrointestinal tract, not protein bound or metabolized

   ii. Requires reaching plasma levels very close to toxic levels for effect, which is reached in 10 to 14 days

   iii. Must monitor blood levels

     ● Therapeutic levels: 0.8–1.5 mEq/L

     ● 1.4 mEq/L may be toxic

     ● Frank toxicity at 2.0; above 2.5 = hemodialysis

   iv. Good kidney function and adequate salt and fluid intake essential; 95% excreted in urine

   v. Peak serum level: 1–3 hours

   vi. Potassium-sparing diuretics have no effects; loop diuretics result in increased serum levels.

e. Side effects

   i. Narrow margin of safety, must monitor blood levels

   ii. Tremor, thirst, anorexia, gastrointestinal distress commonly occur at therapeutic levels

   iii. Seizures and coma

   iv. Polyuria and polydipsia

   v. Edema

   vi. Acne

   vii. Benign leukocytosis

   viii. Hypothyroidism

   ix. Nephrotoxic

   x. Diabetes insipidus

f. Long-term lithium use has adverse effects on renal function.

g. Compliance often difficult, patient may value manic experiences

h. Teratogenic, produces cardiac malformations (Ebstein anomaly tricuspid valve)

Valproic Acid

a. For acute mania, rapid cycling bipolar disorder, impulse control

b. Mechanism of action: augmentation of GABA in CNS

c. Monitor blood levels

d. Hepatotoxic (liver function impaired)

e. Side effects

    i. Sedation

    ii. Mild tremor

    iii. Gastrointestinal distress

    iv. Occasional agranulocytosis

f. At toxic levels: confusion, coma, cardiac arrest

g. Teratogenic (neural tube defect)

Carbamazepine: Second-line Treatment

a. For acute mania, rapid cycling bipolar disorder, impulse control

b. Mechanism of action:

    i. Blocks sodium channels in neurons with action potential

    ii. Alters central GABA receptors

c. Monitors blood levels and signs of rash

d. Side effects

    i. Similar to valproic acid, plus nausea, rash, mild leukopenia

    ii. Occasional agranulocytosis

    iii. Aplastic anemia

e. Toxic levels: atrioventricular block, respiratory depression, coma

ANXIOLYTICS (ANTIANXIETY)

Benzodiazepines

a. Used for anxiety, acute and chronic alcohol withdrawal, convulsions, insomnia, "restless legs," akathisia, panic disorder

b. Mechanism of action: depresses CNS at limbic system, RAS, and cortex

c. Binds to GABA-chloride receptors; facilitates action of GABA

d. Pharmacokinetics

    i. All undergo hepatic microsomal oxidation, except for lorazepam, oxazepam, and temazepam, which undergo glucuronide conjugation

    ii. Well-absorbed orally

e. Adverse effects

    i. CNS depression (sedative effect)

    ii. Paradoxical agitation

    iii. Confusion and disorientation, especially in elderly

    iv. Overdose: apnea and respiratory depression (not for use with patients with sleep apnea)

    v. Withdrawal: insomnia, agitation, anxiety rebound, gastrointestinal distress; abrupt withdrawal can bring on seizures

f. Diminishes effectiveness of ECT

g. Lowers tolerance to alcohol

h. Crosses placenta and accumulates in fetus, withdrawal symptoms in newborn

i. Passed on in breast milk with observable effects

j. Oral contraceptives decrease metabolism of benzodiazepines

Buspirone

i. For anxiety

ii. No anticonvulsant or muscle-relaxing properties

iii. Affects serotonin, not GABA

iv. >7 days for effect

v. Some sedation

vi. Low abuse potential

vii. No withdrawal effects

viii. Not potentiated by alcohol

Review Questions

108. Following his arrest for disturbing the peace, a 35-year-old man is referred for psychiatric evaluation. During the initial interview, he talked rapidly and paced around the room. He reported that he had slept little in the past few days, but that he felt "great". "It's not always like this," he confided. "Sometimes I just feel so bad I can hardly move." During the most common subsequent treatment for this disorder, which of the following side effects would the patient be most likely to experience?

    (A) Insomnia

    (B) Memory loss

    (C) Tardive dyskinesia

    (D) Acne

    (E) Retarded ejaculation

109. A 36-year-old woman is brought to see her physician by her family. The family reports that over the past year she has had trouble controlling her movements. Symptoms include frequent and discrete brisk movements that cause jerks of the pelvis and limbs as well as facial frowns, grimaces, and smirks. The most likely diagnosis for this patient would be

    (A) Pick disease

    (B) Wilson disease

    (C) Parkinson disease

    (D) Huntington disease

    (E) Creutzfeldt-Jakob disease

110. Over a 5-week period, a previously healthy 55-year-old female has developed headaches, progressively severe word-finding difficulty, and confusion. She speaks incoherently and is unable to follow commands, repeat phrases, or name objects. What is the most likely site of the lesion?

    (A) Frontal lobe

    (B) Temporal lobe

    (C) Occipital lobe

    (D) Parietal lobe

    (E) Cerebellum

111. Following an automobile accident, a 46-year-old male is brought to the hospital suffering from head trauma. Over the next week, his medical record notes the appearance of auditory hallucinations, delusions, thought disorders, and poor verbal comprehension. These symptoms are most consistent with a lesion in the

    (A) frontal lobe

    (B) dominant parietal lobe

    (C) nondominant parietal lobe

    (D) dominant temporal lobe

    (E) nondominant temporal lobe

112. A 32-year-old male presents at the local clinic complaining of abdominal cramps, sweating, runny nose, vomiting, and muscle aches. Examination shows that his pulse is rapid and pupils are dilated. He states that he "feels just awful" and that he has had these symptoms for about 24 hours. The most likely pharmacologic treatment would be

(A) none

(B) diazepam

(C) carbamazepine

(D) clonidine

(E) trazodone

113. A 58-year-old chronic alcoholic is evaluated and found to have difficulty with recall of recent events although long-term memories seem intact. The patient appears confused and insists that he has met the physician before, although this is not the case. These symptoms are the result of a syndrome that can result from neuronal damage to the

(A) cerebellum

(B) hippocampus

(C) hypothalamus

(D) reticular activating system

(E) thalamus

114. A 32-year-old schizophrenic patient has been taking a standard course of neuroleptic medication for the past year. This medication has been very effective at controlling his delusions and hallucinations. However, during a regular checkup the patient was found to be suffering from dry mouth and constipation. The patient reports that it is hard to read because his vision is blurry, and then lapses into delirium. These symptoms are most likely produced by blockage of what receptors?

(A) Dopamine

(B) Histamine

(C) Muscarinic

(D) Norepinephrine

(E) Serotonin

115. A 24-year-old woman was recently diagnosed with undifferentiated schizophrenia and placed on a standard drug regimen. About 2 weeks into her treatment, she experiences disturbing extrapyramidal side effects. The most likely side effect to appear at this time would be

(A) akathisia

(B) akinesia

(C) physical tremors

(D) Pisa syndrome

(E) tardive dyskinesia

116. Patients placed on which of the following medications most likely should have blood drawn and checked on a weekly basis?

    (A) Clozapine

    (B) Haloperidol

    (C) Olanzapine

    (D) Risperidone

    (E) Thioridazine

117. A 46-year-old man who was being treated for depression is brought to the emergency department complaining of headache at the base of the skull, chest pains, and stiff neck. Physical exam shows that his nose is bleeding, his pupils are dilated, and his blood pressure is extremely high. He reports vomiting repeatedly in the past few hours. Based on this initial presentation, the physician suspects that the patient has recently eaten which of the following foods?

    (A) Avocados

    (B) Cottage cheese

    (C) Hamburger

    (D) Raw eggs

    (E) French fries

    (F) Fried chicken

    (G) Dried figs

Answers

108. **Answer: D.** Lithium has been associated with side effects leading to lethargy (hypothyroidism), edema (lithium is a salt), acne, and seizures.

109. **Answer: D.** Age of onset and description indicate the onset of Huntington chorea.

110. **Answer: B.** Temporal lobe is associated with language, memory, and emotional expression.

111. **Answer: D.** Lesions of the dominant temporal lobe result in euphoria, auditory hallucinations, thought disorder, and poor verbal comprehension.

112. **Answer: D.** The man is suffering from opiate withdrawal. The drug on the list to treat the withdrawal is clonidine.

113. **Answer: E.** The man most likely is suffering from Korsakoff syndrome, in which chronic thiamin deficiency leads to neuronal damage in the thalamus as well as the frontal lobes.

114. **Answer: C.** The patient displays the symptoms of anticholinergic intoxication. This is the result of blockage of the muscarinic receptors.

115. **Answer: B.** Difficulty completing simple movements or common skills occurs relatively early in the course of treatment. Tremors and akathisia appear after about 1 to 2 months. Tardive dyskinesia rarely occurs before the patient is on the medication for at least 3 months.

116. **Answer: A.** Because of the risk of agranulocytosis with clozapine, blood must be monitored weekly.

117. **Answer: A.** The patient is suffering from a hypertensive crisis that is likely the result of consuming tyramine-containing food while on MAOIs for his depression. Tyramine can be acquired from cheese, dried fish, sauerkraut, sausage, chocolate, or avocados.

SELECTED IMPORTANT COURT CASES

Karen Ann Quinlan: Substituted Judgment Standard

In the Quinlan case, Karen Ann was in a persistent vegetative state, being kept alive only by life support. Karen's father asked to have her life support terminated according to his understanding of what Karen Ann would want. The court found that "if Karen herself were miraculously lucid for an interval . . . and perceptive of her irreversible condition, she could effectively decide upon discontinuance of the life support apparatus, even if it meant the prospect of natural death."

The court therefore allowed termination of life support, not because the father asked, but because it held that the father's request was most likely the expression of Karen Ann's own wishes.

Substituted judgment begins with the premise that decisions belong to the competent patient by virtue of the rights of autonomy and privacy. In this case, however, the patient is unable to decide, and a decision-maker who is the best representative of the patient's wishes must be substituted. In legal terms, the patient has the right to decide but is incompetent to do so. Therefore, the decision is made for the patient on the basis of the best estimate of his or her subjective wishes.

Note the key here is *not* who is the closest next of kin, but who is most likely to represent the patient's own wishes.

Brother Fox *(Eichner vs Dillon)*: Best Interest Standard

The New York Court of Appeals, in its decision of *Eichner vs Dillon,* held that trying to determine what a never-competent patient would have decided is practically impossible. Obviously, it is difficult to ascertain the actual (subjective) wishes of incompetents.

Therefore, if the patient has always been incompetent, or no one knows the patient well enough to render substituted judgment, the use of substituted judgment standard is questionable, at best.

Under these circumstances, decisions are made for the patient using the **best interest standard**. The object of the standard is to decide what a hypothetical "reasonable person" would decide to do after weighing the benefits and burdens of each course of action.

Note here the issue of who makes the decision is less important. All persons applying the best-interest standard should come to the same conclusions.

SELECTED IMPORTANT COURT CASES (*Continued*)

Infant Doe: Foregoing Lifesaving Surgery, Parents Withholding Treatment

As a general rule, parents cannot withhold life- or limb-saving treatment from their children. Yet, in this exceptional case they did.

Baby Boy Doe was born with Down syndrome (trisomy 21) and with a tracheoesophageal fistula. The infant's parents were informed that surgery to correct his fistula would have "an even chance of success." Left untreated, the fistula would soon lead to the infant's death from starvation or pneumonia. The parents, who also had two healthy children, chose to withhold food and treatment and "let nature take its course."

Court action to remove the infant from his parents' custody (and permit the surgery) was sought by the county prosecutor. The court denied such action, and the Indiana Supreme Court declined to review the lower court's ruling. Infant Doe died at 6 days of age, as Indiana authorities were seeking intervention from the U.S. Supreme Court.

Note that this case is simply an application of the best-interest standard. The court agreed with the parents that the burdens of treatment far outweighed any expected benefits.

Roe vs Wade (1973): The Patient Decides

Known to most people as the "abortion legalizing decision," the importance of this case is not limited to its impact on abortion.

Faced with a conflict between the rights of the mother versus the rights of the putative unborn child, the court held that in the first trimester, the mother's rights are certainly paramount, and that states may, if they wish, have the mother's rights remain paramount for the full term of the pregnancy.

Because the mother gets to decide, even in the face of threats to the fetus, by extension, all patients get to decide about their own bodies and the health care they receive. In the United States, the locus for decision-making about health care resides with the patient, not the physician.

Note that courts have held that a pregnant woman has the right to refuse care (e.g., blood transfusions) even if it places her unborn child at risk.

Tarasoff Decision: Duty to Warn and Duty to Protect

A student visiting a counselor at a counseling center in California states that he is going to kill someone. When he leaves, the counselor is concerned enough to call the police but takes no further action. The student subsequently kills the person he threatened. The court found the counselor and the center liable because they did not go far enough to warn and protect the potential victim.

The counselor should have called the police and then should also have tried in every way possible to notify the potential victim of the potential danger.

In similar situations, first try to detain the person making the threat, next call the police, and finally notify and warn the potential victim. All three actions should be taken, or at least attempted.

LEGAL ISSUES RELATED TO MEDICAL PRACTICE

This section lays out a set of rules that constitute the general consensus of legal opinion. Apply these rules to individual situations as they arise.

Rule #1: Competent patients have the right to refuse medical treatment.
- Incompetent patients have the same rights, but must be exercised differently (via a surrogate).
- Patients have an almost absolute right to refuse. Patients have almost absolute control over their own bodies. The sicker the patient, the lesser the chance of recovery, the greater the right to refuse treatment.

Rule #2: If patient is incompetent to make decisions, physician may rely on advance directives.
- Advance directives can be oral.
- Living will: written document expressing wishes
  - Care facilities must provide information at time of admission
  - Responsibility of the institution, not the physician
  - Only applies to end-of-life care
- Health power of attorney: designating the surrogate decision-maker
  - "Speaks with the patient's voice"
  - Beats all other decision rules
- In end-of-life circumstances, if power of attorney person *directly* contradicts the living will, follow the living will.

Rule #3: Assume that the patient is competent unless clear behavioral evidence indicates otherwise.
- Competence is a legal, not a medical issue.
- A diagnosis, by itself, tells you little about a patient's competence.
- Clear behavioral evidence would be:
  - Patient is grossly psychotic and dysfunctional
  - Patient's physical or mental state prevents simple communication
- If you are unsure, assume the patient is competent. The patient does not have to prove to you that he is competent. You have to have clear evidence to assume that he is not.

Rule #4: When surrogates make decisions for a patient, they should use the following criteria and in this order:
- Subjective standard
  - Actual intent, advance directive
  - What did the patient say in the past?
- Substituted judgment
  - Who best represents the patient?
  - What would patient say if he or she could?
- Best-interest standard
  - Burdens versus benefits
  - Interests of patient, not preferences of the decision-maker

Note

The COMLEX Requires You to Know:

- The best response to presented ethical and legal dilemmas

- These questions must be answered by applying the standards of ideal ethical professional conduct.

- This section is not intended to provide legal advice, but merely to guide you in answering questions on the exam.

Note

Family matters only to the degree that reflects the patient's wishes. Family's own wishes are not relevant.

Rule #5: Feeding tube is a medical treatment and can be withdrawn at the patient's request.
- Not considered killing the patient, but stopping treatment at patient's request.
- A competent person can refuse even lifesaving hydration and nutrition.

Rule #6: Do nothing to actively assist the patient to die sooner.
- Active euthanasia and assisted suicide are on difficult ground.
  - Passive, i.e., allowing to die = OK
  - Active, i.e., killing = NOT OK
- On the other hand, do all you can to reduce the patient's suffering (e.g., giving pain medication).

Rule #7: The physician decides when the patient is dead.
- If the physician thinks continued treatment is futile (the patient has shown no improvement), but the surrogate insists on continued treatment, the treatment should continue.
- If there are no more treatment options (the patient is cortically dead), and the family insists on treatment, there is nothing the physician can do; treatment must stop.

Rule #8: Never abandon a patient.
- Lack of financial resources or lack of results are never reasons to stop treatment of a patient.
- An annoying or difficult patient is still your patient.
- You can not ever threaten abandonment.

Rule #9: Keep the physician–patient relationship within bounds.
- Intimate social contact with anyone who is or has been a patient is prohibited. AMA guidelines say, "for at least 2 years."
- Do not date parents of pediatric patients or children of geriatric patients.
- Do not treat friends or family.
- Do not prescribe for colleagues unless a physician/patient relationship exists.
- If patients are inappropriate, gently but clearly let them know what acceptable behavior would be.
- Any gift from a patient beyond a small token should be declined.

Rule #10 Stop harm from happening
- Beyond "do no harm," you must stop anyone from hurting himself or others.
- Take whatever action is required to prevent harm.
- Harm can be spreading disease, physical assault, psychological abuse, neglect, infliction of pain or anything which produces notable disress.
- You must also protect your patient, or anyone not your patient, from being hurt by another.

Rule #11: Always obtain informed consent.

- Full, informed consent requires that the patient has received and under-stood five pieces of information:
  - Nature of procedure
  - Purpose or rationale
  - Benefits
  - Risks
  - Availability of alternatives
- Four exceptions to informed consent:
  - Emergency
  - Waiver by patient
  - Patient is incompetent
  - Therapeutic privilege (unconscious, confused, physician deprives patient of autonomy in interest of health)
- Gag clauses that prohibit a physician from discussing treatment options that are not approved violate informed consent and are illegal.
- Consent can be oral.
- A signed paper the patient has not read or does not understand does NOT constitute informed consent.
- Written consent can be revoked orally at any time.

Rule #12: Special rules apply with children.

- Children younger than 18 years are minors and are legally incompetent.
- Exceptions: emancipated minors
  - If older than 13 years and taking care of self, i.e., living alone, treat as an adult.
  - Marriage makes a child emancipated, as does serving in the military.
  - Pregnancy or giving birth, in most cases, does not.
- Partial emancipation
  - Many states have special ages of consent: generally age 14 and older
  - For certain issues only:
    - Substance drug treatment
    - Prenatal care
    - Sexually transmitted disease treatment
    - Birth control

Rule #13: Parents cannot withhold life- or limb-saving treatment from their children.

- If parents refuse permission to treat child:
  - If immediate emergency, go ahead and treat.
  - If not immediate, but still critical (e.g., juvenile diabetes), gener-ally the child is declared a ward of the court and the court grants permission.
  - If not life- or limb-threatening (e.g., child needs minor stitches), listen to the parents
- Note that the child cannot give permission. A child's refusal of treat-ment is irrelevant.

Rule #14: For the purposes of the COMLEX, issues governed by laws that vary widely across states cannot be tested. This includes elective abortions (minor and spousal rights differ by locality) and legal age for drinking alcohol (vary by state).

Rule #15: Good Samaritan Laws limit liability in nonmedical settings.
- Not required to stop to help
- If help offered, shielded from liability provided:
  - Actions are within physician's competence
  - Only accepted procedures are performed.
  - Physician remains at scene after starting therapy until relieved by competent personnel
  - No compensation changes hands

Rule #16: Confidentiality is absolute.
- Physicians cannot tell anyone anything about their patient without the patient's permission.
- Physician must strive to ensure that others *cannot* access patient information.
- Getting a consultation is permitted, as the consultant is bound by confidentiality, too. However, watch the location of the consultation. Be careful not to be overheard (e.g., not elevator or cafeteria).
- If you receive a court subpoena, show up in court but do not divulge information about your patient.
- If patient is a threat to self or other, the physician MUST break confidentiality
  - Duty to warn and duty to protect (Tarasoff case)
  - A specific threat to a specific person
  - Suicide, homicide, and abuse are obvious threats.
  - Infectious disease should generally be treated as a threat, but be careful. Here issue is usually getting the patient to work with you to tell the person who is at risk
  - In the case of an STD, the issue is not really whether to inform a sexual partner, but how they should be told. Best advice: Have patient and partner come to your office.

Rule #17: Patients should be given the chance to state DNR (Do Not Resuscitate) orders, and physicians should follow them.
- DNR refers only to cardiopulmonary resuscitation.
- Continue with ongoing treatments.
- Most physicians are unaware of DNR orders.
- DNR decisions are made by the patient or surrogate.
- Have DNR discussions as part of your first encounter with the patient.
- Do not ask the patient about "do not resuscitate" wishes. Explain details of what is entailed.

Rule #18: Committed mentally ill patients retain their rights.
- Committed mentally ill adults legally are entitled to the following:
  - They must have treatment available.
  - They can refuse treatment.
  - They can command a jury trial to determine "sanity".

- They lose only the civil liberty to come and go.

- They retain their competence for conducting business transactions, marriage, divorce, voting, driving

- The words "sanity" and "competence" are legal, not psychiatric, terms. They refer to prediction of dangerousness, and medicopsychological studies show that health care professionals cannot reliably and validly predict such dangerousness.

Rule #19: Detain patients to protect them or others.

- Emergency detention can be effected by a physician and/or a law enforcement person for 48 hours, pending a hearing.

- A physician can detain; only a judge can commit.

- With children, special rules exist. Children can be committed only if:

  - They are in imminent danger to self and/or others.

  - They are unable to care for their own daily needs.

  - The parents have absolutely no control over the child, and the child is in danger (e.g., fire-setter), but not because the parents are unwilling to discipline a child.

Rule #20: Remove from patient contact health care professionals who pose risk to patients.

- Types of risks

  - Infectious disease (TB)

  - Substance-related disorders

  - Depression (or other psychological issues)

  - Incompetence

- Actions

  - Insist that they take time off

  - Contact their supervisors if necessary

- The patient, not professional solidarity, comes first.

Rule #21: Focus on what is the best ethical conduct, not simply the letter of the law.

The best answers are those that are both legal and ethical.

Practice Questions

- Should physicians answer questions from insurance companies or employers? (Not without a release from the patient)

- Should physicians answer questions from the patient's family without the patient's explicit permission? (No)

- What information can the physician withhold from the patient? (Nothing. If patient may react negatively, figure out how to tell patient to mitigate negative outcome)

- What if the family requests that certain information be kept from the patient? (Tell the patient, but <u>first</u> find out <u>why</u> they don't want the patient told)

- Who owns the medical record? (Health care provider, but patient must be given access or copy upon request)

What should the physician do in each of these situations?

- Patient refuses lifesaving treatment on religious grounds? (Don't treat)

- Wife refuses to consent to emergency lifesaving treatment for unconscious husband citing religious grounds? (Treat, no time to assess substituted judgment)

- Wife produces card stating unconscious husband's wish to not be treated on religious grounds? (Don't treat)

- Mother refuses to consent to emergency lifesaving treatment for her daughter on religious grounds? (Treat)

- What if the child's life is at risk, but the risk is not immediate? (Court takes guardianship)

- From whom do you get permission to treat a girl who is 17 years old? (Her guardian)

From whom does the physician obtain consent in each case?

- A 17-year-old girl's parents are out of the country and the girl is staying with a babysitter? (If a threat to health, the physician can treat under doctrine of *in locum parentis*)

- A 17-year-old girl who has been living on her own and taking care of herself? (The girl herself)

- A 17-year-old girl who is married? (The girl herself)

- A 17-year-old girl who is pregnant? (Her guardian)

- A 16-year-old daughter refuses medication but her mother consents, do you write the prescription? (Yes)

- The 16-year-old daughter consents, but the mother refuses? (No)

- The mother of a minor consents, but the father refuses? (Yes, only one permission needed)

- When should the physician provide informed consent? (Always)

- Must informed consent be written? (No)

- Can written consent be revoked orally? (Yes)

- Can you get informed consent from a schizophrenic man? (Yes, unless there is clear behavioral evidence that he is incompetent)

- Must you get informed consent from a prisoner if the police bring in the prisoner for examination? (Yes)

Review Questions

118. A 7-year-old girl is brought to the hospital by a woman who has been entrusted with her care while the girl's parents are in Mexico for vacation. The girl has sustained a non-life-threatening but serious injury during play that has almost completely severed one of her fingers from her left hand. The consensus of the physicians is that with prompt action the finger can be reattached with minimal permanent loss of movement for the child. Without prompt action, the use of the finger is likely to be lost. However, the attending physician is concerned about proceeding without the permission of the parents. The best course of action would be to

    (A) try to contact the parents to get their permission to perform the procedure

    (B) seek a legal injunction allowing the operation

    (C) operate at once, citing the doctrine of therapeutic privilege

    (D) seek the consent for the operation from the woman in whose care the girl was left

    (E) seek further confirmation from additional specialists in this type of surgery

119. During the second year of residency training, you discover that the chief resident on your rotation is using amphetamines on a regular basis in order to stay alert when on call. When you mention your concern to the resident, he tells you, "Mind your own business. I'm not one of your patients." At this point, your best action would be to

    (A) monitor the chief resident over the next few weeks to be sure that there is no danger to patient care

    (B) talk with other residents and see if they share your concern

    (C) contact the hospital ethics committee for advice and guidance

    (D) contact the American Medical Association

    (E) seek legal counsel

    (F) schedule a meeting to speak with the residency program director

    (G) lodge a complaint with the state licensing board

    (H) ask the nursing staff if they have noticed anything unusual about the chief resident

120. While riding the hospital elevator to visit one of his patients, an internal medicine physician overhears two residents discussing a surgical case. The case involves a 45-year-old male who received a lymph node biopsy. The biopsy was negative. However, during the procedure, the resident performing the surgery nicked the large intestine. The mistake was noticed and quickly corrected. The resident was overheard to say, "It's all taken care of. We didn't think we needed to worry the patient by mentioning this little glitch." After overhearing this conversation, what action should the physician take?

(A) Ask the nurse for the patient's chart to confirm that the mistake was benign

(B) File a formal complaint with the hospital ethics committee

(C) File a formal complaint with the state licensing board

(D) Look up the patient and check on how he is doing

(E) Reprimand the residents on the spot and demand to speak with their supervisor

(F) No harm was done, the physician need do nothing

(G) Speak with the chairman of internal medicine

(H) Speak with the chairman of surgery

(I) Tell the residents that they need to inform the patient and suggest the best method to have the discussion

121. A 42-year-old woman has an annual physical exam, including a mammogram. She announces with great excitement that she will be getting married in 3 months and invites her physician to attend the wedding. A week later, the results of the mammogram reveal a previously undetected mass. At this point, what action should the physician take?

(A) Call the patient immediately and inform her of the findings of the mammogram

(B) Have a nurse with experience in this area call the patient and discuss the findings

(C) Make an appointment to discuss the mammogram finding with the patient within a week of receiving the results

(D) Postpone informing the patient of the findings until after the wedding so as not to upset her

(E) Schedule the patient for a confirmatory mammogram after the wedding

(F) Schedule an appointment to discuss the findings with the patient and her fiancé before the wedding

122. A 68-year-old man is seen by his physician for a monthly appointment to monitor his diabetes. The physician provides encouragement with his diet and adjusts his medication dosage. Several days later, the patient's wife telephones the physician and asks about her husband's condition and what she should do to keep him on his diet. What action should the physician take?

(A) Have the nursing staff call her back and explain the dietary regime

(B) Give her an internet address where information about diabetes can be found

(C) Obtain permission from her husband before discussing his diabetes with her

(D) Schedule an appointment to discuss the issues she raises face-to-face

(E) Ask her if her husband requested that she call

(F) Offer her a referral to another physician so she can be checked for diabetes

123. A 75-year-old man is diagnosed with severe blockage in several cardiac arteries. The standard procedure for such cases is by-pass surgery that has a high rate of success. Pharmacologic options are also available, but at best will merely maintain the patient and will not remove the life-threatening blockage. Life expectancy for the pharmacologic intervention is substantially shorter than the surgical one. When presented with these available treatment options and the associated life expectancies, the patient declines the surgery and wants to be treated by pharmacologic means. The physician strongly disagrees with the patient's decision. Faced with this decision, the physician's next course of action should be to

(A) meet with the patient's family and try to convince them to change the patient's mind

(B) review the treatment options again with the patient and tell him to take a week to think it over

(C) schedule the patient for a consultation with a colleague and ask the colleague to advise the patient to choose the surgery

(D) schedule the patient for psychological evaluation

(E) start the pharmacological treatment

(F) tell the patient that you cannot agree with his choice, and cannot continue to be his physician if he insists on it

(G) tell the patient that you are required to select the treatment option with the best outcome and schedule him for surgery

124. A 54-year-old man, who makes his living as a bus driver, was sent by his company for a physical exam. The physical exam turns up nothing abnormal, although the man reports ongoing fatigue. When questioned in detail, the man professes no difficulty going to sleep. In fact, he often finds himself nodding off during the day. He also reports hallucinations as he is falling asleep and sometimes is unable to move when he wakes up in the morning. The physician suspects that the man suffers from a sleep disorder. When informed of this diagnosis, the patient requests that this information be kept confidential from his employer. At this point, the physician's best course of action is to

(A) arrange for pharmacologic treatment for the patient and maintain his confidentiality

(B) do not inform the employer, but negotiate with the patient to take time off from work on medical leave pending outcome of treatment

(C) inform his employer of his diagnosis and begin treatment

(D) refer him to a local sleep center for full evaluation and inform the employer based on the results of this workup

(E) try to obtain the patient's permission to inform the employer and schedule him for treatment

(F) schedule him for a psychiatric consult to rule out malingering

125. A 66-year-old man recently diagnosed as having prostate cancer is scheduled for an appointment to discuss his treatment options. The attending physician designates a second-year resident to meet with the patient and to obtain informed consent before proceeding with treatment. The resident meets with the patient and returns with signed informed consent forms, indicating that the patient has elected the radiation option to treat his cancer. Reviewing the conversation with the resident, the attending physician discovers that the resident did not mention a relatively new surgical procedure as a possible treatment option. At this point, what action should the attending physician take?

(A) Convene a seminar of all residents in this rotation and review the informed consent rules

(B) Exclude the resident from obtaining informed consent from patients until he has reviewed the informed consent rules

(C) Have all of the residents on the rotation accompany you while you visit the patient and demonstrate the right way to obtain informed consent

(D) Informed consent has been obtained, but instruct the resident that in the future he should mention the surgical procedure as an option to the patient

(E) Informed consent has been obtained; schedule the patient for the radiation treatment to which he has consented

(F) Instruct the resident to go back and talk to the patient again, this time mentioning the new surgical procedure

(G) Visit the patient personally and obtain informed consent again, this time mentioning the new surgical procedure

Answers

118. **Answer: C.** The physician may exercise therapeutic privilege and assume *in locum parentis* responsibility.

119. **Answer: F.** The program director is the one with the authority and responsibility to address the substance use issues.

120. **Answer: I.** The dual goals of training the residents and making sure the patient gets the information need to be met here. The issue is not to reprimand, but to better teach the residents.

121. **Answer: C.** You need to deliver the bad news, in a timely manner, and in person.

122. **Answer: C.** Confidentiality is absolute. You are not to discuss the case with her without the husband's explicit permission.

123. **Answer: E.** The patient makes medical decisions, not the physician. The options and consequences have been explained and the patient has made his choice. Begin treatment. Note that the surgical option is still available should the patient change his mind.

124. **Answer: C.** The patient likely suffers from narcolepsy, which can be debilitating and certainly makes him dangerous behind the wheel of a bus. There is a clear risk, so confidentiality must be breached to prevent harm. This is not a negotiation with the patient. The physician is obligated to act.

125. **Answer: F.** Patients must be told about all available options for informed consent to be valid. The resident should complete the job he started and go back to talk to the patient again. Getting the attending physician involved complicates the relationship with the patient and undermines the resident's confidence for handling this and similar situations.

NONGOVERNMENT METHODS OF PAYMENT FOR SERVICES

a. <u>Fee-for-service</u>: payment is rendered after service is delivered. Economic incentive is to do more so more can be billed.

   i. Physicians make money when more treatment is provided.

   ii. Danger = overtreatment

b. <u>Standard insurance (indemnity insurance)</u>

   i. Insurance company helps patient pay for health care in exchange for a periodic payment by patient (*premium*),

   ii. Patient shares in payment by means of:

- <u>Deductible</u>: patient pays a certain amount before insurance assistance begins
  - Annual deductible: patient pays certain amount each year
  - Per-occurrence deductible: patient pays certain amount each time services are rendered
- <u>Copayment</u>: remainder of bill is divided between patient and insurance company
  - Copayment calculation takes place only after deductible is satisfied
  - Common copayments may be:
    1. Patient 20%/insurance 80% or
    2. Patient 30%/insurance 70%

   iii. <u>Blue Cross Blue Shield</u>: nonprofit insurance company

- Blue Cross covers hospital charges
- Blue Shield covers physician services
- Coverage comes with deductibles and copayments
- Premiums intended to cover only:
  - Benefits
  - Administrative costs
  - Catastrophic losses

c. <u>Health maintenance organization (HMO)</u>: prepaid group practice

    i. Either hires physicians or contracts with physicians to provide services

    ii. Payment by *capitation*: a fixed payment is made each month

- Members pay a fixed amount per month.
- Physicians are paid for the number of patients they are responsible for, not for how much they do for each patient. The same payment is made whether services are used or not.
- No additional (or only minimal) payment is made when services *are* used.
- Physicians make money when patients stay well and do not need to use services.
- Incentives:
  - Under treatment
  - More likely to foster preventive medicine

Appendix Table 1. Types of HMOs

Type	Payment to Physicians	Who owns Facilities	Importance of HMO patients to practice
Staff Model	Salary	HMO	Only patients
Group Model	Fixed capitation, profit sharing	HMO	Core
Network Model	Negotiated capitation	Practice	Less important
Individual Practice Association (IPA)	Many contracts, negotiated fee schedules	Practice	Secondary

d. <u>Preferred provider organization (PPO)</u>: fee-for-service at a discount

    i. Insurance company contracts to provide services at a present price or discount

    ii. Discount is substantial, often 30% below standard fees for primary care and 50% below standard fees for specialists

    iii. In exchange for discount, insurer agrees to provide incentives for patient to use contracted providers

    iv. Provider makes money on volume, i.e., less money per patient but more patients. Efficiency is rewarded.

    v. Provider is limited in ability to raise prices.

    vi. Insurance company conducts utilization review to be sure that only appropriate services are delivered and billed.

    vii. Providers may "bid for patients," seeking greater volume by offering deeper discounts.

GOVERNMENT METHODS OF PAYMENT FOR SERVICES

a. <u>Medicare</u>: Federal government program that makes health care payments to those on Social Security

    i. Program pays health care costs for the:

- Elderly (age >65)
- Disabled
- Dependents of disabled

    ii. Part A pays for hospital care; part B pays for physician services.

    iii. Annual deductibles and copayments are applicable.

    iv. Patient can use up Medicare benefits.

    v. If providers accept "assignment," they must accept Medicare-set fees only.

    vi. Covered services include: hospital stays; laboratory work-ups; non-self-administered drugs; ambulatory surgery; physical, speech, and occupational therapy; rehabilitation; kidney dialysis; ambulance transport; diabetes testing equipment; pneumococcal and hepatitis B vaccination. Some prescription coverage is available for an added fee.

    vii. Services *not* covered: routine physicals; eye/ear examinations for glasses/hearing aids; immunizations; routine foot care; custodial (nursing home) care; most self-administered drugs.

b. <u>Medicaid</u>: health care payments for those on welfare

    i. Joint state/federal program

    ii. Covers all care, including hospital stays, physician services, medication, and nursing homes. However, Medicaid payments to providers are generally far below standard fees.

    iii. If poor and over age 65, Medicare is first used, then Medicaid

    iv. No deductibles, copayments, or fees

    v. Each state sets eligibility, services covered, and administration, hence wide differences across the United States.

c. <u>Diagnostic-related groups (DRGs)</u>

DRGs are payment categories used to classify patients (especially Medicare patients) for the purpose of reimbursing hospitals for each case in a given category, There is a fixed fee, regardless of the actual costs incurred, since patients within each category are clinically similar and are expected to use the same level of hospital resources. DRGs have been used in the United States since the early 1980s to determine how much Medicare pays the hospital for services. They are assigned based on diagnosis, procedure, age, sex, discharge status, and presence of complications or comorbidities (see below).

    i. Limits what the government will pay (but does not set prices)

    ii. Prospective payment is set by taking national median cost to treat each of approximately 500 different diagnoses.

     iii. Payment is determined by adding or subtracting from this median cost according to a formula that includes:

- Principal and up to four secondary diagnoses
- Principal procedures
- Patient's age
- Patient's gender
- Patient's discharge status
- Prevailing wage rate in the area
- Extra payments for teaching hospitals
- Extra payments also for "outliers": patients costing far beyond usual expenses

     iv. Consequences of DRGs

- More outpatient treatment
- Quicker discharges from hospital
- Serial admissions (new payments after 31 days)
- Inflation in number of diagnoses
- Preferences for certain diagnoses and procedures that pay more
- Upcoding: recording a diagnosis that pays more (which is illegal)

     v. DRGs generally do not apply to psychiatric, pediatric, or physical rehabilitation cases.

d. Resource-based relative-value scale (RBRVS)

RBRVS is a program used to determine how much money providers should be compensated. It is used by Medicare and HMOs. This program assigns a relative value to procedures and services performed, and is adjusted by geographic region.

     i. Sets government payments to physicians (and insurance companies, as well)

     ii. Pays fairly well, but takes capacity to set fees away from individual providers

     iii. Payments are made using a formula that includes:

- Amount of time, work, skill, and effort required
- Typical costs of physician's practice (including malpractice premiums)
- Typical cost of physician's postgraduate (residency, fellowship) training
- Typical office overhead

     iv. Consequences of RBRVS

- Higher payments to primary care; lower payments to procedure-based specialties
- Higher payments for cognitive work (talking with and thinking about the patient)

Social Sciences

Basic Science of Patient Safety 17

INTRODUCTION

Case 1: Care done well

A 3-year-old girl falls into an icy fishpond in a small Austrian town in the Alps. She is lost beneath the surface for 30 minutes before her parents find her on the pond bottom and pull her up. CPR is started immediately by the parents on instruction from an emergency physician on the phone, and EMS arrives within 8 minutes. The girl has a body temperature of 19° C and no pulse. Her pupils are dilated and do not react to light. A helicopter takes the patient to a nearby hospital where she is wheeled directly to an operating room. A surgical team puts her on a heart-lung bypass machine, her body temperature increases nearly 10 degrees, and her heart begins to beat. She requires placement on extracorporeal membrane oxygenation. Over the next few days her body temperature continues to rise to normal, and the organs start to recover. She suffered extensive neurologic deficits; however, by age 5, after extensive outpatient therapy, she recovers completely and is like any other little girl again.

Case 2: Failure of the medical system

A newborn baby boy is first noted to be jaundiced through visual assessment hours after delivery, but a bilirubin test is not done. At the time of discharge from the hospital, the child is described as having 'head to toe jaundice,' but a bilirubin test had still not been done, nor had his blood type or Coombs test been performed. The parents are instructed that the jaundice is normal and they should not worry, and to simply place the infant in the window for sunlight. A few days later the baby's mother calls the newborn nursery stating that her son is still yellow, lethargic, and feeding poorly. She is asked if she is a "first-time mom" and then assured that there was no concern. The mother continues to notice that the child is not well. At age 5 days, the mother's concerns are acknowledged and a pediatrician admits the baby boy to the pediatric unit. On day 6 in the afternoon, the child has a high pitched cry, respiratory distress, and increased tone. He also starts to arch his neck in a way that is characteristic of opisthotonos. The child is ultimately diagnosed with classic textbook kernicterus, resulting in permanent brain damage.

The 2 real cases above represent the reality of our current health care system and the issues of patient safety. In one case a series of complex processes result in an excellent outcome, while in another a patient suffers preventable injury.

What are the factors that cause a good versus poor outcome? The field of patient safety seeks to answer this question and take steps to prevent future patients from being harmed by medical errors.

Patients are at risk for sustaining harm from the health care system and do so at an alarmingly high rate. Injury can range from minor to severe incidents, including death. The cause of these adverse events is not usually intentional injury (i.e. someone intending to harm patients), but rather is due to the complexity of the health care system combined with the inherent capability of human error.

The prevalence of medical errors in the United States is a significant and ongoing problem. Media reports of catastrophic injury resulting in disability or death due to medical care often reach news headlines, and are a significant concern to patients, families, and members of the health care team. The causes of these errors are varied, and can include failures in the administration of medication, performing surgery, reporting laboratory results, and diagnosing patients, to name a few.

Ensuring patient safety is the responsibility of every member of the health care team. To do so requires an understanding of safety science and quality improvement principles. Patients, providers, payers, and employers are all stakeholders in improving patient safety. Applying these principles to the study of medical errors can help health care professionals learn from past errors and develop systems that prevent future errors from harming subsequent patients. Systems in health care delivery can be redesigned to create safeguards and safety nets which make it difficult for members of the health care team to make errors that harm patients. The goal of health care should be to learn the strategies and systems that are currently being put into place to improve patient safety.

SCOPE OF THE PROBLEM

In 1999 the Institute of Medicine (IOM) published its landmark publication, 'To Err is Human: Building a Safer Health System,' reporting that at least 44,000 people—and perhaps as many as 98,000—die in hospitals each year as a result of medical errors that could have been prevented. This exceeds deaths attributed to breast cancer, motor vehicle collisions, and HIV. Approximately 1 in 10 patients entering the hospital will suffer harm from an adverse event.

Patient harm from preventable medical errors is a serious concern in health care. The impact of these errors can have dramatically negative effects on patients, their families, and the health care personnel involved. In addition to the toll on human suffering, medical errors also present a significant source of inefficiency and increased cost in the health care system.

Medical errors are the eighth leading cause of wrongful death in the United States. The problem is not limited to this country, however; medical errors are a global problem.

Some of the more common contributors to medical errors and adverse patient events are as follows:

Medication errors represent one of the most common causes of preventable patient harm. An estimated 1.5 million deaths occur each year in the United States due to medication error. The IOM estimates that 1 medication error occurs per hospitalized patient each day.

Common causes of medication error

- Poor handwriting technique on a prescription pad or order form, resulting in a pharmacist or nurse administering the wrong drug or wrong dose
- Dosing or route of administration errors
- Failure to identify that a given patient is allergic to a prescribed medication
- Look-alike or sound-alike drugs (e.g., rifampin/rifiximin)

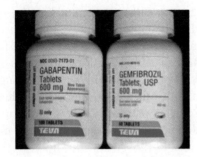

Figure 17-1. 'Look-Alike' Medications

Strategies that help to reduce or prevent medication errors are as follows.

- The **5 Rs** help to confirm several key points before the administration of any medication.
  - Right drug
  - Right patient
  - Right dose
  - Right route
  - Right time

- Computerized physician order entry (CPOE) involves entering medication orders directly into a computer system rather than on paper or verbally. The computer software (i.e. electronic health record) can automatically check for prescribing errors or allergies.

Hospital-acquired infections (HAI) affect 5-15% of all hospitalized patients and 40% of patients in ICU. The World Health Organization (WHO) estimates that the mortality from health-care-associated infections ranges from 12–80%.

HAI can occur in many forms, the most common of which in hospitalized patients is **urinary catheter-related infection** (UTI). UTI accounts for 40% of all HAI; >80% of these infections are attributable to use of an indwelling urethral catheter. Adhering to strict indications for using indwelling catheters, maintaining sterile technique during catheter insertion and exercising prompt removal of the catheter when it is no longer required can help reduce the risk of a urinary catheter-related infection.

Central line associated bloodstream infection (CLABSI) is another common HAI, and among one of the most common infections observed in patients admitted to critical care units. It is estimated that 70% of hospital-acquired bloodstream infections occur in patients with central venous catheters. Symptoms include fever, chills, erythema at the skin surrounding the central line site and, in severe cases, hypotension secondary to sepsis.

These infections can be associated with significant morbidity and mortality, increased length of hospital stay, and increased hospital cost. Checklists have been developed which provide best practices for the placement of central lines that lower the risk of infection (e.g., hand washing, gloving and gowning, sterile barriers, and early removal of central lines when possible).

Hospital-acquired pneumonia (HAP) is an infection that occurs more often in ventilated patients, typically ≥48 hours after admission to a hospital. These ventilator-associated pneumonias (VAP), a subtype of HAP, tend to be more serious because patients are often sicker and less able to mount effective immune responses. HAP is the second most common nosocomial infection. Common symptoms include coughing, fever, chills, fatigue, malaise, headache, loss of appetite, nausea and vomiting, shortness of breath, and sharp or stabbing chest pain that gets worse with deep breathing or coughing. Several methods have been undertaken to prevent HAP, including infection control (e.g. hand hygiene and proper use of gloves, gown and mask), elevation of the head of the bed in ventilated patients, and other measures to reduce the risk of aspiration.

Surgical site infections (SSI) occur following a surgical procedure in the part of the body where the surgery took place. Some SSIs are superficial and limited to the skin, while others are more serious and involve deep tissue under the skin, body cavities, internal organs, or implanted material (e.g. knee or hip replacements). Symptoms include fever, drainage of cloudy fluid from the surgical incision or erythema and tenderness at the surgical site. Most superficial SSIs (e.g., cellulitis) can be treated with appropriate antibiotics, whereas deeper infections (i.e., abscess) require drainage. Pre-operative antibiotics have been effective in reducing the rate of SSIs.

Patient falls are a common cause of injury in hospitals and other health care settings such as nursing homes. Over 1/3 of elderly people age >65 fall each year. Researchers estimate that >500,000 falls happen each year in U.S. hospitals, resulting in 150,000 injuries. Approximately 30% of inpatient falls result in injury, with 4–6% resulting in serious injury. Injuries can include bone fractures, head injury, bleeding, and even death. Injuries from falls also increase hospital costs.

Assessing a patient's fall risk helps to identify high-risk patients who can benefit from preventative resources. Some risk factors include advanced age (age >60), muscle weakness, taking >4 prescription medications (especially sedatives, hypnotics, antidepressants, or benzodiazepines), impaired memory, and difficulty walking (e.g. use of a cane or walker). Interventions such as increased observation, nonslip footwear, and making the environment safe all play a role in preventing injury from falls.

Unplanned readmissions occur when patients unexpectedly return to the hospital <30 days after being discharged. According to a *New England Journal of Medicine* study analyzing close to 12 million Medicare beneficiaries, nearly 20% of those discharged were readmitted within 30 days. Several factors can lead to a hospital readmission, such as poor quality of care or breakdowns in communication during a transition of care (e.g. hospital to rehabilitation center). Readmissions may also occur if patients are discharged from hospitals prematurely, are discharged to inappropriate settings, or if they do not receive adequate information or resources to aid in recovery.

For example, a 79-year-old patient treated for congestive heart failure (CHF) returns to the hospital 10 days after discharge with exacerbation of CHF. It was discovered that upon release the patient had failed to fill the prescription for the diuretic started during the initial hospitalization. Improving communication, patient education and providing appropriate support to patients at risk for readmissions are all strategies to reduce unplanned readmissions.

CAUSES OF MEDICAL ERROR

The miraculous recovery of the little girl after the drowning event in case 1 highlights the incredible complexity of our modern health delivery system. There were numerous steps that were required to get right in the care of the patient. Unfortunately, these steps are not always followed as well as they were in that case. Machines break down, a team can't get moving fast enough, or a simple step is forgotten or the wrong step applied. The greater the number of steps required, the greater the risk of something going wrong. Couple that with the fact that human beings are prone to error, especially when working under less-than-ideal circumstances, and it is no wonder that medical errors pose such a threat to health care.

The complexity of the health care system, together with the potential for mistakes due to human nature, is the primary reason that patients experience medical errors. Understanding medical error and the science of patient safety can help us design a health care system capable of getting it right every time.

The potential for human error is amplified by poor working conditions. This includes poor workplace conditions (e.g., overworked staff, time pressures, lack of safety protocols or lack of appropriate supervision), as well as poor individual conditions (e.g., fatigue, stress or illness).

The following is a mnemonic to help assess the fitness of a health care professional to attend to patient care.

> **IM SAFE**
>
> **I:** Illness (Are you suffering from an illness that is degrading your performance?)
>
> **M:** Medications (Are you taking medications that may impair your judgment?)
>
> **S:** Stress (Are you adequately managing the stressors in your life?)
>
> **A:** Alcohol (Are you using alcohol in excess with negative consequences?)
>
> **F:** Fatigue (Are you getting enough rest?)
>
> **E:** Eating (Are you maintaining a healthy diet?)

For example, one study on physician performance found that being awake 24 hours was equivalent to having a blood alcohol level of .10 (legally intoxicated by most standards) (Dawson & Reid, 1997).

Communication and teamwork failures are another leading cause of adverse patient events. Lack of appropriate communication creates situations where medical errors are likely to occur. These errors have the potential to cause severe injury and unexpected patient death. Errors at the time of transitions or handoffs are among the most common communication errors in healthcare. Handoffs occur frequently between nurses and between residents in teaching hospitals, but also among attending faculty (e.g., on-call physicians, hospitalists, ED staff). Using techniques of structured communication (e.g., SBAR, call-backs) can help safeguard against errors. Poor teamwork and lack of

Note

Errors are bound to occur due to a combination of a complex health care system and the reality of human fallibility.

coordination between members of the patient care team also result in medical errors. A growing recognition of the need for improved teamwork in health care has led to the application of teamwork training principles, originally developed in aviation, to a variety of clinical settings. Recognized barriers to effective teamwork include:

- Inconsistency in team membership
- Lack of time
- Lack of Information Sharing
- Hierarchy
- Defensiveness
- Conventional Thinking
- Complacency
- Varying Communication Styles
- Conflict
- Lack of Coordination
- Distractions
- Fatigue
- Workload
- Misinterpretation of Cues
- Lack of Role Clarity

Teamwork training attempts to reduce the potential for patient harm by developing effective communication skills, a supportive working environment, and an atmosphere in which all team members feel comfortable speaking up when they suspect a problem. Team members are trained to cross-monitor; check each other's actions, offer assistance when needed, and address errors in a nonjudgmental fashion (i.e. watch each other's backs). Huddles, Briefs and Debriefs are essential components of teamwork training; as is providing feedback, especially after critical incidents. Remember, a chain is only as strong as its weakest link.

TYPES OF MEDICAL ERROR

Types of Errors

Diagnostic

- Error or delay in diagnosis
- Failure to employ indicated tests
- Use of outmoded tests or therapy
- Failure to act on results of monitoring or testing

Treatment

- Error in the performance of an operation, procedure, or test
- Error in administering the treatment
- Error in the dose or method of using a drug
- Avoidable delay in treatment or in responding to an abnormal test inappropriate (not indicated) care

Preventive

- Failure to provide prophylactic treatment
- Inadequate monitoring or follow-up of treatment
- Other
  - Failure of communication
  - Equipment failure
  - Other system failure

Source: Leape, Lucian; Lawthers, Ann G.; Brennan, Troyen A., et al. *Preventing Medical Injury*. Qual Rev Bull. 19(5): 144–149, 1993

Errors can be categorized as slips, lapses, or mistakes.

- **Slips** can be thought of as actions not carried out as intended or planned e.g. injecting a medication intravenously when you meant to give it subcutaneously. Slips are observable.
- **Lapses** are missed actions and omissions (e.g. forgetting to monitor and replace serum potassium in a patient treated with furosemide for acute congestive heart failure). Lapses are generally not observable (i.e. one cannot directly 'see' a lapse of memory).

Both slips and lapses are actions that do not 'go as intended.'

- **Mistakes** are a specific type of error brought about by a faulty plan or incorrect intentions; the intended action is wrong (e.g. extubating a patient prematurely based on misapplication of guidelines, or treating a patient for a suspected pneumonia when the patient was misdiagnosed and actually has a pulmonary embolism).

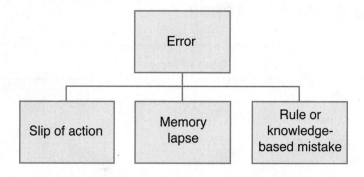

Figure 17-2. Types of Error

It is important to differentiate errors (slip, lapse, or mistake) from violations.

- **Violations** are deliberate actions, whereby someone does something and knows it to be against the rules (e.g. deliberately failing to follow proper procedures). A health care professional may consider that a violation is well-intentioned; however, it would still technically constitute a 'violation' rather than an error. For example, a physician may decide to forgo entering a patient's allergies into the electronic record due to time constraints in starting treatment. If this act led to an adverse medication reaction due to a missed allergic reaction, it would technically be considered a violation and not an error.

Errors may result in adverse events or near-misses.

- **Adverse events** are harms or injuries that result directly from medical care, not from negative outcomes due to the patient's disease or medical condition.
- **Near-misses** are errors that occur but do not result in injury or harm to patients because they are caught in time or simply because of luck.

Diagnostic errors account for at least 17% of preventable errors in hospitalized patients. Diagnostic errors can be categorized as no-fault, system-related, and cognitive.

- **No-fault errors** may happen when there are masked or unusual symptoms of a disease, or when a patient has not fully cooperated in care.
- **System-related** errors include technical failure, equipment problems and organizational flaws.
- **Cognitive errors** frequently result from a diagnosis that was wrong, missed, or unintentionally delayed due to clinician error.

The following are examples of common cognitive errors.

A wrong diagnosis may occur when the clinician holds on to a particular diagnosis (usually the initial one, in a phenomenon called **anchoring bias**) and becomes dismissive to signs and symptoms pointing to another diagnosis. For example, a 65-year-old man presents with epigastric pain, and emesis, and he sits leaning forward. He has a history of alcoholism. The patient is likely to be diagnosed with pancreatitis. However, holding on to this diagnosis to the exclusion of any other diagnosis—despite the patient's denial of alcohol use for several years, normal blood levels of pancreatic enzymes, and abnormal EKG which is ignored—would be an anchoring error.

Confirmation bias, looking for evidence to support a pre-conceived opinion, rather than looking for evidence that refutes it or provides greater support to an alternative diagnosis, may accompany an anchoring error. Clinicians should regard conflicting data as evidence for the need to continue to seek the true diagnosis (e.g. in the case above; acute MI) rather than as anomalies to be disregarded.

Availability bias is the tendency to assume a diagnosis based on recent patient encounters or memorable cases (i.e., the most cognitively "available" diagnosis).

It is estimated that thousands of hospitalized patients die every year due to diagnostic errors. Missed or delayed diagnoses (particularly of cancer) are a prominent reason for malpractice claims. Poor teamwork/communication between clinicians and a lack of reliable systems for common outpatient clinical situations (e.g., triaging acutely ill patients by telephone and following-up on test results) have been identified as predisposing factors for diagnostic error.

SYSTEMS APPROACH TO MEDICAL ERROR

Health professionals dedicate their lives to the care of patients. Most are highly trained and competent; however, the nature of health care is extremely complex, and people, despite good intentions, are still capable of making errors.

Although hospitals, clinics, and doctor's offices take many steps to keep their patients safe, medical errors can, and do, occur. Rather than penalize individuals who make honest mistakes, the goal of patient safety is to redesign systems to be more fool-proof and able to compensate for human error.

Bad Apples/Blame Culture: When a medical error occurs, the bad apple approach seeks to identify who is responsible for the error and take punitive action against that individual. However, this approach does not improve safety. It creates a culture of fear and doesn't address the root cause of the error.

Only 5% of patient harm is due directly to incompetence or poor intentions. People need to be accountable, but systems changes are needed to truly transform care. Unfortunately, health care has a long tradition of a blame culture. Blaming people who make errors does not get to underlying causes or help to prevent the error from happening to someone else in the future.

The most effective approach to reducing harm from medical error is to find out *how* the error happened, rather than who did it, and then fix the system to prevent errors from causing injury to patients. Improvements in patient safety will be hindered as long as there is a focus on blaming individuals.

SYSTEMS APPROACH TO FAILURE

An understanding of medical error requires an understanding of the systems failures underlying the majority of adverse patient events. Health care is a complex system. Errors that harm patients tend to have multiple causes that are ingrained in this complex system. James Reason, a pioneer and leader in the research area of human error and organizational processes, describes the **Swiss Cheese Model** of accident causation; it is a model used in risk analysis and risk management in complex systems including health care.

The Swiss cheese model encompasses the understanding that patient harm often results from multiple, upstream or proximal errors. In the Swiss cheese model, each 'slice' represents a barrier, and each hole is a failure in the system due to either active or latent failures. Under normal circumstances one of the barriers works to prevent patient harm (e.g. the nurse catches that the medication ordered is the wrong dose before giving it to the patient); however, occasionally the perfect storm scenario arises where the holes line up and allow an error to reach the patient resulting in harm.

For example, if the hazard were wrong-site orthopedic surgery, slices of cheese might include policies for identifying sidedness on radiology imaging, a protocol for signing the correct site when the surgeon and patient meet in the preoperative area, and a second protocol for reviewing the medical record and checking the previously marked site in the operating room. Many more layers exist but the point is that no single barrier is foolproof. They each have "holes," hence, the Swiss cheese.

In some serious events such as wrong site surgery, even though the holes will only align infrequently, the result is still unacceptable patient injury. For instance, in an emergency situation, all 3 of the surgical identification safety checks mentioned above may fail or be bypassed, resulting in the surgeon meeting the patient for the first time in the operating room already under anesthesia. A hurried x-ray technologist might mislabel a film (or simply hang it backward and a hurried surgeon may not notice), confirming the surgical site with the patient may not take place at all (e.g. if the patient is unconscious) or, if it takes place, be rushed and offer no real protection.

Under the blame culture traditionally present in health care, a person may be reprimanded for an error but the holes in the system are not addressed; making it quite probable that the same error will be committed by someone else in the future leading to more patient harm. The goal is to examine the system and develop methods to redesign care so that the holes are removed.

Note

Approximately 80% of medical errors or adverse patient events are system-derived.

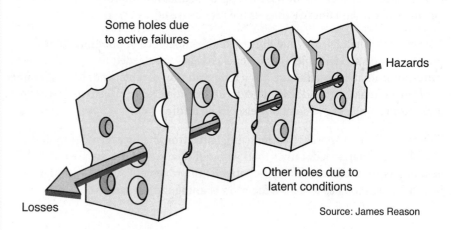

Figure 17-3. Successive Layers of Defenses, Barriers, and Safeguards

Other industries with complex systems, such as aviation and nuclear power plants, have successfully employed systems engineering to drastically improve safety and reliability. These industries have also made changes to improve communication, teamwork, and the culture of safety.

Another example of lessons learned from systems engineering is the automobile safety industry. Most motor vehicle collision (MVC) deaths are due to driver error or deliberate misbehavior (e.g. speeding, running a red light, failure to wear a seatbelt, etc.). The death toll from MVC in the past several decades has declined significantly. Drivers today are not necessarily safer drivers than before; however, design changes in cars (e.g. collapsible steering columns, airbags) and safe highway design (e.g. improved lighting, deformable lampposts) have resulted in drastic reductions in mortality from MVCs.

Likewise, the goal in patient safety is to prevent errors from resulting in harm to patients. Health care must create safety nets that absorb mistakes before they reach patients. Some examples of system-based redesigns for patient safety include protocols to ensure proper patient identification, such as the following:

- Using at least 2 methods such as patient name and date of birth to confirm patient identify prior to the administration of medications
- Using a standardized pre-operative checklist to help operating room staff review critical information prior to surgery (e.g. pre-operative antibiotics)
- Removing look-alike drugs from the nursing unit in order to prevent medication errors

ERROR DISCLOSURE AND REPORTING

Many victims of medical errors never learn that the mistake occurred, because the error is simply not disclosed. Healthcare professionals have traditionally shied away from discussing errors with patients, due to fear of precipitating a malpractice lawsuit, issues of professional embarrassment or discomfort with the disclosure process. It is both an ethical and professional responsibility to ensure that errors resulting in patient harm are disclosed and reported.

The first priority after an event which causes patient harm is to care for the patient's medical needs. **Disclosure** of the error is another important early action. Following an adverse event, patients and families want to hear an apology and to know what is being done to prevent the error from harming someone else in the future. They may also require emotional and social support. Honesty and transparency are essential. There is no role for covering up an error (e.g. altering documentation to conceal the error) or withholding information from the patient or family. Such practices are unethical and betray the professional responsibility we have to patients. Studies have demonstrated that a timely and sincere apology may actually reduce the likelihood of a lawsuit.

Often the most senior physician responsible for the patient and most familiar with the case will make the official disclosure. An error disclosure should include the following 3 elements:

- Accurate description of the events and their impact on the patient
- Sincere apology showing care and compassion
- Assurance that appropriate steps are being taken to prevent the adverse event from happening to another patient in the future

Reporting allows for errors to be studied so that system-based improvements can be made to help prevent such errors from harming patients in the future. Reporting errors is essential for error prevention and provides opportunities to improve processes of care by learning from failures of the health care system. In order to be effective, reporting must be safe. Individuals who report incidents must not be punished or suffer other ill-effects from reporting. The fear of punitive retaliation or other negative consequences will serve as an impediment to incident reporting. The identities of reporters should not normally be disclosed to third parties.

Other barriers to error reporting include the belief that that no corrective action will be taken and having an overly burdensome reporting system. To overcome these barriers, reported events should be reviewed and acted upon in a timely fashion, and the system for reporting errors should be made as straightforward as possible.

One other recognized barrier to error reporting is failure to recognize that an error has occurred. For example, an interventional cardiologist accidentally orders the wrong dose of medication during a cardiac catheterization; however, the nurse who has worked with this cardiologist for years knows the correct dose intended and makes the appropriate adjustment. No harm has occurred but it would be wrong not to realize that an error did happen.

Health care professionals need to be educated about medical error identification, including the identification and importance of near-misses. Although near-misses (errors that occur but fortunately do not result in patient harm) do not generally need to be disclosed to patients, they should still be reported to the system so that they, too, can be studied. One person's near-miss may be the next person's fatal error. Estimates of the scope of medical errors likely do not reflect the numerous near-misses that do not result in patient harm.

It is important to have a culture that promotes error reporting and error analysis in order to enhance health systems. Every error represents an opportunity to improve a process; however, in order to improve, these errors must be recognized and made known so that system-wide learning and performance can take place.

ANALYSIS OF MEDICAL ERRORS

A systematic approach for understanding the cause of adverse events and identifying flaws in the system which can be corrected to prevent harm in the future is called **root cause analysis** (RCA). RCA is *retrospective* in nature; the focus is on systems and process rather than individual blame. The question asked is, "**how did this happen?**," not "whose fault is this?" The goal is to determine why an event happened and what can be done to prevent it from happening again. RCA is not applicable to negligence or willful harm.

A classic tool used in RCA is the **Fishbone** or **Ishikawa diagram** (also known as a **Cause and Effect diagram**), which analyzes a complex system and identifies possible causes for an effect or problem. This type of diagram is used to explore and display all the possible causes of a particular error.

Note

Estimates are that voluntarily reported medical errors only reflect 10–20% of actual errors.

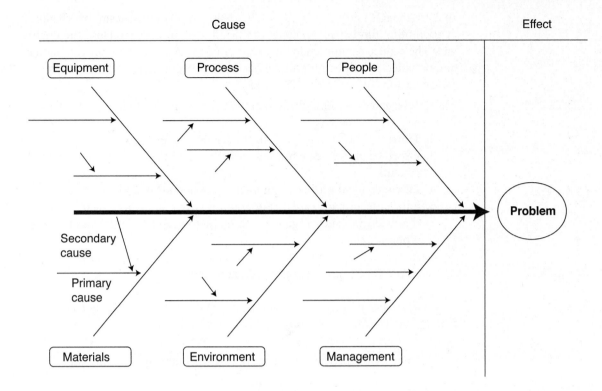

Figure 17-4. Sample Fishbone (Ishikawa) Diagram

The RCA allows the team to identify problems in the system or process of care. The end product of the RCA process is a list of recommended actions to prevent the recurrence of the adverse event in the future. Recommendations commonly consist of one or more of the following actions: standardizing equipment, using double checks or backup systems, employing forcing functions that physically prevent users from making common mistakes, making changes to the physical set-up, updating or improving technology, using cognitive aids (e.g. checklists or mnemonic devices), simplifying a process, educating staff or implementing new safety policies.

In contrast to the retrospective nature of RCA, the prospective failure mode effects analysis (FMEA) is an engineering approach which seeks to anticipate and prevent adverse events through safety design. The goal of FMEA is to prevent patient problems before they occur. FMEA is a systematic and proactive approach that seeks to identify possible failures in the system and potential weaknesses in order to develop strategies to prevent the failures from occurring.

PRINCIPLES OF QUALITY IMPROVEMENT

> 'Every system is perfectly designed to get the results it gets.'
>
> Source: Don Berwick, M.D.

A key principle of quality improvement is to design systems capable of identifying, preventing, absorbing and mitigating errors. Some everyday examples of safety design outside of health care are seatbelt alarms in cars, heat-sensitive fire sprinkler systems, and tip-over switches which automatically turn off space heaters that have accidentally fallen over.

In 2001, the IOM published a report, "Crossing the Quality Chasm" which aimed at promoting fundamental changes in health care in order to close the quality gap. The report recommended a redesign of the American health care system and provided principles for guiding quality improvement. Specifically, the report defined 6 aims of health care (STEEEP):

1. **Safe**: avoidance of injuries to patients from the care that is intended to help them
2. **Timely**: reduce waits and harmful delays in care
3. **Effective**: provide care based on scientific knowledge likely to benefit patients
4. **Efficient**: avoid waste in equipment, supplies, ideas, and energy
5. **Equitable**: provide care that does not vary in quality because of personal characteristics such as gender, ethnicity, geographic location, and socio-economic status
6. **Patient-centered**: provide care that is respectful of and responsive to individual patient preferences, needs, and values

Another significant initiative in quality improvement is the Institute for Health Care Improvements (IHI) Triple Aim that describes an approach to optimizing health system performance using new designs to pursue 3 dimensions (i.e. "Triple Aim").

- Improve the patient experience of care (including quality and satisfaction)
- Improve the health of populations
- Reduce per capita cost of health care

Measures of Quality

There are 3 traditional categories of measures used in quality improvement: structure, process, and outcomes.

- **Structure** relates to the physical equipment, resources, or facilities (e.g., number of ICU beds in a hospital).

- **Process** relates to how the system works (e.g. how often nurses use bar coding to identify patients prior to administering medication).

- **Outcomes** represent the final product or end result in patient care (e.g. infection rate in pediatric hematology patients admitted to the hospital). Outcomes are often difficult to assess in quality improvement, and many people often use process measures as a surrogate for outcomes. For example, it may be difficult to accurately track all HAI (*outcomes measure*), so rates of compliance with hand washing are monitored instead (*process measure*).

A fourth type of measure introduced to quality improvement is the concept of a balancing measure. **Balancing measures** ask whether changes made to improve one part of the system cause an unanticipated decrease in performance in another part of the system (e.g. did an initiative aimed at increasing the efficiency of discharging patients from the hospital lead to more patients being sent home without appropriate follow-up instructions).

Models of Quality Improvement

One example of a common quality improvement model is a combination of building and applying knowledge to make an improvement by asking 3 questions and using the **PDSA** (plan, do, study, act) cycle developed by W. Edwards Deming, a pioneer and influential leader in quality control.

1. What are we trying to accomplish?
2. How will we know whether a change is an improvement?
3. What changes can we make that will result in an improvement?

This model takes the simple concept of "trial and error" and transforms it into the PDSA model that can be used to make improvements in health care.

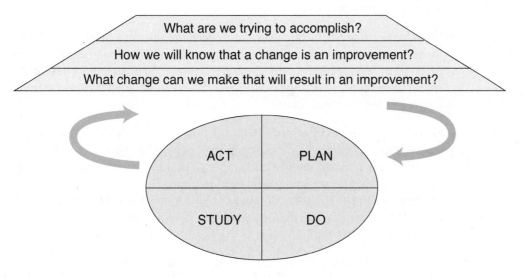

Figure 17-5. The Model for Improvement

Source: Langley, Nolan, Nolan & Provost 1999

- **Plan**: plan a change or a pilot test of a new intervention or innovation
- **Do**: carry out the plan
- **Study**: evaluate the results
- **Act**: decide what actions should be taken to improve (i.e. implement the new intervention or start over with a new plan based on the prior results)

Six Sigma is another model for quality improvement with origins from the manufacturing industry. The term comes from the use in statistics of the Greek Letter (sigma) to denote Standard Deviation from the mean. Six sigma is equivalent to 3.4 defects (or errors) per million. This system uses specific steps to reduce variation and improve performance.

- DMAIC (define – measure – analyze – improve - control): an improvement system for **existing processes** falling below specification
  - **Define**: Define the problem in detail.
  - **Measure**: Measure defects (in terms of "defects per million," or Sigma level).
  - **Analyze**: Do in-depth analysis using process measures, flow charts and defect analysis to determine the conditions under which defects occur.
  - **Improve**: Define and test changes aimed at reducing defects.
  - **Control**: What steps will you take to maintain performance?

Lean (also called Lean Enterprise or Toyota Production System) is an improvement process that seeks to improve value from the patient's perspective, by reducing waste in time and resources that do not enhance patient outcomes. This includes certain lab tests, imaging studies or care services that may be commonly performed, but in reality do not actually help the patient. For example, a preoperative EKG obtained on a healthy 21 year-old with no cardiac symptoms undergoing a small outpatient procedure can be considered a wasteful test that does not help the patient.

Flowcharts allow health care teams to understand the steps involved in the delivery of patient care service. A flowchart is a visual illustration of all the steps or parts of a process in patient care. There are 2 types of flowcharts: **high-level flowcharts** (more conceptually focused, 'big picture') and **detailed flowcharts** (more focused on specific, fine points).

Flowcharts are more accurate and effective when all representative members of a health care team actively participate in their design. They help health-care providers achieve a shared understanding of a clinical process and use that knowledge as the basis for designing new ways to improve services. Specifically, they can help to identify steps that do not add value to the process (e.g. unnecessary duplication of services), to determine areas of delay in care, and to discover failure points in the system.

Pareto charts are used to describe a large proportion of quality problems being caused by a small number of causes. It is based on the classic 80/20 rule from economics, where 80% of the world's wealth is described to be in the hands of an elite 20% of the population.

The Pareto principle applied to health care states that the **majority of patient safety errors stem from only a few recurring contributing factors**, which should serve as the focus the problem-solving efforts. In essence, it is a method of prioritizing problems, highlighting the fact that most problems are affected by a few factors and indicating which problems to solve and in what order. A Pareto chart includes the multiple factors that contribute to an effect arranged in descending order (according to the magnitude of their effect). The ordering is an important step because it helps the team concentrate efforts on those factors that have the greatest impact

Run charts (or time plots) are graphs of data collected over time which can help determine whether an intervention or enhancement in the patient care process has resulted in true improvement over time or rather if it simply represents a random fluctuation (that might be incorrectly interpreted as a significant improvement). Run charts are created by plotting time along the X-axis (e.g. minutes, hours, days, months) and the quality measure on the Y-axis (e.g. number of infections, wait times, falls). The median (or 50th percentile) is measured using baseline historical data and then compared to outcomes measured following the quality improvement intervention.

Run charts help identify whether there is a true trend vs. a random-pattern. A shift in the process signaling a significant change in quality can be identified, for example, by observing ≥6 consecutive points above or below the median, or by ≥5 consecutive points all increasing or decreasing.

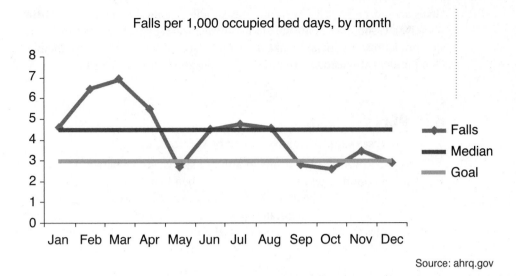

Figure 17-6. Sample Run Chart Plotting Patient Falls

A Shewhart (or control chart) applies formal statistical calculations (statistical process control) to determine whether the observed rise and fall of a quality measure over time is within a predictable range of variation or is an indication of a significant change in the system. Control charts use upper and lower control limits (sometimes called "natural process limits") which indicate the threshold at which the process output is considered statistically 'unlikely,' and are drawn typically at 3 standard errors from the center line.

A **convenience sample** is the study group or population used in the test of a quality improvement initiative. Using convenience sampling is an efficient and simple method to test an intervention. This is not the same process often used in randomized controlled trials, and thus may not be an accurate reflection of the larger group. Ideally, however, the sample will have approximately similar characteristics to the larger population.

LEADING CHANGE IN PATIENT SAFETY

Patient safety is the professional responsibility of everyone on the patient care team. In order to effect change in the quality of health care, health care professionals must utilize leadership principles. Changing behavior is difficult, and there are always multiple barriers to change efforts. To be effective in leading transformation, change efforts need to create a sense of urgency, be data-driven, team-based, specific, and measurable.

Successful leadership can be achieved even without a formal position of authority. Strategies for effectively influencing change include the following:

- Gathering compelling data
- Adopting a 'systems' view of the problem
- Getting buy-in from administrative leadership or a powerful clinical ally
- Developing ideas to solve the problem
- Formulating an action plan

Goals should be SMART (**s**pecific, **m**easurable, **a**chievable, **r**ealistic, and **t**ime-sensitive). Good leaders are able to organize a team, articulate clear goals, manage conflict resolution, and make decisions based on the input of team members. Good leaders also lead by example and model good patient safety behavior.

KEY DEFINITIONS

- **Adverse event:** any injury caused by medical care
  - An adverse event results in unintended harm to a patient by an act of commission or omission, rather than by the underlying disease or condition of the patient. Identifying something as an adverse event does not imply error, negligence, or poor quality care. It simply indicates that an undesirable clinical outcome resulted from some aspect of diagnosis or therapy, not an underlying disease process.

- **Adverse reaction:** occurs when unexpected harm results from a justified action
  - An adverse drug reaction occurs when the correct process was followed for the context in which the medication was used.

- **Authority gradient:** command hierarchy of power or balance of power, measured in terms of steepness
  - First used in aviation to describe the phenomenon where pilots and copilots failed to communicate effectively in stressful situations due to the significant difference in their perceived expertise or authority. Hierarchies which exist in medicine are also subject to causing errors. Most health care teams require some degree of authority gradient; otherwise roles are blurred and decisions cannot be made in a timely fashion. However, within a hierarchy, tools of effective clinical communication and teamwork can overcome risks to patient safety.

- **Brief:** short planning session prior to the start of a clinical activity, in order to achieve team orientation, establish expectations, anticipate problems, and plan for contingencies

- **Checklist:** algorithmic listing of actions to be performed in a given clinical setting, with the goal to ensure that no critical step will be forgotten
  - Though a seemingly simple intervention, checklists have played a leading role in the most significant successes of the patient safety movement, including the near-elimination of central line–associated bloodstream infections in many intensive care units. Checklists have also been used in the operating room to ensure that OR teams are well-oriented and that evidence-based standards known to reduce complications are followed (e.g. use of pre-operative antibiotics).

- **Closed-loop communication:** a type of communication whereby, when a request is made of team members, someone specifically affirms out loud that he or she will complete the task and states out loud when the task has been completed
  - For example, during a cardiac resuscitation a physician orders a medication to be given intravenously and the nurse verbally confirms receipt of the order and verbally confirms when the medication has been administered as requested.

- **Debrief:** information exchange process designed to improve team performance and effectiveness, held after a clinical event in order to review and learn

- **Error:** failure of a planned action to be completed as intended or the use of a wrong plan to achieve an aim (i.e. an act of commission or doing something wrong); also includes failure of an unplanned action that should have been completed (i.e. an act of omission, or failing to do the right thing)

  – For example, ordering a medication for a patient with a documented allergy to that medication is an **error of commission**. Failing to prescribe a proven medication with major benefits for an eligible patient (e.g. low-dose unfractionated heparin for venous thromboembolism prophylaxis for a patient after hip replacement surgery) is an **error of omission**. Errors of omission are more difficult to recognize than errors of commission but are thought to represent a larger scope of the problem in patient safety.

  Errors can also be defined in terms of active or latent as coined by Professor James Reason, one of the founders in the field of safety science. According to Professor Reason, **active errors** occur at the point of contact between a human and some aspect of a larger system (e.g., a human–machine interface). They are generally readily apparent (e.g., pushing an incorrect button, ignoring a warning light) and almost always involve someone at the frontline. Active errors or active failures are sometimes referred to as errors at the 'sharp end,' figuratively referring to a scalpel. In other words, errors at the sharp end are noticed first because they are committed by the person closest to the patient. This person may literally be holding a scalpel (e.g., an orthopedist operating on the wrong leg) or figuratively be administering any kind of therapy (e.g., a nurse programming an intravenous pump with the wrong medication dose) or performing any aspect of care.

  Latent errors (or latent conditions), in contrast, refer to less apparent failures of organization or design that contribute to the occurrence of errors or allow them to cause harm to patients. To complete the metaphor, latent errors are those at the other end of the scalpel—the 'blunt end'—referring to the many layers of the health care system that affect the person "holding" the scalpel. For example, policies that allow a patient to enter an operating room and start an operation before confirming the patient's identify, intended procedure and site of surgery are considered latent errors that can result in wrong patient or wrong site surgery.

- **Forcing function:** aspect of a design which prevents a specific action from being performed or allows its performance only if another specific action is performed first

  – For example, automobiles are now designed so that the driver cannot shift into reverse without first putting a foot on the brake pedal. One of the first forcing functions identified in health care was the removal of concentrated potassium from general hospital wards. This action is intended to prevent the inadvertent preparation of intravenous solutions with concentrated potassium, an error that had produced small but consistent numbers of deaths for many years.

- **Handoffs:** the process whereby one health care professional updates another on the status of ≥1 patients for the purpose of taking over their care
  - An example includes a resident physician who has been on call overnight telling an incoming resident about the patients admitted who require ongoing management. Nurses commonly conduct a handover at the end of their shift, updating the oncoming nurse about their status of the patients and tasks that need to be performed. Handoffs are a potential source of patient safety failure from the lack of important information being conveyed or misinformation being conveyed.

- **Harm/hazard:** harm is the impairment or any negative effect on the structure of function of the body (e.g., disease, injury, suffering, disability, death); hazard is a circumstance, agent or action with the potential to cause harm

- **Huddle:** an often impromptu problem-solving meeting conducted in order to assess a critical situation, reestablish situation awareness, reinforce plans already in place, and determine the need to adjust the plan

- **Iatrogenic:** an adverse effect of medical care, rather than of the underlying disease (literally "brought forth by healer," from Greek *iatros*, for healer, and *gennan*, to bring forth)

- **Incident reporting:** collecting and analyzing information about an event which could have harmed (near-miss) or did harm (adverse event) a patient in a health care setting

- **Medication error:** any preventable event which may cause or lead to unintended and incorrect medication use or patient harm, while the medication is in the control of the health care professional or patient
  - Medication error occurs when a patient receives (a) the wrong medication, or (b) the right medication but in the wrong dosage or manner (e.g. given orally instead of IV, correct medication given at the wrong time).

- **Medication reconciliation:** process of avoiding unintended inconsistencies in medication regimens which can occur with any transition in care (e.g. hospital admission, transfer to ICU, discharge to rehab center) by reviewing the patient's current medication regimen and comparing it with the regimen being considered for the new setting of care
  - Medical reconciliation helps to ensure that the intended medications are continued, and that medications that are supposed to be discontinued are not inadvertently continued. For example, medical reconciliation performed prior to discharging a patient from the hospital can detect if medication changes were made during the hospital stay that need to be continued once the patent is home (e.g. intravenous antibiotics started in the hospital during the treatment of pneumonia which are intended to be continued orally at home).

- **Near-miss (or close call):** error or other incident which does not produce patient injury, but only because of intervening factors or pure chance
  - This good fortune might reflect robustness of the patient (e.g., a patient with penicillin allergy receives penicillin, but has no reaction) or a fortuitous, timely intervention (e.g., a nurse happens to realize that a physician wrote an order in the wrong chart).

- **Patient safety**: The WHO defines patient safety as 'the reduction of risk of unnecessary harm associated with health care to an acceptable minimum (2009)
  - The Agency for Healthcare Research and Quality uses the definition that 'patient safety is a discipline in the health care sector that applies safety science methods toward the goal of achieving a trustworthy system of health care delivery. Patient safety is also an attribute of health care systems; it minimizes the incidence and impact of, and maximizes recovery from, adverse events.

- **Quality assurance (QA):** an older term, not likely to be used today; QA was reactive, retrospective, policing, and in many ways punitive; often involved determining who was at fault after something went wrong

- **Quality improvement (QI):** involves both prospective and retrospective reviews; is aimed at improvement— measuring where you are and figuring out ways to make things better; specifically attempts to avoid attributing blame and to create systems to prevent errors from happening

- **Read backs (or call-backs)**: when a listener repeats key information so that the transmitter can confirm its correctness
  - To address the possibility of miscommunication when information is conveyed verbally, many high-risk industries use protocols for mandatory read-backs. For example, a laboratory technician calling a physician with a critical lab value may request that the physician read back the critical lab value to ensure it was received correctly.

- **Root cause analysis (RCA):** structured process for identifying the causal or contributing factors underlying adverse events or other critical incidents
  - Initially developed to analyze industrial accidents, RCA is now widely employed in error analysis within health care. A central tenet of RCA is to identify underlying problems that increase the likelihood of errors, while avoiding the trap of focusing on mistakes by individuals. RCA seeks to explore all the possible factors associated with an incident by asking what happened, why it happened, and what can be done to prevent it from happening again.

- **SBAR:** a form of structured communication first developed for use in naval military procedures; it stands for situation (what is going on with the patient?), background (what is the clinical background or context?), assessment (what do I think the problem is?), recommendation/request (what would I do to correct it?)
  - It has been adapted for health care as a helpful technique for communicating critical information that requires immediate attention and action concerning a patient's condition. It promotes patient safety by helping individuals communicate with shared expectations in a concise and structured format which improves efficiency and accuracy.

- **Sentinel event:** adverse event in which death or serious harm to a patient has occurred; used to refer primarily to events that were not at all expected or acceptable (e.g., an operation on the wrong patient or body part)

- **Violation:** intentional or deliberate deviation from safe operating procedures, standards, or policies
  - A violation is different from an error, which is an unintentional action. Unlike errors which are honest mistakes due to human nature, intentional violations are behaviors for which individuals need to be held accountable.

- **Wrong-site procedure:** operation or procedure done on the wrong part of the body or on the wrong person; it can also mean the wrong surgery or procedure was performed
  - Wrong-site procedures are rare and preventable, though they do still occur. A standard system to confirm the patient, site, and intended procedure with the medical team and patient before starting the procedure is a widely employed method of reducing or eliminating wrong-site procedures.

Chapter Summary

- Studies demonstrate that a considerable number of patients are harmed from preventable medical errors. Most instances of patient harm, however, are the result of bad systems and not bad people.

- Blaming individuals rarely brings about the type of substantial improvement in safety that is required.

- A systems-based approach is an effective method for reducing harm and increasing the safety of patient care. This includes a supportive environment where errors are openly reported, studied, and used to redesign health care delivery.

- Improving patient safety requires a commitment from all members of the health care team.

- Basic concepts for building a safer health care system include:

  - Standardizing care whenever possible

  - Reducing reliance on memory (e.g. using checklists for important steps)

  - Using systems-based approaches to build safety nets into the health care delivery process to compensate for human error

  - Openly reporting and studying errors (i.e. learn from error)

  - Engaging with patients (i.e. patient education is a powerful tool to prevent errors and improve quality)

  - Communicating effectively and functioning as an effective team

Key Points

- Medical errors result from the complexity of health care combined with the reality of the inherent fallibility of human nature. Although accountability and responsibility are important, simply blaming people for errors they did not intend to commit does not address underlying failures in the system and is an ineffective way of improving safety.

- The majority of errors or adverse events are system derived and redesigning systems in health care delivery hold the greatest potential for advancing patient safety and quality improvement.

- Improving communication, teamwork and the culture of safety are effective methods in improving patient safety.

- Safety is a team effort: requiring everyone on the care team to work in partnership with one another and with patients and families.

Review Questions

126. A 64-year-old man is admitted to the hospital for treatment of bacterial pneumonia. The treating clinician forgets to ask about allergies and the patient is unaware that his severe allergy to penicillin is not known to the treatment team. The patient receives a dose of intravenous penicillin and suffers an anaphylactic response but is successfully resuscitated by the medical team. Which of the following is the most accurate description of the medical error?

    (A) Slip resulting in a near miss

    (B) Violation resulting in a near miss

    (C) Lapse resulting in an adverse event

    (D) Violation resulting in patient injury

    (E) Non-preventable adverse event

127. A new intern who is not being supervised is asked to see a patient who is being discharged following treatment of a lower extremity deep vein thrombosis. The intern prescribes a six month course of warfarin without reviewing the patient's other medications. Unknown to the intern, the patient is taking an antibiotic which increases the anticoagulant activity of warfarin. The pharmacy computer system is broken and the drug is filled manually, which does not enable the computer system to alert to the drug –drug interaction. An overworked nurse fails to check for drug interactions during the medication reconciliation and gives the patient the prescription upon discharge. The patient fills the prescription at a local drug store and suffers a significant bleeding complication requiring re-hospitalization and surgery.

    According to James Reason's Swiss cheese model of error, which one of the following would be the most effective approach to preventing this adverse event in the future?

    (A) Identifying and correcting the single overarching failure in the health care system responsible for the adverse event

    (B) Identifying and weeding out the individuals involved in this medical error

    (C) Applying a systemic approach to eliminating all causes of human error

    (D) Building successive layers of safety barriers into the system that prevent medical error from resulting in patient harm

    (E) Initiating a campaign to remind clinicians to be more vigilant and to follow established safety protocols

128. As a member of the clinical team you are interested in developing a new system to more closely monitor blood glucose levels of diabetic patients admitted to the hospital for vascular wound care. In order to assess the impact of this new system on patient quality, you and your team conduct a PDSA cycle. Which of the following statements is correct regarding the PDSA cycle?

    (A) The PDSA cycle begins with full scale implementation

    (B) The PDSA cycle consists of small, rapid test of new initiatives

    (C) Changes from PDSA are based on expert intuition, and do not require data collection or interpretation

    (D) PDSA is a means of analyzing past errors in order to design system based interventions

    (E) The PDSA cycle requires a randomized control trial

129. A 23-year-old man with a history of depression is admitted to the inpatient psychiatry ward after the third attempt at suicide with an intentional drug overdose. The patient has been stabilized medically; however, is under 24-hour monitoring by the nursing staff due to repeated attempts at self-harm. During change of shift, there is a mistake in communication and no one is assigned to the patient. The mistake is noticed 15 minutes into the new shift, and a member of the nursing team is assigned to watch the patient. Fortunately, during the 15-minute period the patient did not make any attempts to harm himself. Which of the following statements about this event is correct?

    (A) This is a sentinel event and should be reported to the medical board

    (B) This is a sentinel event and should be reported to the hospital and family

    (C) This is a near miss and should be reported to the hospital

    (D) This is a near miss and should be reported to the patient and family

    (E) This is a near miss and no reporting is required since the patient was not harmed

130. A nurse practitioner receives a phone call from the mother of one of the pediatric patients in the practice who frequently suffers from ear infections. The mother typically sees the physician and receives antibiotics to treat her child's condition. Given that it is a weekend and the office is closed, the nurse practitioner phones in the antibiotic prescription based on the mother's recollection of the name of the medication used in the past. The prescription is filled at a new pharmacy that does not have the patient's prior medical records on file. The child suffers an allergic reaction after which it is discovered that the wrong antibiotic was ordered. Which of the following statements is correct regarding root cause analysis (RCA)?

    (A) RCA involves a retrospective, systems approach to error analysis

    (B) RCA is a prospective approach to systems redesign

    (C) RCA involves only the individual(s) directly involved in the error

    (D) RCA is only performed for errors resulting in patient death

    (E) Due to privacy laws the results of RCA are confidential and not shared

131. A critical and respiratory care unit is attempting to decrease their rate of ventilator-acquired pneumonia. The team develops a new clinical protocol to help reduce hospital acquired pneumonia in ventilated patients. The protocol includes several new activities which have not previously been followed uniformly in the unit. The changes includes head of bed elevation, daily oral care, daily assessment of readiness to extubate and having access to infectious disease specialists for consultation in the treatment of ventilator-associated pneumonia.

Which one of the following represents an outcomes measure of quality?

(A) Measure the compliance rate in following guidelines for head of bed elevation over a 3 month period following the new protocol

(B) Determine the number of infectious disease specialists available for consultation during a 3 month period following the new protocol.

(C) Monitor the number of patients who self-extubate prematurely during the daily assessment of readiness to extubate over a 3 months period following implementation of the new protocol

(D) Monitor the number of infections over 3 months following implementation of the new protocol

(E) Determine the wait time for starting antibiotics in patients with suspected ventilator-associated pneumonia.

132. A geriatric team is interested in decreasing the number of patient falls in their nursing home. After convening as a group to discuss possible interventions, a new system of identifying patients at high-risk for falling and providing these patients with fall prevention interventions is implemented. Following this intervention, the rate of patient falls per month is followed for 12 months on a run chart. No baseline data was collected. Which of the following best describes the results of the run chart?

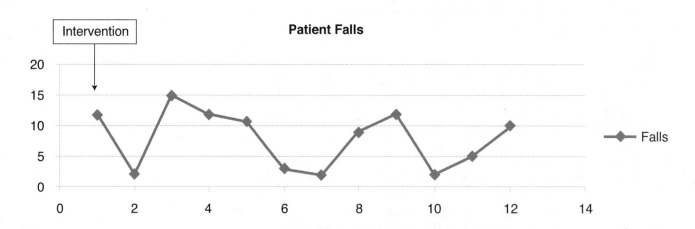

(A) The intervention led to a significant decrease in patient falls
(B) The intervention led to a significant increase in patient falls
(C) The intervention resulted in no change in patient falls
(D) The impact of the intervention is subjective
(E) The impact of the intervention is inconclusive

133. An 85-year-old woman is being transferred to an acute rehabilitation facility following a hospital admission for hip replacement surgery. Postoperatively during her hospital stay she was started on deep vein thrombosis (DVT) prophylaxis medication with plans to continue the medication upon discharge. The intern and nurse discharging the patient failed to convey this new medication to the receiving treatment team at the rehabilitation center. The patient is not continued on her anticoagulation medication and sustains a DVT leading to a fatal pulmonary embolus 3 weeks after transfer. Which of the following actions will facilitate quality improvement and the prevention of a similar error in the future?

(A) Determine which staff member(s) failed to order the medication

(B) Develop a process to increase the use of medication reconciliation

(C) Send a memo to all staff about the importance of DVT prophylaxis

(D) Educate patients about the dangers of DVT following hip surgery

(E) Conduct monthly audits to monitor medication errors at transitions of care

Answers

126. **Answer: C.** A lapse is an internal event that generally involves a failure in memory; as opposed to a slip which is an observable action commonly associated with attentional or perceptional failures resulting in an unintended execution of a correctly intended action. The result of the described error was harm to the patient in the form of anaphylaxis with the need for resuscitation, and therefore is categorized as an adverse event. An adverse event is any harm or undesirable clinical outcome resulting from medical care as opposed to the underlying disease process, and does not have to result in permanent disability or death. A violation is a deliberate act of not following policy or procedures, which was not the situation in this scenario. A near miss is an event or a situation that does not produce patient harm, but only because of intervening factors or good fortune. The adverse event described is the result of an error and is completely preventable.

127. **Answer: D.** The most effective approach to improving patient safety and quality is to address system-level causes of failure. In the Swiss-cheese model, safety barriers are recognized as having unintended weaknesses (i.e. holes) which can occasionally align and allow an error to result in patient harm. In order to improve patient safety, the system must be redesigned to have effective safety barriers capable of preventing errors from resulting in patient harm. Attempting to penalize individuals who make honest errors or eliminate the potential for human error yields limited results.

128. **Answer: B.** The PDSA Cycle is a systematic series of steps for gaining valuable learning and knowledge for the continual improvement of a product or process The PDSA cycle consists of developing a plan to test an intervention (Plan), carrying out the intervention (Do), observing and measuring the impact of the intervention (Study), and determining what modifications should be made to the system or process as a result of the study observations (Act). These interventions are small scale, rapid tests of new initiatives. Interventions with promising results are then selected for larger scale implementation. They do not require the rigor of randomized controlled trials. These 4 steps are repeated over and over as part of a never-ending cycle of continual improvement.

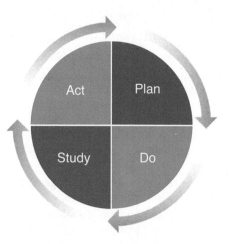

129. **Answer: C.** The event described is a near miss; there was an error which fortunately did not result in patient harm. Most near misses need not be disclosed to patients or families; however, they should be reported to the hospital in order for the error to be studied in an attempt to learn how to prevent it in the future. A sentinel event is an adverse event resulting in serious or permanent injury to a patient.

130. **Answer: A.** The root cause analysis is a retrospective approach to error analysis. It is typically performed for errors resulting in significant patient harm, but can be performed for any adverse event that a team wishes to review. The RCA process usually involves the individual(s) involved in the event as well as any other members of the team typically involved in the care delivery process related to the event. Although the details such as the names of the individuals involved in the event are not shared publically, the general findings of the RCA can be shared throughout the system in order to improve the quality of the system.

131. **Answer: D.** The number of infections over 3 months following implementation of the new protocol is an outcomes measure. Compliance rates in following guidelines are a process measure. The number of infectious disease specialists would be a structure measure. The number of patients prematurely self-extubating would be a balancing measure. Wait times for starting antibiotics is another process measure.

132. **Answer: E.** A run chart provides a dynamic display of a process over time. Run charts help to determine using minimal mathematical complexity if interventions made in a process or system over time lead to improvements. Run charts also provide the foundation for the more sophisticated method of statistical analysis using control charts. The run chart allows a team to understand the stability of a process as well as determine any shifts, trends or runs which may indicate changes based on interventions. However, without a baseline for comparison, one cannot determine from this run chart whether or not any significant change has occurred.

133. **Answer: B.** Quality assurance (QA) is an older term describing a process that is reactive and retrospective in nature. It is a form of 'policing' to ensure that quality standards have been followed. It often relies on audits and traditionally has focused on punitive actions for failures in quality. It often involved determining who was at fault after something went wrong. QA has not proven to be very effective in transforming care. The goal of quality improvement (QI), on the other hand, is to achieve improvement by measuring the current status of care and then developing systems-based approaches to making things better. It involves both prospective and retrospective reviews and specifically attempts to avoid attributing blame. Rather, QI seeks to create systems to prevent errors from happening. In the case above, developing a process to increase the use of medication reconciliation would be following the principles of QI. The other interventions are QA-based and/or simply not as effective in creating and sustaining a positive change.

Index

Note: Page numbers followed by *f* and *t* indicates figures and tables respectively.

A

Abandonment of patient, 198
Abuse
    of child. *See* Child abuse
    of domestic partner, 113–114
    of elderly, 114, 114*t*
    substance. *See* Substance-related disorders
Accident causation model, 223–224, 224*f*
Accuracy, screening tests, 10
Acetylcholine (ACh), 177–178
    sleep and, 127
Acting out, as defense mechanism, 91, 94*t*
Addition, mutually exclusive events and, 19
Adherence, to treatment, 135–136
Adjusted (standardized) rate, 7
Adjustment disorder, 156–157
Adolescents
    child-development principles and, 108
    developmental milestones in, 107*t*
    pregnancy among, 65–66
    sexual behavior among, 65
    sexually transmitted diseases in, 66
    sleep-wake cycle and, 125*f*, 125*t*
    suicide among, 44–45
Adults, attachment and loss in, 108–109. *See also* Grief
Advance directives, 197
Adverse events
    contributing factors, 216–218
    medical errors causing, 222
Age/Aging
    disease rates correlated with, 8*t*
    facts about, 110–111
    leading cause of death by, 52*t*
    sexuality and, 70
    sleep-wake cycle and, 125*f*, 126
Agnosia, 172
Agraphia, 172
Al-Anon, 57
Alcohol consumption
    effects of, 55–57
    medical complications of, 56–57
    sleep and, 126
Alcoholics Anonymous, 57

Alcoholism, 55–57
Alexia, 172
α (type I) error, 27
Alzheimer disease. *See* Primary degenerative neurocognitive
    disorder of the Alzheimer type (DAT)
2-(aminomethyl)phenylacetic acid (AMPA),
    role in schizophrenia, 146
Amnesia, 157
Amphetamine, effects and treatment for abuse of, 58*t*
Amygdala, 176
Anabolic steroids, 59
Analysis of variance (ANOVA), 29*t*, 31
Anchoring bias, diagnostic error and, 222
Angel dust (PCP), effects and treatment of, 58*t*
Anhedonia, 144
Anorexia nervosa, 151, 152*t*
Anorgasmia, antidepressant use and, 185
Antianxiety medications, 189–190
Anticholinergic effects
    of antipsychotics, 181
    of cyclic antidepressants, 184
Antidepressants, 184–186
    electroconvulsive therapy and, 186–187
    types of, 184–186
    use considerations, 184
    other drugs used as, 187
Antipsychotics
    adverse effects of, 181–183
    extrapyramidal reactions to, 182, 182*t*
    potency of, 183*t*
    typical and atypical, 183–184, 183*t*
    use considerations, 181
Antisocial personality disorder, 159, 160*t*
Anxiety
    defenses generated by, 90–93, 94*t*
    and learning relationship, 82, 82*f*
Anxiety disorders, 152–153
Anxiolytics, 189–190
Aphasias, 172–173
Apraxia, 172
    constructional, 173*f*
Aripiprazole, 184
Arousal disorders, sexual, 68
Assisted suicide, 198
"At risk" population, 3, 4
Attachment, and loss, 108–109
Attack rate, 4

Attention deficit hyperactivity disorder (ADHD), 144
Attention processing deficits, in schizophrenia, 147
Attributable risk (AR), 15
Autism spectrum disorders, 143–144
Availability bias, diagnostic error and, 223
Aversive conditioning therapy, 79, 81t
Avoidant personality disorder, 159, 160t

B

Bad apples approach, to medical error, 223
Balancing measures, in quality improvement, 228
Barbiturates
    effects and treatment for abuse of, 58t
    and sleep, 127
Barriers
    in medical error reporting, 225–226
    in systems approach to failure, 223–224, 224f
Basal ganglia, 177
Bed-wetting, 130
Behavior
    alcoholism treatment and, changes in, 57
    brain and, 173f, 174–177
    learning and, 75–78
Behavior patterns, type A, 99
Behavior therapy/modification
    based on classical conditioning, 79, 81t
    based on operant conditioning, 79–80, 81t
Bender Visual Motor Gestalt Test, 102
Benton Visual Retention Test, 102
Benzodiazepines, 189–190
    effects and treatment for abuse of, 58t
    and sleep, 127
Bereavement. *See* Grief
Best interest standard, 197
    Baby Boy Doe case, 196
    in *Eichner vs. Dillon*, 195
β (type II) error, 27
Bias
    in diagnostic error, 222–223
    in research studies, 12–13, 14t, 17
Biofeedback therapy, 80, 81t
Biostatistics
    descriptive, 21–24
    inferential, 24–28
    probability. *See* Probability
Bipolar disorder, 150, 150t
Birth defects, 53
Blame culture approach, to medical error, 223
Blocking, as defense mechanism, 88, 94t
Blue Cross Blue Shield, 209
Body dysmorphic disorder, 154
Borderline personality disorder, 158–159, 160t
Brain
    abnormalities in schizophrenia, 147
    and behavior, 173f, 174–177
Brain lesions, 174–175
    and memory, 176t
Breathing-related sleep disorder, 128
Broca aphasia, 172
Brother Fox *(Eichner vs. Dillon)*, 195
Bruxism, 130

Bulimia nervosa, 151, 152t
Bupropion, 187
Buspirone, 190

C

Caffeine, effects and treatment for absue of, 58t
CAGE questions, 56
Cancer rates, 51
    incidence and death, 51t
Cannabis, effects and treatment for abuse of, 58t
Capitation payments, 49, 210
Carbamezepine, 189
Cardiovascular effects
    of antipyschotics, 182
    of cyclic antidepressants, 185
Case-control study, 14, 15f
    differentiating from other observational studies, 17t
    odds ratios in, 16
        colorectal cancer and family history, 16t
        lung cancer and smoking, 16t
Case-fatality mortality rate, 8t
Case report observational study, 14
Case series report observational study, 14
Cataplexy, 127
Catatonic symptoms, in schizophrenia, 145
Categorical scale, 28t, 29
Cause and Effect diagram, in root cause analysis, 226–227, 227f
Cause-specific mortality rate, 8t
Central line associated bloodstream infection (CLABSI), 217–218
Central nervous system (CNS) effects
    of antipsychotics, 182, 182t
    of commonly abused substances, 59f
    of cyclic antidepressants, 185
Central tendency, 21–22, 21f
    skewed, 21, 22f
Cerebellum, 177
Child abuse, 111–112, 114t
    sexual, 113
Child development
    intellectual disability, 143, 143t
    milestones in, 103–105, 104f, 106t–107t
    principles of, applying, 108–111
Children. *See also* Infants
    attachment and loss in, 108
    autism spectrum disorders in, 143–144
    concept of illness and death in, 110
    development. *See* Child development
    discipline of, 108
    DSM 5 diagnoses in, 143–144
    as homicide victims, 113f
    legal and ethical issues related to, 199
    mentally ill, detention of, 201
Chi-square, 29t, 31
    for nominal data, 31t
Chlamydia, 66
Circumcision, female, 113
Clang associations, 144
Classical conditioning, 75–76, 75f
    behavior therapy/modification based on, 79, 81t
Clinical trials. *See* Intervention studies
Closed-ended questions, in physician-patient communication, 134

Clozapine, 184
Codeine, effects and treatment for absue of, 58t
Cognitive errors, in diagnosis, 222
Cohort study, 14, 15f
    differentiating from other observational studies, 17t
Coining, 112
Communication, medical errors and, 219–220, 223
Community trial, 18
Competency of patient
    advance directives and, 197
    assumption of, 197
Computerized physician order entry (CPOE), 217
Conduction aphasia, 173
Confidence intervals, 25–26
    for relative risk and odds ratios, 26
Confidentiality, 200
Confirmation bias, diagnostic error and, 223
Confounding bias, 13
    effects associated with, 14t
Confrontation, in physician-patient communication, 134
Constructional apraxia, 173f
Continuous reinforcement, in operant conditioning, 77
Control chart, for quality improvement, 231
Control group, in intervention study, 17
Convenience sample, for quality improvement, 231
Conversion disorder, 155
Copayment, 209
Coprophilia, 67
Copying task, ability by age, 104, 104f
Coronary prone behavior pattern, 99
Correlation analysis, 30, 30f
Cortex
    frontal, 174
    occipital, 175
    parietal, 175
    temporal, 170, 174
Cortical abnormalities, in schizophrenia, 147
"Crossing the Quality Chasm" (IOM report), 228
Cross-over study, 18, 18f
Cross-sectional study, 14, 15f
    differentiating from other observational studies, 17t
Crude mortality rate, 8t
Crude rate, 7
Cyclic antidepressants, 184–185
Cyclothymia, 148, 148t

D

Death
    causes by age group, 52
    child's concept of, 110
    determination of, 198
    non-genetic causes of, 51t
    patterns among minorities, 53t
    sudden, in infants, 53, 128
    unexplained, in child age <1, 53, 128
    in U.S., leading causes of, 47, 52
    wrongful, medical error as cause of, 216
Death rate, in U.S., 47, 52
Decision-making
    by patient, 196
    by surrogate, 197

Deductible, 209
Defense mechanisms
    anxiety defenses, 90–93, 94t
    defined, 87
    immature defenses, 88–89, 94t
    mature defenses, 93–94, 94t
    Narcissistic defenses, 87–88, 94t
Defenses, in systems approach to failure, 223–224, 224f
Delirium, neurocognitive disorder vs., 167, 167t–168t
Delta sleep, 121f, 123f
    sleep deprivation and, 124
Delusions, 144
Dementias. See Neurocognitive disorders
Deming, W. Edward, 228
Denial, as defense mechanism, 88, 94t
Dependent personality disorder, 160, 160t
Depersonalization disorder, 157
Depression
    behavioral models of, 81–82
    bipolar disorder, 150, 150t
    grief vs., 109t
    major depressive disorder, 149–150, 150t
    persistent depressive disorder, 148
    with seasonal pattern, 149
    sleep and, 127
Descriptive statistics, 21–24
Design bias, in research study, 13
    effects associated with, 14t
Desire disorders, sexual, 68
Detailed flowcharts, for quality improvement, 230
Detention, of mentally ill, 200–201
Development
    in adolescent, milestones in, 107t
    in child. See Child development
    general patterns in, 103
    in infant, 103–105, 104f, 106t–107t
    pubic hair, 107t
Diagnostic and Statistical Manual – DSM 5. See DSM 5 (Diagnostic and Statistical Manual 5) diagnoses
Diagnostic error, 221
    biases in, 222–223
    categories of, 222
Diagnostic-related groups (DRGs), 211–212
Direct questions, in physician-patient communication, 134
Discipline, of children, 108
Disclosure, of medical error, 225
Discrete performance anxiety, 153
Disease rates, 3–8
    and age correlation, 8t
    calculation for, 3
    cancer, 51
    mandatory reportable diseases, 50t
Displacement, as defense mechanism, 94t
Dissociation, as defense mechanism, 93, 94t
Dissociative identity disorder, 157
Distribution curves, skewed, 21, 22f
Distributions, 21–24
Disulfiram therapy, for alcoholism, 57, 57f
Divorce rate, 43
    age at marriage and, 44
DMAIC (define,measure, analyze, improve, control) model, for quality improvement, 229

DNR (Do Not Resuscitate) orders, 200
Domestic partner abuse, 113–114, 114t
Dopamine, 178
    in mesolimbic pathway, 55
    sleep and, 126, 127
Dopamine hypothesis, in schizophrenia, 146
Double-blind randomized controlled clinical trial, 17
Drawings, projective, 102
DSM 5 (Diagnostic and Statistical Manual 5) diagnoses, 143–160
    adjustment disorder, 156–157
    anxiety disorders, 152–153
    in childhood, 143–144, 143t
    dissociative disorders, 157
    eating disorders, 151, 152t
    factitious disorder, 156, 156f
    hoarding disorder, 154
    malingering, 156, 156f
    mood disorders, 145–150, 150t
    obsessive-compulsive disorder, 154
    personality disorders, 157–160, 160t
    schizophrenia, 144–148
    somatic symptom disorders, 155–156, 156f
    trauma and stress-related disorders, 154–155
Duloxetine, 187
Duty to warn/protect, 196, 200
Dying patients, dealing with, 109

E

Eating disorders, 151, 152t
Echolalia, 144
Echopraxia, 144
Ego-dystonic homosexuality, 69
    defense mechanisms and, 87
Ego-syntonic homosexuality, 69
Eichner vs. Dillon, 195
Ejaculation, in sexual response cycle, 66t
    premature, 69
Elderly
    abuse of, 114, 114t
    and aging, facts about, 110–111
    sleep-wake cycle in, 125f, 126
    suicide among, 111, 111f
Electroconvulsive therapy (ECT), 186–187
Electroencephalography (EEG), of sleep stages, 123f
Emergency detention, 201
Enkephalins, 179
Enuresis, 130
Epidemiology, 3–8
    mood disorders, 150t
    neurocognitive disorders, 168
    substance-related disorders, 60
    suicide, 45–46, 46t
Erectile disorder, in males, 68
Error
    in hypothesis testing, 27
    in medical care. *See* Medical error(s)
    in medication, 216–217, 217f
    in research studies, 14
    statistical, 27
Ethical issues. *See* Legal and ethical issues

Euthanasia, 198
    active, 198
Excessive daytime sleepiness (EDS), 127
Exhibitionism, 67
Experimenter expectancy, 12
    effects associated with, 14t
Exposure therapy, 79, 81t
Extinction
    in classical conditioning, 76
    in operant conditioning, 77
Extinction therapy, 80, 81t
Extrapyramidal (EP) reactions, to antipsychotics, 182, 182t

F

Facilitation, in physician-patient communication, 134
Factitious disorder, differentiating between somatic symptom
        disorder and, 156, 156t
Fading therapy, 80, 81t
Failure, systems approach to, 223–225, 224f
Failure mode effects analysis (FMEA), 227
Falls, in health care settings, 218
Family life, 43–44
FDA approval, for intervention study, 17
Feeding tubes, 198
Fee-for-service payments, 209
    PPOs and, 210
Females
    elderly, suicide rates among, 111f
    orgasm disorder in, 68
    sexual interest arousal disorder in, 68
    sexuality and aging in, 70
Fetal alcohol syndrome (FAS), 56
Fetishism, 67
Figures, copying ability by age, 104, 104f
Fishbone diagram, in root cause analysis, 226–227, 227f
5 Rs strategy, in medication administration, 217
Flight of ideas, 144
Flowcharts, for quality improvement, 230
Fluphenazine, 183
Frontal cortex, 174
Frontal/temporal disease, 170
Frotteurism, 67
Fugue state, 157
Functional neurological symptom disorders, 155

G

Gamma amino-butyric acid (GABA), 180
Gender dysphoria, 68t
Gender identity, 68t
Generalized anxiety disorder (GAD), 152
Genetics, contribution to alcoholism, 56
Genitopelvic pain disorder, 69
Global aphasia, 173
Glue sniffing, effects and treatment for, 58t
Glutamate, role in schizophrenia, 146
Glutamic acid, 179
Gonorrhea, 66
Good Samaritan Laws, 200
Grief
    depression vs., 109t
    Kubler-Ross stages of, 109

H

Hallucinations
  defined, 144
  hypnagogic and hypnopompic, 127
Hallucinogens, effects and treatment for absue of, 58*t*
Haloperidol, 183
Halstead-Reitan Battery, 102
Harm to patient. *See also* Medical error(s)
  prevention of, 198, 216
  risk of, 216
Hashish. *See* Cannabis
Hawthorne effect, 12, 14*t*
Health belief model, 136
Health care delivery systems
  complexity of, 219
  outcomes in, case studies, 215–216
  payment methods in, 49
    government, 211–212
    non-government, 209–210
  utilization trends, 48–49
Health care professionals
  fitness for patient care, 201, 219
  medical error identification by, 226
  practice questions concerning, 201–202
  rules of conduct for, 197–201
  substance-related disorders among, 60
Health maintenance organization (HMO), 210
  types of, 210*t*
Health power of attorney, 197
Helplessness, learned, 81
Hemineglect/Hemi-inattention, 173*f*
Hemispheric dominance, 172
Heroin, effects and treatment for absue of, 58*t*
Herpes simplex virus, type 2 (HSV-2), 66
High-level flowcharts, for quality improvement, 230
Hippocampus, 176
Histrionic personality disorder, 158, 160*t*
HIV/AIDS, 49–50
  neurocognitive disorder associated with, 171–172
Hoarding disorder, 154
Holmes and Rahe scale, 99
Homicide, child victims of, 113*f*
Homicide rate, by age, 47*f*
Homosexuality, 69–70
Hospital-acquired infections (HAI), 217–218
Hospital-acquired pneumonia (HAP), 218
Hospitalization trends, 48, 49
  for mentally ill, 47
Human papilloma virus (HPV), 66
Humor, as defense mechanism, 93, 94*t*
Huntington chorea, 170–171
Hydrocephalus, normal pressure, 171
Hypertensive crisis, MAOI use and, 185–186
Hypothalamus, 176
Hypothesis testing, 26–27
Hypoxyphilia, 67

I

Identity formation, in teenagers, 108
Illness, child's concept of, 110
Illness anxiety disorder, 155

Illusions, 144
Immature defenses, 88–89, 94*t*
Impotence, 68
Imprinting, 105
IM SAFE mnemonic, 219
Incidence
  calculating, lung cancer example, 7*f*
  factors affecting, 6*t*
  prevalence vs., 5
Incidence rate, 3
  calculation for, 3
  considerations in, 3–4
Indemnity insurance, 209
Independence, probability and, 19
Infants
  developmental milestones in, 103–105, 104*f*, 106*t*–107*t*
  mortality rate, in U.S., 47, 52, 53
  sleep-wake cycle in, 125*f*, 126
Infections, hospital-acquired, 217–218
Inferential statistics, 24–28
Information processing deficits, in schizophrenia, 147
Informed consent, 199
Inhalants, effects and treatment for absue of, 58*t*
Insomnia, 129
Institute for Health Care Improvements (IHI) "Triple Aim" initiative, 228
Institute of Medicine (IOM)
  "Crossing the Quality Chasm," 228
  medication error estimate by, 216
  "To Err is Human: Building a Safer Health System" (IOM report), 216
Instrumental conditioning. *See* Operant conditioning
Insurance payments, 209–210
Intellectual disability, 143
  in fetal alcohol syndrome, 56
  IQ score and, 100
  levels of, 143*t*
Intellectualization, as defense mechanism, 91, 94*t*
Intelligent quotient (IQ), 100–101
  calculation methods, 100
  distribution in general population, 100*t*
  tests measuring, 101
Intermittent reinforcement, in operant conditioning, 77–78
Interval scale, 28*t*, 29
Interval schedules, in reinforcement, 77–78
Intervention studies, 17–18
Introjection (Identification), as defense mechanism, 89, 94*t*
Ishikawa diagram, in root cause analysis, 226–227, 227*f*
Isolation of affect, as defense mechanism, 90–91, 94*t*

K

Ketamine. *See* Hallucinogens
Klüver-Bucy syndrome, 176
Knowledge-based mistake, medical error and, 221, 222*f*
Korsakoff syndrome, 177
Kubler-Ross stages of grief, 109

L

Lapse in memory, medical error and, 221
Late-look bias, 13
  effects associated with, 14*t*

Leading questions, in physician-patient communication, 134
Lead-time bias, 12, 13f
    effects associated with, 14t
Lean (Lean Enterprise/Toyota Production System) model, for
        quality improvement, 229, 230
Learned helplessness, 81
Learning
    and anxiety relationship, 82, 82f
    behaviorist model of, 75–78
Learning-based therapies. *See* Behavior therapy/modification
Legal and ethical issues
    best interest standard, 195, 196
    practice questions concerning, 201–202
    related to medical practice, 197–201
    substituted judgment standard, 195
Life events, stressful, 99
Life expectancy, in U.S., 47, 52
Limbic system, 175–177
    abnormalities in schizophrenia, 147
Lithium, 188
Living will, 197
Loose associations, 144
Loss, attachment and, 108–109. *See also* Grief
Low birth weight, 53
Loxapine, 182
LSD. *See* Hallucinogens
Luria Nebraska Battery, 102

M
Major depressive disorder, 149–150
Males
    biologic, gender identity and preferred sexual partner of, 68t
    elderly, suicide rates among, 111f
    hypoactive sexual desire disorder in, 68
    premature ejaculation in, 69
    sexual erectile disorder in, 68
    sexuality and aging in, 70
    sexual response cycle in, 66t
Malingering, differentiating between somatic symptom disorder
        and, 156, 156t, 164
Mandatory reportable diseases, 50–51
Mannerisms, 144
Marijuana. *See* Cannabis
Marital status, well-being index scores for, 43
Marriage, 43
    age at, divorce rate and, 44
Masochism, 67
Masturbation, 69
Matched pairs *t*-test, 29, 31, 31t
Mature defenses, 93–94, 94t
MDMA (Ecstasy), 59f
Mean, 21
    standard deviation and, 23f, 24f
Measurement bias, 12
    effects associated with, 14t
Median, 21
Medicaid, 211
Medical error(s)
    actual vs. reported, 226
    analyzing, 226–227
    categories of, 221, 222f

causes of, 219–220
    contributing factors, 216–218
    disclosure and reporting of, 225–226
    near-misses vs., 226
    prevalence of, 216
    reducing. *See* Quality improvement
    systems approach to, 223–225
    types of, 221–223
Medicare, 49, 211
    hospital readmission rates, 218
Medication errors
    causes of, 217, 217f
    IOM estimate of, 216
    reduction strategies, 217
Melatonin, sleep deprivation and, 125
Memory, brain lesions and, 176t
Memory lapse, medical error and, 221, 222f
Mental illness
    detention of children with, 201
    health care delivery and, 48
    patient rights and, 200–201
Mescaline. *See* Hallucinogens
Mesolimbic pathway, substance-related disorders and, 55
Meta-analysis, 13
Metabolic effects, of cyclic antidepressants, 185
N-methyl-D-aspartate (NMDA), role in schizophrenia, 146
Minnesota Multiphasic Personality Inventory (MMPI), 101–102
Minorities, cause of death among, 53f
Mirtazapine, 187
Mistakes, as medical error, 221, 222f
Mode, 21
Modeling behavior, 78
Monoamine oxidase inhibitors (MAOIs), 186
Mood disorders, 148t
    epidemiology of, 150t
    subtypes, 148–150
Mood stabilizers, 188–189
Morbidity, 50–53
    morbidity rate defined, 6
Mortality rate(s), 52, 52t
    defined, 6
    from health care-associated infection, WHO estimates, 217
    types of, 8t
    in U.S., 47
Motor vehicle collision (MVC) deaths, patient safety analogy and,
        224–225
Moxibustion, 112
Multiplication, independent events and, 19
Mutism, 144
Mutual exclusion, probability and, 19, 20f

N
Naltrexone therapy, for alcoholism, 57
Narcissistic defenses, 87–88, 94t
Narcissistic personality disorder, 158, 160t
Narcolepsy, 127
Near-misses
    medical errors causing, 222
    vs. medical errors, 226
Necrophilia, 67
Negative predictive value, 10

Negative reinforcer, in operant conditioning, 76
Neologisms, 144
Neurocognitive disorders, 168–172
    Alzheimer type vs. vascular type, 170t
    delirium vs., 167, 167t–168t
    HIV-related, 171–172
Neurofeedback therapy, 80, 81t
Neuroleptics. *See* Antipsychotics
Neurological effects, of antipyschotics, 181–182
Neurologic exams, dysfunctions on, 173f
Neuropsychologic tests, 102
Neurotransmitters, 177–180. *See also individually named*
    neurotransmitters
    in bipolar disorder, 150
    in major depressive disorder, 149
    in schizophrenia, 146
    sleep-associated, 127
New England Journal of Medicine, readmission to hospital study, 218
"New events," 3
Nicotine, effects and treatment for absue of, 58t
Nightmares, 129t
Night terrors, 129t
No-fault errors, in diagnosis, 222
Nominal data, *Chi*-square analysis for, 31t
Nominal scale, 28t, 29
Non-neurological effects, of antipyschotics, 182–183
Norepinephrine (NE), 178
    sleep and, 127
Normal pressure hydrocephalus, 171
NREM (non-rapid eye movement) sleep, 121, 122
    changes over life cycle, 125f
Nucleus accumbens, drugs working in, 55
Null hypothesis, 26
    error types and, 27
    types of, 26
Number Needed to Harm (NNH), 15
Number Needed to Treat (NNT), 15

O

Objective personality tests, 101–102
Objects, phobias associated with, 153
Observational learning, 78
Observational studies
    analyzing, 15–16
    differentiating, 15f, 17t
    types of, 14–15
Obsessive-compulsive disorder, 154
Obsessive-compulsive personality disorder, 159–160, 160t
Occipital cortex, 175
Occupational therapy (OT) programs, for elderly, 111
Odds ratio (OR)
    in case-control studies, 16
        colorectal cancer and family history, 16t
        lung cancer and smoking, 16t
    confidence intervals for, 26
Olanzapine, 184
One-tailed null hypothesis, 26
One-way ANOVA, 29t, 31
Open-ended questions, in physician-patient communication, 134
Operant conditioning, 76–78, 76f
    behavior therapy/modification based on, 79–80, 81t

Opiate, effects and treatment for absue of, 58t
Ordinal scale, 28t, 29
Organic disorders
    aphasias, 172–173
    delirium vs. neurocognitive disorders, 167, 167t–168t,
        168–172, 170t
    hemispheric dominance, 172
    involving brain and behavior, 173–177
    Tourette's disorder, 167
Orgasm disorders
    in females, 68
    in males, 69
Outcomes, in quality measurement, 228
Oxycodone, effects and treatment for absue of, 58t

P

Pain disorders, sexual, 65, 66, 69
Pain management, behavioral approaches to, 82–83
Paint thinner, inhaling, effects and treatment for abuse of, 58t
Panic disorder, 152–153
Paranoid personality disorder, 157–158, 160t
Paranoid presentation, in schizophrenia, 145
Paraphiliac disorders, 67
Parents, withholding treatment by, 199
    Baby Boy Doe case, 196
Pareto charts, for quality improvement, 230
Parietal cortex, 175
Parkinson disease, 171
Partial reinforcement, in operant conditioning, 77–78
Passive-aggressive, as defense mechanism, 92, 94t
Patient
    relationship with physician. *See* Physician-patient relationships
    risks toward, 201, 216
    treatment adherence by, 135–136
Patient falls, in health care settings, 218
Patient harm. *See also* Medical error(s)
    prevention of, 198, 216
    risk of, 201, 216
Patient rights
    decision making and, 196
    limitations on, 197
    of mentally ill, 200–201
Patient safety, 215–232
    ensuring, responsibility for, 216
    health care professionals posing risk to, 201
    improving, strategies for, 231–232. *See also* Quality
        improvement
    medical errors compromising. *See* Medical error(s)
    motor vehicle collision deaths analogy and, 224–225
    system-based redesign examples for, 225
Pavlovian conditioning. *See* Classical conditioning
PDSA (plan, do, study, act) model, for quality improvement, 228–
    229, 229f
Pearson correlation, 29t, 30
Pedophilia, 67
Penetration disorder, 69
Period prevalence, 5
Perseveration, 144, 173f
Persistent depressive disorder, 148
Personality disorders, cluster characteristics, 157–160, 157–160t
    anxious and fearful, 159–160, 160t

dramatic and emotional, 158–159, 160t
    odd or eccentric, 157–158, 160t
Personality tests, 101–102
Pervasive developmental disorders. *See* Autism spectrum disorders
Phases, of intervention study, 17
Phencyclidine (PCP), effects and treatment for abuse of, 58t
Phobias
    school phobia, 105
    social anxiety disorder, 153
    specific, 153
Physical health, and psychologic adjustment to stress, 99–100
Physician-patient relationship
    general rules about, 131–134
    legal and ethical issues related to, 198
Physician-patient relationships
    dying patients, 109
    elements in, 134–135
    good, significance of, 135
Physicians. *See* Health care professionals
Pneumonia, hospital-acquired, 218
Point prevalence, 5
Pons, 177
"Pooled *t*-test," 30
Positive predictive value, 10
Positive reinforcer, in operant conditioning, 76
Post-test probabilities, 10–11
Poverty of speech, 144
Power, statistical, 28
Power of attorney, for health decisions, 197
Predictive values, screening tests, 10
Preferred provider organization (PPO), 210
Prefrontal cortical (PFC) impairment, 147
Pregnancy, teenage, 65–66
Premature ejaculation, 69
Pressured speech, 144
Pre-test probabilities, 9–10
Prevalence
    calculating, lung cancer example, 7f
    factors affecting, 6t
    and incidence, relationship between, 5
    of medical errors, 216
    point vs. prevalence, 5
    vs. incidence, 5
"Prevalence pot," 5, 5f
Prevalence rate, 4–5
    calculating, 3
Preventive errors, 221
Primary degenerative neurocognitive disorder of the Alzheimer
    type (DAT), 168–169
    vascular neurocognitive disorder vs., 168–169, 170t
    warning signs of, 168
Prion disease, 170
Probability(ies)
    post-test, 10–11
    pre-test, 9–10
    rules governing, 19–20
Process, in quality measurement, 228
Professional personnel. *See* Health care professionals
    and patient relationships. *See* Physician-patient relationships
Projection, as defense mechanism, 87–88, 94t
Projective drawings, 102
Projective personality tests, 102

Proportionate mortality rate (PMR), 8t
Psychologic adjustment, to stress, 99–100
Pubic hair development, 107t
Punishment, in operant conditioning, 77
p-value
    in hypothesis testing, 26–27, 27f
    meaning of, 28
Pygmalion effect, 12, 14t

Q

Quality, measures of, 228
Quality improvement
    measures used in, 228
    models of, 228–231
    principles of, 227–228
    strategies for influencing, 231–232
Question types, in physician-patient communication, 134
Quetiapine, 184
Quinlan, Karen Ann, 195

R

Random error, 14
Randomized controlled clinical trial (RCT), 17
Range, 22
Rapport, in physician-patient relationships, 135
Rates, disease. *See* Disease rates
Rationalization, as defense mechanism, 91–92, 94t
Ratio scale, 28t, 29
Ratio schedules, in reinforcement, 78
Reaction formation, as defense mechanism, 92, 94t
Readmission to hospital, unplanned, 218–219
Recall bias, 13
    effects associated with, 14t
Receiver Operating Characteristic (ROC) curves, 10
Redirection, in physician-patient communication, 134
Refusal of care
    patient competency and, 197
    patient rights and, 196
Regression, as defense mechanism, 89, 94t
Reinforcement/reinforcers
    in operant conditioning, 76–77
        schedules, 77–78, 78t
        secondary, 78
        spontaneous recovery and, 78
        types of, 76–77, 77t
    organic factors affecting, 82
    response-contingent, depression and, 82
Relative risk (RR), 15
    confidence intervals for, 26
Reliability, 12
REM (rapid eye movement) sleep, 121, 122, 123f
    changes over life cycle, 125f
    narcolepsy and, 127
    sleep deprivation and, 124
Repeated measures ANOVA, 29t, 31
Reporting, of medical error, 225–226
Repression, as defense mechanism, 90, 94t
Research studies
    bias in, 12–13, 14t
    interventional (clinical trials), 17–18
    observational, 14–17

Resource-based relative-value scale (RBRVS), 212
Respondent conditioning. *See* Classical conditioning
Responses, to stimuli in classical conditioning, 75–76, 75*f*
Reticular activating system (RAS), 176
Risk factors, for suicide, 46*t*
Risk(s)
    relative. *See* Relative risk (RR)
    of suicide, 46*t*
    toward patient, 201, 216
Risperidone, 183
Roe vs. Wade, 196
Root cause analysis (RCA), of medical error, 226–227, 227*f*
    failure mode effects analysis vs., 227
Rorschach Inkblot Test, 102
Rule-based mistake, medical error and, 221, 222*f*
Run charts, for quality improvement, 230, 231*f*

S

Sadism, 67
Safeguards, in systems approach to failure, 223–224, 224*f*
Safety, of patient. *See* Patient safety
SANDman mnemonic, 127
Scales
    arrangement of, 29
    types of, 28–29, 28*t*
Scatterplots, 30, 30*f*
Schizoid personality disorder, 158, 160*t*
Schizophrenia
    attention and information processing deficits in, 147
    brain abnormalities in, 147
    clinical presentation, 145
    good prognosis in, predictors for, 146
    long-term course in, 148
    neurochemical issues in, 146
    overview, 144–145
    type I (positive symptoms), 145
    type II (negative symptoms), 145
Schizotypal personality disorder, 158, 160*t*
School phobia, 105
Screening tests, 9–11
    in healthy and diseased populations, 11*f*
    results in 2 x 2 table, 9*t*
    ROC curves, 11*f*
Seasonal affective disorder (SAD), 149, 157
Sedative-hypnotics. *See* Barbiturates; Benzodiazepines
Selection bias, 12
    effects associated with, 14*t*
Selective serotonin re-uptake inhibitors (SSRI), 185–186
Sensitivity, in screening tests, 9
    ROC curves, 11*f*
Sentence Completion Test, 102
Separation anxiety, 105
Separation anxiety disorder, 105
Separation from partner, data on, 43
Serotonin (5-HT), 179
    in mesolimbic pathway, 55
    role in schizophrenia, 146
    sleep and, 127
Serotonin syndrome, SSRI use and, 185–186
Sexual abuse, of child, 113
Sexual arousal disorders, 68

Sexual behavior, in U.S., 65–67
Sexual desire disorder, male hypoactive, 68
Sexual dysfunctions, 68–69
Sexual effects
    of antipyschotics, 183
    of cyclic antidepressants, 185
Sexuality, and aging, 70
Sexually transmitted diseases, 66
Sexual pain disorders, 69
Sexual response cycle
    in female, 67*t*
    in male, 66*t*
Shaping therapy, 79–80, 81*t*
Shewhart control charts, for quality improvement, 231
Sick role components, 134
Six Sigma model, for quality improvement, 229
Skewed curves, 21, 22*f*
Skinner experiment. *See* Operant conditioning
Sleep
    biochemical changes in first hours of, 124*t*
    biologic rhythms of, 122
    in bipolar disorder, 150
    changes over life cycle, 125*f*
    chemical and psychiatric correlates of, 126–127
    developmental aspects of, 125*f*, 126
    disorders of, 127–130
    facts about, 122
    lack of, effect on performance, 124, 219
    in major depressive disorder, 149
    neurotransmitters associated with, 127
    stages of, 123*f*
    types of, 121, 121*f*
Sleep apnea, 128
Sleep deprivation, 124–125
    effects of, 219
Sleep disorders, 127–130
Sleep latency, 122
Sleep-wake cycle, 122
    developmental aspects of, 125–126, 125*f*, 125*t*, 126*t*
    narcolepsy and, 127
    sleep stages in, 123*f*
Sleep-walking, 130
Slips/slip of action, medical error and, 221, 222*f*
SMART goals, in patient safety, 232
Smooth pursuit eye movements (SPEM), 147
SN-N-OUT mnemonic, 9
Social anxiety disorder, 153
Social learning, 78
Socioeconomic status (SES), 44
Somatic symptom disorder(s), 155–156
    differentiating from factitious disorders and malingering, 156, 156*t*
    functional neurological, 155
    with predominant pain, 156
Somatization, as defense mechanism, 89, 94*t*
Somnambulism, 130
Spearman correlation, 30
Specificity, in screening tests, 9–10
    ROC curves, 11*f*
Specific rate, 7
Speech
    poverty of, 144
    pressured, 144

SP-I-N mnemonic, 10
Splitting, as defense mechanism, 88, 94*t*
Standard deviations, 22–23, 23*f*, 24*f*
Standardized (adjusted) rate, 7
Stanford-Binet Scale, 101
Statements, in physician-patient communication, 134
Statistical errors, 27
Statistical inference, 26–28
Statistical power, 28
Statistical tests, 29–31
STEEP mnemonic, 228
Steroids, abuse of, 59
Stimuli, in classical conditioning, 75–76, 75*f*
Stimulus control therapy, 80, 81*t*
Stranger anxiety, 105
Stress
    physical health and, 99–100
    physiologic responses to, 100
Stress-related disorders, 154–155
Structure, in quality measurement, 228
Subjective standard, 197
Sublimation, as defense mechanism, 93, 94*t*
Substance P, 179
Substance-related disorders. *See also individually named substances*
    among physicians, 60
    CNS effects of, 59*f*
    common substances abused, 58*t*
    epidemiology of, 60
    helpful hints of, 60*t*
    physiology of, 55
    signs suggestive of, 60*t*
Substituted judgment standard, 195, 197
Sudden infant death syndrome (SIDS), 53, 128
Suicide, 44–48
    among elderly, 111, 111*f*
    among teens, 44–45
    assisted, 198
    clinical issues, 47–48
    epidemiology of, 45
    in major depressive disorder, 149
    methods, 44
    risk factors for, 46*t*
    statistics on, 44
Suicide rate, in U.S., 44
    by age, 47*f*
Suppression, as defense mechanism, 93–94, 94*t*
Surgical site infections (SSI), 218
Surrogate, decision-making by, 197
Survival rates, false estimate of, 12, 13*f*
Swiss Cheese Model, of accident causation, 223–224, 224*f*
Syphilis, 66
Systematic desensitization therapy, 79, 81*t*
Systematic error, 14
System-related errors, in diagnosis, 222
Systems approach, to medical error, 223–225

T

Tanner stages of pubic hair development, 107*t*
Tarasoff Decision, 196, 200
Tardive dyskinesia (TD), antipyschotics and, 182
Teamwork, poor, medical errors and, 219–220, 223

Teenagers. *See* Adolescents
Teeth-grinding, 130
Temporal cortex, 174
    frontal/temporal disease, 170
Tests
    screening. *See* Screening tests
    statistical, 29–31
Thalamus, 176
Thematic Aperception Test (TAT), 102
Thioridazine, 183
Time plots, for quality improvement, 230, 231*f*
"To Err is Human: Building a Safer Health System"
    (IOM report), 216
Tourette's disorder, 167
Toyota Production System model, for quality improvement, 230
Transcortical aphasia, 173
Transference, 94
Transsexual, 68*t*
Transvestite fetishism, 67
Trauma, disorders associated with, 154–155
Trazodone, 187
Treatment
    errors in, 221
    legal and ethical issues related to, 197–201
    parents withholding, 199
        Baby Boy Doe case, 196
    patient adherence to, 135–136
"Triple Aim" (IHI initiative), 228
t-tests, 30–31
    matched pairs, 29*t*, 31, 31*t*
    "pooled," 30
Two-tailed null hypothesis, 26
Two-way ANOVA, 31
2 x 2 Table, screening results in, 9*t*
Type A behavior pattern, 99
Type I error, 27
Type II error, 27

U

Undoing, as defense mechanism, 92, 94*t*
Unplanned readmissions, 218–219
Urinary catheter-related infections (UTI), 217
Urophilia, 67

V

Validity, 12
Valproic acid, 188–189
Variability measures, 22–23
Variance, 22
Vascular neurocognitive disorder, 169
    Alzheimer type neurocognitive disorder vs., 170*t*
Venlafaxine, as antidepressant, 187
Ventral tegmental area, drugs working in, 55
Verbigeration, 144
Victim-perpetrator relationship
    in child homicide, 113*t*
    in child sexual abuse, 113
    in elder abuse, 114
Violations, medical error and, 222
Voyeurism, 67

W

Wechsler Adult Intelligence Scale, Revised (WAIS-R), 101
Wechsler Intelligence Scale for Children, Revised (WISC-R), 101
Wechsler Memory Scale, 102
Wechsler Preschool and Primary Scale of Intelligence (WPPSI), 101
Well-being index scores, 43
Wernicke aphasia, 172
Wilson disease, 171
Withdrawal symptoms, commonly abused substances, 58*t*
Withholding of treatment, by parents, 199
    Baby Boy Doe case, 196
Workplace conditions, medical error and, 219
World Health Organization (WHO), health care-associated
        infection estimates, 217
Wrongful death, medical error as cause of, 216

Z

Ziprasidone, 184
Zoophilia, 67